Beyond Complicity

Beyond Complicity

Why We Blame Each Other Instead of Systems

Francine Banner

UNIVERSITY OF CALIFORNIA PRESS

University of California Press
Oakland, California

Library of Congress Cataloging-in-Publication Data

Names: Banner, Francine, author.
Title: Beyond complicity : why we blame each other
    instead of systems / Francine Banner.
Description: Oakland, California : University of
    California Press, [2024] | Includes bibliographical
    references and index.
Identifiers: LCCN 2023022710 | ISBN 9780520394230
    (hardback) | ISBN 9780520399464 (paperback) | ISBN
    9780520394247 (ebook)
Subjects: LCSH: Conspiracy—Law and legislation—
    United States. | Conspiracy—Social aspects—United
    States. | Accomplices—Social aspects—United
    States. | Criminal justice, Administration of—
    United States. | Blame—Social aspects—United
    States. | Responsibility—Social aspects—United
    States. | United States—Politics and government—
    21st century.
Classification: LCC KF9479 .B36 2024 | DDC 345.73/02—
    dc23/eng/20230614
LC record available at https://lccn.loc.gov/2023022710

Manufactured in the United States of America

32 31 30 29 28 27 26 25 24 23
10 9 8 7 6 5 4 3 2 1

publication supported by a grant from
The Community Foundation for Greater New Haven
as part of the **Urban Haven Project**

CONTENTS

ACKNOWLEDGMENTS

I would like to thank the University of Michigan-Dearborn Office of Research and Sponsored Programs for their generous support of this project. Thanks also to Maura Roessner, Sam Warren, and the staff at UC Press, for guiding this project to completion. I shared initial drafts of several chapters at conferences, including the Detroit Mercy Law Review Women and the Law conference and U.S. Feminist Judgments Project's Feminist Legal Theory Summer Series, and I am grateful to participants in these events for their thoughtful and critical input. I would also like to thank the reviewers of the manuscript, particularly the reviewers who provided insight on early drafts. Thanks to their comments, this is a much better product.

On a more personal level, I would like to thank several people not only for their contributions to this project, but for their support and encouragement. Thank you to my friend Riaz Tejani for moving my work forward in important ways; and to Michal Buchhandler-Raphael for your extensive and careful comments when this book was still in its nascent stages. Elizabeth Brown, thank you for your support, enthusiasm, and skilled edits as the project developed. Hopefully you see many of your suggestions reflected here. To

Amos Guiora, abundant thanks for asking such thoughtful questions regarding accountability and growth. And to Gray Cavender, my mentor and friend, in the words you once shared with me from Toni Morrison, "Look. How lovely it is, this thing we have done— together."

Introduction

After January 2021, when years of violent rhetoric culminated in a dramatic insurrection at the US Capitol, the world questioned who was responsible. As the president was impeached, charged with high crimes and misdemeanors, the list of others who might have enabled, fomented, or encouraged the attack grew long. It included not only the president's advisors, friends, and family members, but politicians who challenged election results, members of the Republican party, everyone who voted for the president, and anyone who failed to vote. News and social media came under fire for having provided platforms that enabled hate and amplified distrust.

Some of the questions raised after the Capitol riots were legal in nature. Trials were held for seditious conspiracy and obstruction of justice. The legal questions were intertwined with moral ones. *How much encouragement must a person have provided in order to have facilitated the downfall of American democracy? Were those who knowingly incited violence more responsible than those who simply went along? Was it too late, after the insurrection, for representatives and cabinet officials to have a moral change of heart?*

In 2017, complicit was the Word of the Year.[1] Nestled among other anxiety-ridden words like xenophobia, misinformation, and gaslighting, the term encompassed the *zeitgeist* for our time. Journalist Lindy West described the selection as

> follow[ing] a chilling but logical evolution. In 2015 the Word of the Year was broad and neutral—"identity"—issues of racial and gender injustice having finally come closer to becoming national priorities ... By the end of 2016, as Trumpism seized the wheel, our national conversation on identity sharpened to a sinister specificity: that year's word was "xenophobia.²

Complicity is not partisan. Ferreting out accomplices is a preoccupation of conservative Oath Keepers, enamored with conspiracy theories that Democrats are colluding to undermine individual liberties. Complicity also pervades conversations in liberal sectors, as activists sift through the detritus of racism, sexism, and homophobia that shape contemporary law and policy, identifying ways in which action and inaction by institutions and individuals might be propping up biased systems and structures.

It is not just politics that raises the specter of complicity. Each new year brings forth new accusations of, if not racism, assault, or sexual harassment, then abuses of power, by high-profile persons. When a bad actor is identified—a Harvey Weinstein, Jeffrey Epstein, or Larry Nassar—this is not the end of the inquiry but the beginning. We search for potential enablers among family, coworkers, neighbors, and friends. Allegations of complicity are levied at actions from the strategic—planning a coup or deliberately covering up predatory violence—to the mundane—using plastic straws or failing to recycle. We sometimes use the term to call out a specific harm or perpetrator. We might identify complicity, for example, in the actions of high-ranking collaborators who supported a dictator's rise to political power, or the profit-motivated partners who purposefully overlooked ethical malfeasance by corrupt entrepreneurs.³

Often, the term suggests not only the facilitation of interpersonal harms, but is a means of recognizing when a person or entity has aided—or has failed to avert—more diffuse or complicated structural problems. Museums confront complicity as they reckon with what should be done with tainted donations; universities disclaim it as they decide whether to dismantle monuments erected in honor of known racists; and corporations worry about being labeled complicit when they consider whether their products, or platforms might be facilitating discrimination.

Complicity describes perpetrator-like behaviors, like deliberately marketing a toxic product or purposefully hiding the crimes of a serial predator, but it also encompasses unwitting ones. Philosophers Corwin Aragon and Alison M. Jaggar describe how an action like stepping in to help a disabled or elderly person across a street might have seemed like a good idea at the time but in retrospect may have done more harm than good; upon reflection, the good Samaritan's actions could seem patronizing, furthering ableist or ageist assumptions about ability and autonomy.[4] The *Serial* podcast offers a critique of "nice white parents" who engage in charitable giving and voluntarism that benefits individuals like them while ignoring the needs of less privileged communities. We can be nice to the wrong people, treating wrongdoers with kindness signaling approval of their misdeeds. We can be ignorant of the ways in which generosity in one area—donating heavily to a well-funded local parent-teacher organization, for example—can lead to deprivation in another. One of the most egregious ways a person can become an accomplice is by staying silent; another is by being unequivocally nice.

The breadth of behaviors that falls under the umbrella of complicity can be baffling. *Complicit* is how we describe Ghislaine Maxwell, convicted of procuring victims for sex trafficker Jeffrey Epstein, and how we categorize governments that tacitly encourage genocide and crimes of war. But it is also how we talk about colleagues who fail to speak up after hearing a racist or sexist joke, or what we might call neighbors who voted for a distasteful candidate in recent elections. The #MeToo and Black Lives Matter social movements have generated a seemingly endless list of politicians, CEOs, and celebrities who have in some way enabled racism or sexism. Behind each new allegation trails a serpentine list of potential aiders and abettors. Everyday people are not immune. When news emerges about any impending crisis or hazard—climate change, election interference, state violence, war, addiction, sexual harassment—questions arise as to whether any of our hands are truly clean.

How did we get to this place, where our lives are circumscribed by the concern that we or others are contributing to harm? What, really, are we personally accountable for? Most importantly, *How can one person intervene and act, especially when we are dealing with large-scale and inherited, structural problems?* These preoccupations are the basis of this book.

UNFOLDING COMPLICITY

The word complicit is not new. For centuries it has been used to describe a range of behaviors that are sometimes illegal but often just immoral or unethical. In the 1200s, Saint Thomas Aquinas highlighted nine ways persons might be culpable as a non-direct perpetrator: "By command, by counsel, by consent, by flattery, by receiving, by participating, by silence, by not preventing, and by not denouncing."[5] The first recorded use of the word in English was in 1656, originating in the Latin *complicare,* meaning "to fold together," and borrowed from the old French word *complice,* meaning partner. Describing "a consenting or partnership in evil," it is one of eleven thousand words that appear in one of the very first dictionaries, Thomas Blount's *Glossographia.* Blount spent more than twenty years working on his glossary in an effort to help aspiring middle-class people like himself understand the "hard" words they were likely to encounter in literature, law, and day-to-day life.[6] Even 350 years ago complicity was a term that was essential to know but difficult to wrap one's head around.

The roots of complicity in law run as deep as those in society. In 1330, Simon de Bereford was hanged for his role in aiding and counseling fellow British nobleman Roger Mortimer in the assassination of King Edward II, although there is no evidence de Bereford was present at the scene of the crime. British legal treatises dating back to the 1100s and 1200s discussed the need to expand accountability for homicide in cases where it was impossible to identify a primary perpetrator, when people on the scene "came with the intention of slaying though they struck no blow," or if people gave advice to a would-be perpetrator, even if they were repulsed by the evildoing that was planned.[7]

The formal legal doctrine of accomplice law can be traced back to *Blackstone's Commentaries of the Law of England*, published in 1765. The *Commentaries*, which strongly influence US law, set out four levels of participation in crime: the principal in the first degree, who directly committed the offense; the principal in the second degree, who was present and aided in the offense's commission; the accessory before the fact, who was "not the chief actor in the offense, nor present at its performance, but [was] someway concerned therein, either before or after the fact committed"; and the accessory after the fact, a person who did not participate but knew a felony was committed and somehow comforted or assisted the principal, such as by covering up the crime.[8]

Most contemporary criminal statutes do away with the distinction between the principal and the accessory before the fact, so that anyone who provides assistance for a crime before it takes place can face the same penalty as the person who actually committed the crime, up to life in prison or—in states that have it and cases where the accomplice assisted in plotting and planning—the death penalty. In theory, accomplice charges impose derivative liability, meaning that the punishment of the helper is logically extended from their role in the completed crime. In reality, however, complicity serves a much broader and more complex function in criminal law, often punishing defendants for relatively minor—and sometimes unintended—roles they played in furthering harm.

Theories of complicity also play a growing role in US civil law. Tort suits abound relating to sexual misconduct, gun violence, and opioid addiction, leading to settlements in the millions, and even billions. Although some lawsuits are filed against direct perpetrators, scrutiny increasingly falls on third parties—the institutions (and their representatives) who ignored claims of sexual misconduct and failed to fire serial predators; the consulting firms that outlined strategies for marketing addictive drugs or downplaying climate change; the technology companies who provided the platforms where hateful speech and misinformation could be disseminated. Increasingly, disclaiming complicity is deployed as a shield; individuals and organizations argue that they cannot ethically engage in activities such as counseling a patient on reproductive healthcare, designing a cake for an LGBTQ+ customer, or providing an insurance plan that covers birth control for employees, because the act could signal support for something they find morally objectionable.

Examining complicity is like taking apart an intricate work of origami. Unfolding complex structures reveals intersecting crease patterns, some which are deeply embedded and others that reveal paths considered but not taken. It is only when a structure is unfolded that we can see places where pathways intersect, sometimes unexpectedly, revealing a foundation that we didn't know existed. Exploring these patterns does not just reveal the missteps of the past; it can tell us something important about who we are now. It can even provide a road map for rebuilding in the future.

While its precise meaning remains elusive, there are essentially two ways complicity functions in society and law today. Complicity can operate to show newfound connections between individuals, systems, and structures—exposing pathways we can build on to create social change. But complicity can also be used to isolate, to call out or shame without proposing a pathway to repair or reform.

COMPLICITY AS ISOLATION

Cultural critics describe US society as having transitioned from a guilt culture, in which people are punished for the bad acts they have done, to a shame culture, where people are more likely to be judged and socially excluded based on their perceived inadequacies as a person.[9] Columnist David Brooks distinguishes, "[i]n a guilt culture you know you are good or bad by what your conscience feels. In a shame culture you know you are good or bad by what your community says about you."[10]

Some argue that shaming serves a key function; it is a necessary ritual that confirms an individual's moral perspective is out of step with the norms of society as a whole.[11] When it seems as if a person is unlikely to arrive at a moral reckoning on their own, it is important to let them know that their views are not in tune. It is only by coming to understand that an action is wrong that a person's outlook and behavior can change.

When waged against individuals, however, accusations of complicity can become a mechanism of social distancing. Since 2020, the process of mass shaming, characterized pejoratively as cancel culture, has proliferated, with some cancellations carried out with a particular venom. A vindictive condemnation of character is on display in subreddits like *I Never Thought Leopards Would Eat My Face* and *Fuck You Karen,* which are dedicated to savoring the comeuppance others face when unjust policies they once supported come back to bite them.[12] At the height of the Covid-19 pandemic, more than half a million people celebrated the Herman Cain Awards, reveling in the circumstances of Covid disbelievers who contracted—or even died from—the virus. Subreddit *Byebyejob* boasts over 600,000 members who gleefully savor the consequences faced by individuals whose racist or otherwise offensive acts have caused them to be fired.[13] As we sort out who among us might be enabling a malignancy like racism or sexism, social media can operate as a "digital pillory," with memes, posts, and tweets used to shame, humiliate, and exclude.[14]

The fear that even the smallest of individual actions may cause harm to—or may be accused of causing harm to—someone else can be paralyzing. Psychologists estimate that about a third of the population will suffer from some kind of anxiety disorder in their lifetime, and new psychological disorders are emerging—Covid Anxiety Syndrome, eco-anxiety—that stem from a growing incapacity to make personal decisions in the face of what seem like overwhelming risks.[15] Fear of social stigmatization or condemnation can stymie productive questions and conversation. Concern that our actions might foster future harms can thwart us from doing good things in the present.

In her final book, *Responsibility for Justice*, social theorist Iris Marion Young contended that the imposition of blame and shame on individuals could not be a useful mechanism for dealing with systemic violence.[16] Shaming punishments, Young argued, were rooted in the typical liability model of justice, which looks backward from the scene of the crime to assign responsibility for wrongdoing.[17] The liability model is not equal to the task of reckoning with the overwhelming, diffuse, and multifaceted risks we face today.

Complicity can serve a more productive function than individual shaming, however. At its best, the concept is engaged not to denigrate or demean, but to make visible the ways in which the decisions of persons or entities are not in silos but instead intersect with larger systems and structures in the world. Allegations of complicity can articulate connections that might previously have been hidden, saying something new about the responsibility of a person, institution, or corporation to the larger social environment.

COMPLICITY AS CONNECTION

We are living in a time when we are reconsidering intersections of individuals, institutions, and the world across a diverse range of contexts—the COVID-19 pandemic, systemic racism, sexual assault and harassment, financial crises, threats to reproductive and LGBTQ+ rights and freedoms, climate change, addiction, and others. Historian Adam Tooze refers to this as a period of "global polycrisis," when we are facing growing economic, sociopolitical, and climate risks that are increasingly diverse and intersecting.[18] While Tooze and others highlight human beings' precarity, as what we once thought was an assured future becomes increasingly uncertain, there are reasons to see this historical moment as one of not only crisis but possibilities.

Across fields from sociology to technology studies to psychology, researchers suggest that we are at an historical moment when human beings' understanding of the responsibility of the individual to the world is changing.[19] Sociologist Ulrich Beck argued that from crisis could come *metamorphosis,* a newfound capacity to see things through a different lens. "[W]hen populations are subjected to devastating events that leave indelible marks on consciousness and affect collective values not only do ... [they] impact on and reorient world-views, they also have the capacity to drive forward radical change."[20] In regard to climate change, philosopher William MacAskill argues, similarly, that we have entered a window of "longtermism," when, due to rapid technological advancements and unprecedented global economic growth, our ability as humans to influence the future—but also our capacity to care about it—are at an all-time high.[21] It is when we are confronted by large-scale problems that we begin to realize the extent to which existing policies and practices have failed us. Out of necessity, we look for new ways of engaging with the world.

There are particular times in history when, as human beings, we have been more prepared than others to examine our interfoldedness with the experiences of people who seem distant from ourselves. Time periods, such as the ending of the trans-Atlantic slave trade in the early 1800s and the post–World War II era of the 1940s through 1960s, ushered in not only rapid political, social, and economic change but, significantly, a growth in human abilities for perception and cognition.[22] The decision to end the system of global enslavement of human beings was not merely economic but also ideological, reflecting a widespread sharing and incorporation of new ideas about inherent rights and liberties that emerged out of Enlightenment philosophies. Similarly, in the aftermath of the Holocaust a new, shared understanding developed about not only humans' capability to do bad things, but—importantly—the power of everyday people to either facilitate harms or intervene to stop them.

Academic disciplines have different ways of describing these societal windows of openness. Anthropologists use the term *liminality* to describe the ambiguous time in which a society is in the middle stage of a rite of passage. Participants in the rite find themselves at a threshold, where they no longer hold their previous status but they have not yet taken on a new cultural identity. In Sociology, a *tipping point* describes this type of moment at which a new belief, practice, or behavior is beginning to spread and take hold in society.[23] Historians use the term *conjuncture* to identify times when economic, political, and social factors coalesce so that once-settled norms and ideas become up for debate, new types of conversations take place, and previously defined categories become open to redefinition.[24] MacAskill calls these moments of "plasticity," marking a contrast to times when societal points of view were rigid or unchangeable.[25]

When we discuss who is enabling, fostering, or facilitating harm, we are looking at problems in a new way, and articulating a different vision of the self as situated within the space of the collective.[26] In these explorations there is a potential to become not only more aware of issues but to become *better* people; thinking through complex questions of accountability has the potential to expand our moral circles, growing the capacity for empathy and our understanding of one another.[27]

On a personal level, examining complicity can encourage powerful self-reflection. Literary theorist Michael Rothberg observes that, although we cling to the appealing narrative of good and evil, in reality, we are all "implicated subjects," meaning that we "are entangled in injustices ... where categories ... [of] innocent and guilty become troubled."[28] When we consider our own and others' potential part in fostering racism, sexism, global inequality, or climate change, we enter an uncomfortable—and often confusing place—where there is not always a clear demarcation between perpetrator and victim. Traditional civil and criminal justice models look backward, focusing on attributing guilt and punishment after the fact. When we evaluate our and others' complicity in structural harms, we are engaging in a more complex inquiry that looks backward—assessing accountability for inherited problems—but is also forward looking, thinking through responsibility for controlling and minimizing harm in the future.

Complicity is an important tool for reckoning with institutional harms and holding corporate, state, and institutional feet to the fire. It is the fear of being deemed complicit that prompted corporations such as Starbucks, McDonald's, and Coke to shutter retail operations in Russia after the 2022 invasion of Ukraine, and caused prestigious nonprofits like the Mayo Clinic and the Kennedy Center to return hundreds of millions in donations from Russian oligarchs. The specter of expanding liability beyond direct perpetration can prompt corporate and institutional settlements with grieving families in response to the opioid epidemic and in the wake of school shootings. Emerging understandings about interconnection can also inspire more prosocial acts from individuals and institutions. In 2022, governments entered into historic agreements on climate change that were based not on the threat of punishment but the realization of a shared and interdependent future.

The book engages a large body of discourse—news and popular media, legal decisions, and academic scholarship from a broad range of disciplines—to explore, through the lens of complicity, the collision of the present with the past. The book points out complicity's utility— connecting the decisions we are making in the current time and place to harms across the globe, and considering what impact they might have on generations to come. The book also illustrates complicity's inutility—the ways in which a growing ambit of personal accountability can end up punishing not only direct perpetrators but those much less worthy of condemnation. A "hard" but essential word in the 1600s, complicity is again a keyword today.[29] The discussions we are having about aiding and abetting across a range of issues signal widespread renegotiation of the boundaries of culpability and accountability.

Much of the existing work on complicity centers on the Holocaust, and it would be impossible to discuss ideas of aiding and abetting without acknowledging the influence that the Holocaust and World War II continue to have on contemporary behaviors and conversations. Out of tragedy, a rich literature emerged analyzing the behavior of states, institutions, and ordinary citizens in the face of previously unimaginable atrocities. While recognizing a deep tradition of scholarship, this project does not draw direct comparisons between the challenges of present-day America and those confronted by European people and nations during the rise and fall of the Third Reich. Rather, the project engages Holocaust scholarship to explore how interrogating complicity may—and may not—lead to individual and social growth.

Also absent from this book is a direct exploration of complicity in the context of the January 6, 2021, insurrection and the allegations and investigations of collusion, conspiracy, and incitement that followed that event. Other scholarly analyses do more justice to discussing the Trump presidency and its ongoing effects on US society than this project could. Although this book does not engage the Trump presidency directly, it might be seen as in conversation with those that do, and the ideas offered herein are hopefully ones that can inspire discussion as we head into the political future.

The six chapters of *Beyond Complicity* explore the isolating and connective impacts of complicity in social and legal contexts.

The first two chapters examine complicity as an organizing principle as society reckons with contemporary issues and problems, including racism, addiction, sexual misconduct, and climate change. Engaging these problems as case studies, the chapters explore how accusations of complicity are a tool of public shaming, a means of distancing and exclusion. Notably, the term has no antonym; once a person has been accused as complicit, there is not a clear path to defending or extracting oneself. Contemporary society is marked by a tortured and tautological culture of accusation and apology.

Yet, these initial chapters also explore complicity as a means of relation, articulating newfound and complex connections between persons or entities and the world. In the wake of the Black Lives Matter and

#MeToo social movements, in the face of climate change, and in (hopefully the final stages of) the global pandemic, the prevalence of complicity as a keyword suggests that many people are making an effort to look beyond their own interests and are recognizing that even small actions can be connected to larger forces in the world.

Chapter 3 shifts to a discussion of legal complicity, beginning with the accomplice charges brought by the state of Minnesota against three former police officers who looked on or assisted principal perpetrator Derek Chauvin in the 2020 killing of George Floyd, an event that sparked a global reckoning with racial justice. Complicity in law shares many features with the social incarnation of the concept. Legal complicity can operate to make visible connections that were previously hidden and to articulate the connection between individual actions and greater harms. More frequently, however, accomplice liability is used to isolate and stigmatize, failing to hold power players accountable while harshly punishing low-level defendants for minor roles in harm creation.

Chapter 4 returns to the discussion of complicity in society, identifying that, although the accomplices convicted in criminal courts often are young, poor, and/or non-White, in this cultural moment in US society it is White women who have become the face of complicity.[30] In a time of rapidly changing social norms, the chapter argues that White women are liminal figures; in public conversations and debates, as a group, White women personify the border of perpetrator and victim, embodying the tensions between being a victim and perpetrator, a passive bystander and an active agent of oppression. The chapter explores the embodiment of complicity in three very visible White women: politician Hillary Clinton, talk show host Ellen DeGeneres, and, lastly, the fictional or referential "Karen," who rose to prominence in memes circulated during the pandemic era. While chapter 3 examines who we actually and legally hold accountable, chapter 4 explores what complicity looks like in the social imagination: Who do we *think* should be held accountable?

Chapter 5 dives more deeply into this moment of liminality, describing US society as at a tipping point, or threshold, in terms who bears accountability for addressing widespread problems of racial and ethnic discrimination and sexual misconduct. In the wake of the #MeToo and Black Lives Matter social movements, complicity is used to identify a growing range of parties and practices that have facilitated not only obvious but less tangible though no less toxic, harms. At the same time, movements toward reforms are meeting powerful intransigence by those in power.

Notably, the conjunctures in which society is open to new ideas do not last forever. The wall of resistance met by reform movements across contexts highlights the fragility of the complicity moment and suggests that the definitions of violence and injury, once expanding, are at risk of being narrowed to exempt state actors and focus on punishing individuals for the harms we do to one another. Whether we emerge from this time as better people—and as an improved society—depends not on just how hard we try to change the status quo—but on how vigorously and creatively those in power push back against us.

The final chapter of the book revisits one of the most powerful complicity narratives that shapes US society today, the myth of the heartless bystander. Using the 1964 murder of Kitty Genovese as a launching point, the chapter traces the emergence of the idea of the uncaring bystander and explores how this inaccurate and incomplete narrative continues to shape the ways in which we interact with one another. The chapter again emphasizes the shortcomings of complicity when it is used as a vehicle for imposing personal shame, and highlights its promise when it is engaged as a means of revealing interconnections among individuals, systems, and structures.

In the art of origami, unfolding complex creations reveals crease patterns. Some are deeply embedded, while others are reminders of paths considered but not taken. The hardest part is that, to discover these patterns, it is necessary to dismantle an existing structure. We have to make a commitment to destroy something we know, with which we have grown comfortable, in order to make something new. We have in our possession the tools not only dismantle but to rebuild. This book offers some gentle suggestions as to how we might move beyond the complicity moment toward forging new ways of interacting with the world—and one another.

ONE

Blood on Our Hands

Accomplices to Racism

At the height of the COVID-19 pandemic philosopher Hugh Breakey offered this hypothetical:

> [S]uppose there's a crowd at the bottom of a cliff. You and thousands of others are at the top, next to an unfortunately placed boulder. If enough of you push the boulder, the people at the bottom will die. You push the boulder. The crowd dies. Have you done wrong? Obviously you have ... Now, ... [s]uppose a boulder is already rolling towards the cliff edge, with the same crowd at the bottom. You sit on the sidelines drinking a martini, while others attempt to stop the boulder. You can't be sure if enough people are acting. Yet you just sit there and watch. Again, you've done wrong—even if they succeed [in stopping it].[1]

It is an example that might resonate, reflecting opinions we've harbored about the actions—or inaction—of neighbors, coworkers, family members, or friends over the past few years. In the wake of the pandemic and Black Lives Matter and #MeToo social movements, and with rising awareness about global inequality and climate change, many of us are revisiting the roles ourselves and others might have played in facilitating racism or sexism, harming the climate, or, however unintentionally, spreading disease. The scenario suggests that accomplices are everywhere, indifference to the fate of others rendering them morally suspect.

It is unlikely the martini drinker in this scenario would be legally guilty; they have not provided the assistance necessary under state and federal criminal laws. It doesn't seem like they have any connection to the victims that would create a legal duty to render aid. In the court of public opinion, however, the onlooker does seem morally corrupt—they have done wrong even if, ultimately, the worst outcome was avoided.

If the observer should have acted to avert disaster, though, what, precisely, should they have done? Our expectation depends on their position and capabilities and our own. There is a lot we don't know. Was the person elderly? Did they have a broken leg? Were they already half in the bag because happy hour started an hour before? Did they have to throw themselves in front of the boulder, or would it be enough to lethargically have begun to rise just as others diverted the rock? What if the person tweeted for others to come to help, or did a TikTok dance to draw attention to the impending tragedy? Was one person's intervention really necessary, we might ask, if others were already helping to diffuse the crisis?

Notably, the observer in the example doesn't seem like a *good* person. They are indifferent to the fate of the people at the bottom of the cliff. They neglect to intervene because they are drinking a martini, not because they are exhausted from working a long shift or distracted by concern for a troubled friend. But, in the end, the harm did not happen. No injury came to the people in the crevasse. It is unclear whether the martini-drinker's silence made any difference at all.

Yet, we might condemn the onlooker anyway. What kind of person would order a cocktail during a catastrophe, we wonder, and what will they do (or not do) when the next hazard emerges? The hypothetical captures the extent to which, today, even ordinary behaviors can be heroic or villainous. During the pandemic, teachers, grocery clerks, and bus drivers became "heroes" on the "front lines" of the war against disease.[2] Advertisers cheekily referred to people who stayed home as "couchpatriots."[3] Those who defied stay-at-home orders to visit family members or eat in restaurants were derided as "quarancheaters."[4] One of the most significant takeaways from the COVID-19 pandemic was that every choice we made—to wear a mask or not, to send a child to school or keep them home, to visit the grocery store or have food delivered—was fraught with consequences not only for ourselves, but for the broader world.

This reflection on human connectedness has been front and center as US society comes to terms with centuries of racism—not only overtly racist beliefs, practices, and behaviors, but less obvious biases inherent in systems and structures, laws, and policies.

On May 25, 2020, George Floyd, a Black forty-six-year-old father of five, was killed after police responded to a call from a teenage convenience store employee reporting that Floyd had used a counterfeit $20 bill to purchase a pack of cigarettes, a minor infraction that ended in an overwhelming display of state violence.[5] What transpired was not uncommon. Similar incidences of police using unwarranted force against unarmed persons, who were often Black or poor, played out over and over again in cities throughout the United States. Typically, the public response to news of an event like this was resignation—the officer was out of line, someone might say, but what could an average person do in the face of widespread and routinized practices of state violence and doctrines like qualified immunity which protect perpetrators from accountability?

In 2020, however, something was shifting. Rather than resignation, the news of Floyd's death inspired protests, and hundreds of thousands of people from all walks of life took to the streets to advocate for justice and reform. For a change, scrutiny did not fall on the victim, but on Derek Chauvin and his fellow law enforcement officers. Society asked new questions: *Why did the police department promote employees who were known to be violent? How did the system allow and enable practices like chokeholds that posed a grave danger to suspects? Should Minneapolis residents have called the police in response to a minor offense?*

The social movement that erupted in 2020 was not only the largest sustained civil rights protest in modern history, but the most geographically expansive and intersectional one, drawing activists from cities and suburbs, and across race, gender, and sexual orientation.[6] This rapid, cohesive mobilization suggested that we were at a conjuncture where traditional conceptions about individual and institutional accountability for the risk of crime were being questioned and challenged.

The discussions about racism taking place today suggest that US society is at a liminal, or tipping point when the definition of racism and the types of behaviors we consider racist are changing. Linguist John McWhorter highlights that the term, once used to describe overt animus, now is understood to encompass acts that are covert, unconscious, and even unintentional, such as thoughtlessly participating in the manufacture of products that enable police brutality, or voting, unquestioningly, for a candidate whose platform bolsters global systems of inequality.[7] The expanding parameters around the definition of racism and adjacent terms like privilege and white supremacy make clear the extent to which our collective understanding of injury and violence has been growing to include a broadening array of not only physical but emotional, psychological, and systemic harms.

In conversations about racism, complicity is a double-edged sword. Allegations of complicity make visible previously hidden connections between behind-the-scenes behaviors and overt harms. They are a means of describing a connection to the larger world, inspiring conversation and debate as to whether and how a person or entity is or should be accountable for causing injury to others.

But labeling a person complicit also can be a means of shaming, a public calling to account for not only actions or speech that are deliberate, but sometimes those that are unintended. Interpersonal finger-pointing has the potential to foreclose conversation rather than inspire it. It can undercut social and emotional growth, condemning and dehumanizing others causing us to become less empathetic and our moral circles to shrink.[8] This push and pull between the structural and the interpersonal has been on display as racism has come to the forefront in public conversations.

INDIVIDUAL ACTIONS, STRUCTURAL HARMS

In summer 2020, in the midst of Black Lives Matter protests, workers at the Ford Corporation sent a letter to the company's chief executive officer. The petition urged the company to stop making vehicles that were "used as accessories to police brutality and oppression."[9] In the letter, employees acknowledged not only the corporation's but their own roles in perpetuating racism, noting, "As an undeniable part of that history and system, we are long overdue to 'think and act differently.'"[10]

Ford was not an outlier. Higher-ups at Trek and Fuji Bicycles received similar pleas calling for divestment from law enforcement, which used bicycles in tactical violence maneuvers against protesters.[11] The focus was not only on individual incidents, but on how "the bike industry on a whole [was] complicit in th[e] racist system of policing," playing "a major part in supporting and upholding violence, oppression."[12] Tech industry workers, too, reflected on their roles in facilitating a range of hazards from disinformation to climate change, signaling a recognition that, rather than neutral tools, streaming services, platforms, and apps are mechanisms that privilege, promote, and amplify particular points of view.[13] Across industries, employees have been revisiting how everyday workers might be perpetuating what Alec Karakatsanis calls "usual cruelties," performing ordinary tasks that all along were contributing to larger social harms.[14]

Employee petitions and protests were among many actions to emerge as the Black Lives Matter movement gained traction in US society. The protests and the pandemic ushered in a phenomenon that economists label The Great Resignation, as more than 4 million Americans left the labor force. While pandemic-related factors such as illness, mental health concerns, and increased caregiving responsibilities were drivers of change, employees also describe leaving jobs based on a sense of moral injury, experiencing a trauma response after years of participating in harm-inflicting organizational cultures.[15]

The changes taking place in the employment sector signal that our collective synapses have been charged so that we are making connections between individual behavior and systemic practices. Bestselling memoirs across industries—finance, entertainment, law—are challenging the "lean in" model popularized by former Facebook chief operating officer Sheryl Sandberg and urging instead that individuals pause and reflect on the role our everyday actions might play in causing harm to others. Employees are recognizing that they can no longer take refuge in compliance. Civil disobedience is not just the province of civil rights activists in Montgomery or Thoreau on Walden Pond but an obligation for all of us.

Nor can corporations themselves claim to be apolitical. In the aftermath of the police involved killing of George Floyd, the damaging of a Target store in Minneapolis became a visceral statement about the ways in which industry is implicated in racism, providing a warning to businesses that they would be held accountable by the public. As the Black Lives Matter movement gained traction, sports teams eschewed racist mascots and logos. Food giant Quaker changed the name of what was formerly Aunt Jemima pancakes, dairy behemoth Land O'Lakes removed an indigenous woman from its advertising, and Mars, Inc. committed to change the Uncle Ben's rice brand. As political debate over diversity, equity, and inclusion have intensified, long-standing American brands like Disney and Budweiser have found themselves in the crossfire, with consumers demanding that the companies visibly pick a side in the so-called culture wars.

Concerns of complicity in racism have been particularly visible in discussions of the US criminal justice system, called to account for long-standing and deeply embedded practices that have disproportionately penalized communities of color. In 2020, protests to eliminate cash bail, reduce fines for low-level offenses, and reallocate funding to police departments highlighted a newly widespread recognition that everyday practices were contributing to surveillance and control of poor and non-White persons and communities.

In response to the groundswell of protests, numerous municipal governments reduced the budget amounts allocated to law enforcement and pledged to redistribute funds to social services. Legislatures weighed referenda eliminating cash bail and decriminalizing or reducing fines and fees for low-level offenses. Primary and secondary schools signed pledges to reduce law enforcement presence, and universities addressed proposals from faculty, staff, and students urging divestment from policing. The American Psychological Association, the professional body that represents all US psychologists, issued an apology for the organization's having been "complicit in contributing to systemic inequities, and [having] hurt many through racism, racial discrimination, and denigration of communities of color, thereby falling short on its mission to benefit society and improve lives."[16] Patterns of connection between institutions and society are evident in the UCLA Divestment Now petition, which describes, "As long as [the university] collaborates with ... police forces, it is *complicit in, and bears responsibility for,* police brutality and racialized state violence ... and will not be a credible home for research, teaching, and community engagement that promote racial justice."[17] These statements expose connections that hadn't before been articulated. They make clear an interfoldedness that was long-hidden or ignored.

EXCAVATING THE FOUNDATION

In 2016, Corey Menafee, a dishwasher at Yale University, broke a windowpane featuring a scene of enslavement.[18] The window had been in the dining hall of Calhoun College, where Menafee worked, for more than a century. The college was named for John C. Calhoun, a US vice president and ardent proponent of slavery. For more than one hundred years, students, staff, and faculty socialized in the shadow of that window, rarely acknowledging its presence, but—as we now understand—profoundly influenced by its imagery. Menafee justified his action with a pragmatic observation: "It's the 21st century, why do I have to go to work and look at this?"[19]

The university's initial response to Menafee's action was not affirming. The employee was arrested and charged with a felony, and his act categorized as vandalism. Yale agreed to drop the criminal charges, but only after Menafee resigned and apologized.[20] The institution insisted that Menafee sign a nondisclosure agreement, silencing his ability to speak publicly about the incident.[21]

Less than ten years later, the institution's response, and particularly the demand that Menafee apologize for and not speak about his gesture of defiance, seems unfathomable. After the protests of summer 2020, universities including Yale rushed to rename buildings to reflect anti-racist ideals. Yale not only apologized to Menafee, but announced the renaming of Calhoun College to honor female mathematician Grace Murray Hopper.[22] In the space of just four years, the university reclassified the employee's behavior from a crime to civil disobedience, and the offensive windowpane became one of hundreds of monuments to white supremacy that were being removed, demolished, and reimagined across state and municipal buildings and university campuses nationwide.

Renaming, by no means a simple process, is the easy part. The dismantling of monuments is the visible edge of a web of complicity by institutions which have participated in centuries of reputation laundering for morally suspect donors, repurposing ill-gotten gains into support for education, the arts, or scholarships for less economically privileged students. Reputation laundering highlights an important quality of complicity—it's sneaky. It is this behind-the-scenes nature that makes us fear that the complicit may be especially resistant to reform.

Allocating institutional accountability for racism raises challenges. There is the specter of mixed motives: *Is it possible to turn bad money to good?* Allegations of upholding white supremacy have put religious institutions, museums, and universities, many of which operate on shoe-string budgets, in a position where they are being asked to return funds to and sever ties with "tainted" donors. These questions are tricky when the donor is problematic—for example, when a contributor to a nonprofit is later convicted of a crime. When the money itself is impure, stemming from centuries of donations from racists, sexists, or climate deniers, questions of complicity are even more complex. Issues of corrupt donations are not new; in the early 1900s, the Congregationalist church debated whether to accept donations from magnate John D. Rockefeller, due to the questionable business practices of Standard Oil.[23] Spoiler: they did.

Recognizing the complicity of institutions, governments, and states in fostering oppression is a vital step forward for anti-racism, but it is replete with challenges. As law enforcement reforms gained traction, opponents capitalized on fear, misrepresenting the defund movement as a call to eliminate all public safety measures. After a wave of policy changes throughout 2020, bills and referenda have stalled, and some law and order candidates have supplanted more progressive ones. When in 2021 violent crime rose in major cities, President Biden—never a fan of the defund movement—enthusiastically rolled out the Safer America Plan, the primary goals of which are to hire more law enforcement officers and invest in crime prevention.[24]

In chapter 5, this book discusses debates that have erupted around critical race theory, or CRT, which are impacting the ways in which elementary, secondary, and college courses are taught nationwide. In 2020, President Trump issued Executive Order 13950 (revoked by President Biden immediately upon his swearing in), which outlawed federal agencies from teaching "divisive concepts," including that "an individual, by virtue of his or her race or sex, bears responsibility for actions committed in the past by other members of the same race or sex."[25] As of fall 2023, more than six hundred bills proposing a ban on teaching CRT in K-12 schools had been put forth across forty-nine states.[26] Many of these bills parroted the language in President Trump's executive order, and a third of them included provisions for withholding federal funds from schools that failed to comply.[27] The governors of Texas and Florida went further, defunding offices dedicated to diversity, equity, and inclusion (DEI) at public universities, on the basis that DEI policies were discriminatory and divisive.

Debates over CRT manifest a widespread and often angry resistance to excavating the nation's history of bias and discrimination, highlighting that the investigation into complicity is a political project.[28] It is a venture which raises questions about what the "true" story of the past is, who is authorized to tell it, and who will be responsible for interpreting its meaning going forward.

Pragmatically, the slowing of anti-racist progress after the eruption of protests in 2020 demonstrates that reforms are easier to institute when demand for a product is high and social pressure is amplified. It is hard to believe that higher-ups at Quaker didn't know for decades that Aunt Jemima pancakes relied on a racist stereotype, or that NASCAR was unaware of the message it was sending by flying a confederate flag at races. The changes that have taken place across corporate America since 2020 are profit-driven. Having white supremacy out in the open is not a good look.

While the anti-racist changes being made by corporations say something positive about public accountability, recent data suggest that change may slow or stop when public pressure subsides and the bottom line is no longer threatened. The reality is stark. In 2020, corporations pledged nearly $70 billion toward anti-racist efforts. As of 2022, less that 1 percent of those funds ($650 million) had been disbursed.[29] Due to a combination of conservative political pressure and cost-cutting measures, in 2023 companies including Amazon, Apple, and Twitter slashed positions dedicated to DEI by more than a third.[30] Starbucks and Walmart, which had expanded their businesses into underserved neighborhoods as a part of strategies to advance racial equity, shuttered stores due in part to safety concerns.[31]

Given the challenges to implementing structural reforms, it is not surprising that many discussions of complicity in racism focus less on fixing problems with institutions or systems and more on calling out individuals, identifying how personal acts and choices may be contributing to harms against persons of color. Some of these conversations are productive, suggesting a rethinking of connections between people and the world. Others, though, highlight complicity's potential for shaming and stigmatizing.

COMPLICITY AS CONNECTION . . . AND DISCONNECTION

Today, many—perhaps most—of our day-to-day conversations take place on social media, where it has become a common practice to call out strangers' bad behavior in videos and memes. Rather than being a passive activity for users, scrolling through and interacting with memes, tweets, and videos creates an opportunity to actively participate in making sense of events and in developing a collective, shared understanding about them. As we consume social media, we reflect on whether behaviors by others reflect positive or negative social norms, and question how representations may or may not reflect our own opinions or behavior. Art historian Mette Mortensen describes this practice as "connective witnessing."[32] Instead of passive observers, when people interact with events on social media, such as commenting on or sharing a video or meme, they are engaging in a "participatory act" during which the witnessing becomes a part of the event itself.[33]

In debating, revisiting, and reconstructing an event or incident, we can change the meaning of the event itself. In recent years, a significant subcategory of the memes and videos shared on forums like Reddit, Instagram, or TikTok has been devoted to critiquing people—often, but not always, White women—who complain to law enforcement about non-White persons engaging in everyday activities, such as barbecuing in a public park, holding a stoop sale, or taking a nap in a university common room. When the actions of alleged racists go viral, hashtags are used to sort the perpetrators into categories, eschewing legal names in favor of labels like "BBQ Becky" or "Permit Patty." In 2020, "Karen" (who is discussed in chapter 4 of this book) became a catchall to describe individuals whose racist or otherwise problematic choices are contributing to systemic and structural harms.

The rampant circulation of videos of Karens, Permit Patties, and BBQ Beckies across social media suggests the collective reckoning that has been taking place in regard to complicity in racism. While the subject of a shared video or meme might be a direct perpetrator, when videos of bad actors go viral, eventually what the offender actually did becomes less relevant than how their actions contributed to bigger, systemic problems.

In May 2020, a video circulated showing a White woman, Amy Cooper, calling 911 to report a fellow visitor in Central Park, a Black male, Christian Cooper (no relation), for allegedly threatening her. In contacts with the police, Amy Cooper repeatedly stated that Christian Cooper was African American and complained, falsely, that Cooper was assaulting her. The widespread online sharing of a video filmed by Christian Cooper during the incident provided an opportunity for connective witnessing. As consumers viewed and commented on the video, conversations focused less on the facts of the event itself and more on the patterns of privilege and oppression that the video revealed, patterns that until that moment had been starkly apparent to Black Americans but were not usually visible to (or perhaps, more accurately, not usually acknowledged by) people who did not face racial discrimination in their daily lives. A blogger described a commitment that many people were making to change their own behaviors: "[T]o say nothing, to do nothing, in the face of these injustices, then we are complicit in this moment of racism, bias and brutality. I will not be [Amy Cooper] ... I will speak out to condemn their behavior and I will call it by its name: racism."[34]

While some people who viewed the viral video were inspired to engage in self-reflection, others put energy into calling Amy Cooper out for her transgression. Commenters lobbied for Cooper, nicknamed the Central Park Karen, to face criminal charges ranging from a misdemeanor to a violent felony like assault or attempted murder, based on the "weaponization" of privilege.[35] Others made death threats against her. The vitriol Amy Cooper faced in the court of public opinion caused Christian Cooper to decide not to cooperate with prosecuting her for the false 911 call: "[S]he's already paid a steep price," Cooper explained, "Bringing her more misery just seems like piling on."[36]

The rapid and widespread public condemnation of Amy Cooper reflects a societal transition from a guilt culture, in which punishments are enacted to encourage people to come to a self-realization about the harm they have done, to a shame culture, where moral education is imposed by a group via ostracism and exclusion. For some the imposition of shame is viewed as necessary and constructive. Cultural critic Touré identifies the connective aspects of complicity in the public shaming of Amy Cooper. He describes the power of the viral video to cause White persons viewing it to "cringe at what their ancestors did ... [and to] understand that modern white power is directly related to those atrocities."[37] It is only when we understand ourselves as flawed that we can change. If a member of a society fails to understand contemporary norms of right and wrong, it can be proper for others to respond to correct them. While "guilt can make a person change one action or habit, shame may push us toward changing our entire outlook on the world."[38] While Christian Cooper resolved not to participate in Amy Cooper's prosecution, his sister Melody felt differently. Drawing a connection between Cooper's 911 call and the 1955 lynching of Emmett Till for allegedly whistling at a White woman in a convenience store, Melody Cooper described, "If there's a chance to send a message to other white women that they can't and shouldn't put Black people at risk in this way, it should be done."[39]

While the shaming taking place on social media has many troubling aspects, if the goal is social growth, it may be necessary—and even healthy—for individuals or communities to be made unsettled or uncomfortable in order to create the conditions where learning can thrive. A primary reason parents and legislators give for banning books, restricting teaching CRT in elementary schools, and dismantling university DEI offices is that issues may be raised that are divisive or unsettling, but it is only when humans are uncomfortable—when we are able to share our ideas and to make mistakes—that learning can occur. Shaming can serve a deterrent function. It also can serve an important symbolic purpose, signaling that, as a society, some beliefs or actions are clearly out of step with current norms.

The calling out of racist behaviors on social media is an indication that, on the whole, we are coming to appreciate a wider range of injuries—from emotional damage to inter-generational trauma to micro-aggressions—that are resulting from forms of violence that previously were invisible in most social discourse. Some of the enforcement regimes that have sprung up may seem unduly punitive or severe, but this lack of proportionality might be seen as a temporary but necessary side effect of moral growth. Over-enforcement is preferable, one might argue, to under-recognition.

There is a pragmatic question, however, as to whether shaming is useful, particularly when it is a mechanism for assigning accountability for the types of risks we confront today—racism, sexism, addiction, climate change—where one person or entity can't be said to have caused the problem, and where there is no solution that is easy or quick. When a court imposes a shaming punishment, such as mandating that a defendant post a public apology online, or stand on a street corner wearing a sign stating, "I stole," it might deter a petty thief from taking another wallet. It is much harder to pinpoint the reformative impacts on a person—or the net positive gain to the world—when a Karen loses their job after having been castigated on social media, or an applicant is denied access to higher education after having shared racist song lyrics in their youth. In such cases it is sometimes unclear whether the object of punishment knew (in a legal or moral sense) that their actions were wrong when they did them. Because it is imposed from outside rather than stemming from self-realization, shame is as likely to result in feelings of indignancy or rage as it is in a desire for reform. It remains unclear whether the objects of public scorn in fact learned a lesson—or if the lesson they learned was the one the shamers intended.

Although the courts purport to be insulated from public opinion, legal and extralegal punishments increasingly intersect. After the Central Park incident, the San Francisco Board of Supervisors introduced the CAREN (Caution Against Racially Exploitative Non-Emergencies) Act, proposing enhanced penalties for fabricating racially biased emergency reports.[40] Other state legislatures drafted bills that criminalized or strengthened charges for filing false or discriminatory police reports. The bevvy of ordinances highlights that a common response to violence today is to advocate for expanding the carceral system. Demands to extend the parameters of legal accountability, however, can suffer from the same problems as a racist 911 call itself, growing the very system Amy Cooper tried to exploit, a system that is set up to unfairly impact the most vulnerable.

Nonetheless we might think—*so what?* Like the martini drinker described at the start of the chapter, many of the people who face criticism online often seem to have it coming. Americans love *schadenfreude*—in German, literally, harmjoy—the smug feeling of amusement we get when others get what's coming to them. This is the feeling shared by many when they have a collective chuckle at the expense of another Karen, or by a million Reddit subscribers when they upvote posts like "Pro war Russian learns he's being conscripted" and "Book ban backfire: Texas school district forced to pull the Bible."

The delight that human beings take in others' comeuppance suggests the less productive side of complicity, which begs questions of what type of punishment is appropriate and how much is enough. Formal legal responses at least theoretically are constrained by principles that the punishment must be proportional to the crime, and that penalties should further goals of deterrence or rehabilitation. There are fewer limits on extralegal punishment; almost no constitutional boundaries circumscribe the retributive effects a person can suffer after a video about them is consumed by millions. Concerns about what adrienne maree brown calls the "destructive power of punitive justice" have led to a more recent movement toward "calling in" versus calling out, encouraging bringing attention to bad behavior through smaller, one-on-one conversations that begin with a conversation with the alleged transgressor, rather than shaming them across social media.[41] These approaches recognize that promoting anti-racist ideals via ostracism and shaming may not be the best way forward and, in fact, can inhibit both individual reckoning and societal repair.

THE OSTRICH PROBLEM

While allegations of complicity against individuals can have connective effects, they have some troubling shortcomings. A big one is that allegations of complicity are waged not just against those who have done intentional acts, but those who act without purpose or knowledge. Today it is not only tangible, racist actions that are being called out, but much less obvious behaviors that are identified as strengthening the sinews that form the corpus of racism.

In criminal courts, judges sometimes give juries something called an ostrich instruction. It means that defendants are not allowed to put their heads in the sand or to close their eyes to a high probability that something nefarious is afoot. While ostrich instructions are used sparingly in the law, the public has much less tolerance for ignorance.

As Black Lives Matter protests erupted in the summer of 2020, activists urged social media users to post content in support of the movement. Influencers faced backlash for posting off-topic posts.[42] Others stepped in hot water by posting links to less-than-supportive resources or engaging hashtags that drew attention away from protests. One example was Natasha Fischer, whose Instagram until June 2020 was devoted entirely to shopping at Trader Joe's and posting photos of merchandise she purchased. Fischer was criticized by subscribers for not posting anti-racist content on her account, and then drew even more ire when, accompanying a post containing links to anti-racist resources, she mistakenly used the conservative hashtag All Lives Matter.[43] Fischer insisted that she supported the ideals of Black Lives Matter but posted hastily because she felt pressured to do so: "I was scared. I didn't know what I did but I saw thousands of comments."[44]

The internet is glutted with celebrity apologies for similarly unwitting blunders. When actors Blake Lively and Ryan Reynolds were called out for having held their 2012 wedding at a South Carolina plantation, they issued a tortured statement describing feeling shame that "in the past" they "allowed [them]selves to be uninformed about how deeply rooted systemic racism is."[45] Other White celebrities rushed to, as Kristen Bell put it, "acknowledge acts of complicity" for having played or voiced non-White or LGBTQ+ characters, decisions that the stars insisted were not intentional acts of racism but what Bell described as a "lack of awareness of . . . pervasive privilege."[46]

Tortured celebrity apologies, like the ostrich instruction itself, suggest that there are different ways of knowing. As psychologists Jennifer Freyd and Pamela Birrell describe, "[W]e can know [things] internally and on the level of sensation or behavior, or we can know them at the level of words."[47] Complicity assumes that each of us has an interior moral compass that can and should be activated to sense bias or discrimination, even when it has not been pointed out to us. We expect human beings to rely on an intrinsic sense of justness, even in the face of opposing social conventions. This sounds good in theory, but in practice it is not the reality. Human beings are constrained by our "bounded awareness"—our perceptions are rooted in our life experiences.[48]

The legion of rushed or canned apologies by celebrities and influencers in the face of accusations of complicity in racism raise an important question about moral accountability: *How much need a person have known then to warrant an apology now?* There is also a problem: the more apologies there are, they less we believe them.[49] When wrongdoing has occurred, behavioral norms demand that the wrongdoer seek forgiveness, yet, in a culture glutted with apologies, we, understandably, doubt their sincerity. The cycle of apology becomes tautological—the more apologies we demand and receive, the fewer of them we believe and the less likely we are to forgive. Our collective skepticism is evidenced by tools like the "celebrity apology generator" a website where one can go to create their own torturous, yet inadequate, statement of remorse.[50]

Once a person is labeled complicit, the road to reform is less than clear. A traditional liability model of punishment would mete out culpability proportional to the level of harm caused by the perpetrator. Once the offender served their sentence or paid their fine, and, ideally, arrived at a place where they were adequately remorseful, they would be deemed to have fulfilled their debt to society. Racism, however, is by no means a completed and contained harm. It is an ongoing one. Imposing a forward-looking model of liability is much more complicated. Tracing patterns of complicity is an effective means of uncovering past wrongdoing, but it does not provide a mechanism for rehabilitation, or a path forward for the accused to extract themselves from the web of accountability in the future.

It is not yet clear whether the cancelled can be rehabilitated. The year 2020 marked a record in the rescinding of college admissions, after universities' review of admitted students' social media accounts revealed that numerous applicants had used racist slurs or posted racist content on social media as teens.[51] The collective will tended in favor of rough justice, identifying college admission as a reward rightfully withheld from those whose actions fostered structural harms. The *New York Times* interviewed a high school student whose athletic scholarship was revoked based on a video of the student singing a song that included a racial slur. By the time she graduated from high school, the offending student had taken down the video, but a screen capture from years prior went viral, causing the university to take action. The person who shared the video expressed satisfaction in teaching his colleague a "lesson."[52] But the lessons being learned through processes of extralegal sanctioning are up for debate. If the primary purpose of college is to educate, what interests are being served by withholding education from those who clearly need it most?

An interesting case is the rescinding of the Harvard admission of Kyle Kashuv, a pro-Trump gun-rights activist and survivor of the 2018 mass shooting at Marjorie Stoneman Douglas High School in Parkland,

Florida. After screen shots circulated documenting Kashuv using racial slurs on social media, the university revoked his admission. Kashuv countered that the screen shots, which were two years old and captured conversations that occurred before the shooting, had been circulated by peers who disagreed with his political views. His apology highlights the complexities of complicity in racism:

> I want to be clear that the comments I made are not indicative of who I am or who I've become in the years since [the shooting].... Harvard deciding that someone can't grow, especially after a life-altering event like the shooting, is deeply concerning. If any institution should understand growth, it's Harvard, which is looked to as the pinnacle of higher education despite its checkered past.... Throughout its history, Harvard's faculty has included slave owners, segregationists, bigots and anti-Semites. If Harvard is suggesting that growth isn't possible and that our past defines our future, then Harvard is an inherently racist institution. But I don't believe that. I believe that institutions and people can grow.[53]

Is Harvard making a move toward righting long-standing wrongs by failing to admit prospective students like Kashuv, who have engaged in racist behaviors? Or is the rescinding of admissions by universities merely a performative gesture that, by displacing blame onto individuals, masks perhaps more insidious, ongoing structural oppressions? As a society, we have yet to answer these questions.

QUIET COMPLICITY

If issues of implication and redemption are difficult to address when a bad act goes viral on social media, they are even more complex when a person is condemned not for an action but a lack of action. In the early 1980s, as the AIDS crisis was decimating the gay community, activists searched for a slogan that would inspire people, the majority of whom were homophobic, to support research efforts on the disease. They settled on a straightforward image, the pink triangle, which had been used to identify homosexual men during the Holocaust. To accompany the illustration they chose an equally stark and striking slogan: SILENCE = DEATH.[54] An activist describes the rallying cry: "We talked about the deadly effects of passivity in crises, communal silence and the nature of political silencing, silence as complicity, and scenarios where bystanders became participants without intending to be."[55]

Today, it is widely accepted that to be silent in the face of oppression is to be complicit, but this was not always the case. Ethicist Victoria Barnett identifies the idea of the active bystander as an outgrowth of Holocaust research that took place in the 1960s and '70s. In the immediate aftermath of World War II, many researchers ignored the roles of citizens of Germany and nearby nations in genocide, assuming that ordinary people were merely following orders of the state.[56] As scholars and allied officials sifted through copious records, however, they began to identify, and then categorize, levels of collaboration by ordinary citizens. By the mid-1960s, researchers began to see witnesses to the war in a way that granted everyday people more agency, and to explore how patterns of behavior by neighbors and coworkers might actively have aided and abetted the crisis.

Over the past half century the idea of bystander accountability has become embedded in the social imagination through the circulation of narratives, like those surrounding the 1964 murder of Kitty Genovese, and the publication of numerous psychological and sociological research studies on witness behavior. There is a widespread belief that to be silent in the face of oppression is to do wrong. President Biden is especially fond of proclaiming that "silence is complicity," engaging the idea in speeches on topics including sexual assault, police-involved violence, COVID-19, anti-Semitism, and support for Donald Trump.[57]

With critiques of silence has come a growing understanding that even being nice or kind can facilitate racism. In *White Fragility*, an anti-racist book that flew off the shelves in 2020, author Robin DiAngelo observes, "There is no neutral place."[58] "Nice, white people who really aren't doing anything other than being nice people are racist. We are complicit with that system."[59] If a person obliges the wrong people, it can signal, if not malintent, then a dangerous obliviousness to the world around them.

As links between what once seemed like innocuous actions and structural harms were coming into stark relief, sales of books like DiAngelo's and Ibram X. Kendi's *How to Be an Anti-Racist* increased exponentially. People whose privilege or position had insulated them from experiencing racial discrimination rushed to understand the many ways they might have supported racist systems. Book clubs dedicated themselves to learning about slavery and redlining. Communities pledged not to bolster inequality by calling 911 for nonviolent offenses. Parent-teacher organizations created plans for wealth redistribution to lower-income school districts. Parents eschewed reading formerly "classic" children's books such as Laura Ingalls Wilder's *Little House on the Prairie* and Dr. Seuss's *And to Think That I Saw It on Mulberry Street*, which contained stereotypical images of persons of color. Many vowed to no longer watch films that contained caricatures or glorified subordination.

As they took stock of their own behavior, many people—most visibly middle- and upper-class White people—began to recognize that ostrich-like actions, even a general lack of interest in how everyday practices contributed to structural harms, could be *toxic*. What seemed like ordinary habits and activities had in fact been manifestations of usual cruelties, seemingly ordinary acts that all along had been instruments of violence. One can see the spatial dynamics of complicity at work in these awakenings. Moral circles were expanding, and we were laying the groundwork for a new vision of the person vis-à-vis the world. The popularity of the term toxic suggests that how we conceptualize the problem of racism has been changing, transforming from an injury that is inflicted from individual to individual into a large scale, public-health crisis, akin to cancer, a nuclear meltdown, or a chemical spill.

SIDE EFFECTS

As with many diseases, attempts to remedy issues of bias and discrimination have created their own problems. The flood of people intent on examining their own complicity and that of others, and the eagerness of those with newfound awareness to step up and speak out, has ushered in new concerns. As society attempts to reckon with structural racism, there is the problem of parachuters, people who jump from one social issue to the next, and confessional allies, who advertise their support of social causes at every opportunity. In June 2020 a group of music artists launched Blackout Tuesday, encouraging social media users to post a black square in lieu of a photo on Facebook and Instagram in solidarity with Black Lives Matter protests. Activists quickly criticized the initiative, pointing out that, rather than helpful resources, individuals clicking on #BLM were being directed to a sea of blank screens.[60] The Blackout Tuesday snafu highlights that members of relatively privileged groups have the tendency to speak *for* less politically powerful groups rather than doing the harder work to create environments in which historically underrepresented voices can be amplified.

As social movements like #MeToo and Black Lives Matter gained steam, activists adopted the language of the previous civil rights era, including the term *woke,* initially engaged by Black Americans as a warning to others to stay vigilant in the face of racist threats.[61] As the term became popular among White allies, woke morphed into a catchall description for generally progressive attitudes, sometimes suggesting a blindness to actual lived experiences of racism. By 2023 conservative politicians adopted woke as a dog whistle, using terms like "woke mob" to signal a threat to "traditional" American values, vaguely and broadly defined. A co-option also happened with the term Karen, first used in African American circles to refer to racist behavior by a particular type of White woman, and eventually used by White people to distance themselves from, and disclaim responsibility for, the bad behavior of other White people.[62]

CONCLUSION

On one hand, contemporary conversations about racism reveal a troubling love of schadenfreude. On the other hand, however, they suggest that thinking through complicity does have the potential to provide a pathway for holding not only individuals but institutions to account for creating and supporting unjust systems. Networks of structural injustice are being made visible, as not only individuals but corporate, state, and institutional actors are called to account for the roles their actions and inaction may have played in facilitating racism.

These conversations are not unique but are the product of a complicity moment, in which similar discussions are taking place across a multiplicity of other issues—sexual assault and harassment, addiction, and climate change. Contentious debates about all of these issues both highlight the significance of complicity as a tool for bringing attention to previously unseen connections and, at the same time, the difficulty of envisioning a path forward beyond complicity toward social change.

TWO

Enabling, Laundering, Greenwashing

Complicity in Addiction, Sexual Misconduct, and Climate Change

Complicity is at the forefront not only in conversations about racism but myriad other social issues and problems. There seems to be no realm of public or private interaction today that is free from allegations that some person or entity has aided and abetted the creation of harm. Individuals and institutions are being called out for not just intentional acts but less visible practices that, although once assumed to be benign, are being identified as contributing to structural or systemic violence.

This chapter continues the discussion of complicity that began in chapter 1 by engaging three more conversations in which questions of accountability are front and center: addiction, sexual misconduct, and climate change. Each case study showcases complicity's contradictions. There are examples of complicity's productive and connective potential, as a broad range of people and entities are being brought to account for illegal or immoral actions or behaviors that were previously ignored or obscured. At the same time, however, the case studies in this chapter show the worst of human nature—how quick we are to rush to judgment, to assign blame for accidental or unwitting behaviors, or to perceive indifference in the face of crises. As we judge ourselves and each other, we don't tend to give much grace.

Significantly, however, the examples in this chapter suggest that the complicity moment is not just about assigning blame. It signals a growth in our capacity for identifying and understanding injury, and a broadening of empathy for other people whose life experiences are very different from our own. Debates about addiction, sexual misconduct, and climate change are contentious, but they suggest that US society is in a unique space where we are not only able to recognize past harms, but we are negotiating the parameters of a less toxic future. Complicity is fueling an expansion in creativity in terms of theories of social and legal accountability, providing a mechanism for holding institutions and governments responsible for past wrongs, and inspiring future repair in revolutionary ways.

ENABLERS: AIDERS AND ABETTORS IN THE OPIOID EPIDEMIC

In the late 1990s the Sackler family was on top of the world. The family had amassed a $13 billion fortune via the company they owned, Purdue Pharma. The company's new drug, an opioid pain reliever called Oxy-Contin, was taking off, with sales of nearly $1 billion every year.[1] The family were darlings of social circles, and they were prolific philanthropists. A person could not go to a museum, theater, or art gallery without seeing the Sackler name.

In the early 2000s, the family's fate took a sharp turn. One of Purdue Pharma's greatest accomplishments was developing and marketing a brand new drug, OxyContin. Based on the company's claims that the drug was not addictive, physicians prescribed it to patients not just for acute pain, but as an analgesic for ordinary ailments—back pain, sore muscles. The combination of Oxy's addictive nature and sales of the drug to healthy people facilitated the rapid development of a black market, as patients sought out Oxy, and doctors began to refuse to refill prescriptions for minor complaints. Despite mounting evidence to the contrary, the company doubled down on its claim that the drug was not addictive.[2] By 2004 more than 3 million Americans were taking Oxy for lifetime non-medical use.[3] Although the drug is now off the market, the demand for synthetic painkillers only has grown. During COVID-19, another quieter epidemic waged in the form of drug overdose deaths, which, fueled by social isolation and disruption to treatment and outreach programs, rose to an all-time high.[4]

As US society confronts what has become an overwhelming hazard of addiction, we are asking what roles individuals and institutions may have played in facilitating the crisis. Accusations land squarely on the Sackler family. In 2020, Purdue Pharma, which filed for bankruptcy in 2019, was fined more than $3 billion—the largest penalty ever against a pharmaceutical manufacturer—after pleading guilty to conspiring to defraud the United States.[5] Additionally, the company is party to a $6 billion settlement among eight states and the District of Columbia, which became a major point of contention in the bankruptcy court. The sticking point was the accountability of individual family members for their contributions to the opioid crisis. Although the Sacklers agreed to contribute personal holdings toward the settlement, they balked at being subjected to future lawsuits by victims or victims' families based on any role in enabling addiction.[6] Ultimately, in a ruling that incensed states' attorneys general, a New York appeals court ruled that members of the family could be shielded from future liability.[7] While the settlement provides that the family must allow any institution or organization in the United States to remove evidence of the Sacklers' financial support from buildings, scholarships, or programs, it also provides that publicity surrounding such removal must not "disparage" the family name.[8]

Artist Nan Goldin's characterization of the family highlights complicity's sneaky quality: "I'm sick of these people behind the scenes, controlling companies and getting away with murder while their faces are never shown."[9] Family members disagree, arguing that they are "scapegoats" being asked to account for a crisis that they might have helped along but did not create.[10] In the family's conception they are martini drinkers sitting at the ledge while the boulder rolls by. They did not create the addiction crisis, which they point out was overtaking the United States well before Oxy came to market, but instead sat back and watched, with no legal or moral duty to intervene as the addiction boulder rolled ever faster toward the ledge.[11]

In the wake of revelations about the addictive properties of Oxy-Contin, not only Sackler family members but a long string of aiders and abettors are being held accountable. Prescribing physicians are serving lengthy prison sentences. Distributors like Walmart and CVS are paying out millions failing to interrupt the flood of pills. Prestigious consulting firm McKinsey, which trumpets its consulting practice as value neutral, has entered into revolutionary multi-million-dollar settlements with states and local governments and school districts relating to the role the company's analyses played in "turbocharging" OxyContin sales.[12]

As with racism, allegations of complicity in fostering addiction are being levied against the reputation launderers, the institutions—prominent museums, hospitals, and universities—who endorsed the Sackler brand by accepting large donations from the family and showcasing their renowned art collection.[13] Demands that institutions return funds and disengage from problematic donors bring up the same question as arises in regard to donations from racists: *Is there an amount of restitution or remorse that is sufficient to remove a person or entity from the sphere of accountability?* They also raise deeper questions about what the moral obligation of institutions should be in the first place. An activist asks, "If museums don't stand for the basic value of human life what do they stand for?"[14] But do museums—or universities or religious institutions—in fact stand for human life, particularly when the body of their historical practices suggests the contrary? It was not until 1998, when museums signed on to the Washington Principles on Nazi-Confiscated Art, making the first formal commitment to returning art confiscated from Jewish families during the Holocaust. Survivors' families continue to bring lawsuits today seeking the return of stolen objects. Harvard and other universities have made efforts to publicize recent investigations into histories of engagement with slavery, making landmark commitments to reparations and repair. At the same time, however, critics point out that the university persists in offering a named fellowship associated with Alfried Krupp, a documented Nazi war criminal.[15]

While arguments about the accountability of family members and other entities and institutions for the crisis of addiction rage on, questions surface regarding the responsibility borne by the rest of us. Oxy may have been the engine, but now synthetic opioid use is so pervasive it has become an epidemic. Should we demand that institutions return "blood money" from pharmaceutical companies even if that money is being reoriented to support causes like clinics or research on treatments? Do we have a responsibility to protest big pharma even as companies create lifesaving drugs like the COVID-19 vaccines? What is each of us obligated to do, morally speaking, to avert more injuries and deaths?

The opioid crisis brings up profound questions about enabling. The Sacklers are egregiously bad actors, but they were not the only ones. What do we do about multinational pharmaceutical corporations, an industry that is rife with profiteering at the expense of the poor and disenfranchised? In the aftermath of COVID-19, pharmaceutical firms and their employees are heroized for their role in developing and distributing vaccines. A significant question remains, however, as to whether these new advancements can clean the hands of an industry tainted not only by the addiction crisis, but by ongoing egregious, profit-driven injustices. The COVID vaccine was the most lucrative medicine ever created, bringing in more than $37 billion in one year for drug manufacturer Pfizer. Despite astronomical profits, arguments over trade deals and intellectual property have resulted in widening inequities in the development and distribution of vaccines and are likely to slow socioeconomic recovery for decades.

Donations from the Sackler family are labyrinthine; they have not just supported tangible products like buildings and art exhibitions, but they undergird the development and application of laws, policies, and practices. While buildings can be renamed, it is impossible to measure the ongoing effects of the $19 million the family gave to the National Academies of Sciences, Engineering, and Medicine, an entity which helped craft the US government's response to the opioid crisis; or to measure how the family's web of influence impacted decision-making by the World Health Organization (WHO), which in 2019 retracted two key reports on opioids based on congressional findings that Purdue Pharma had infiltrated the WHO by creating and funding front organizations which allowed the company covertly to participate in setting the WHO's global healthcare agenda.[16]

Examining the opioid crisis not only provides insight into the insidious nature of complicity, but the discourse of addiction itself is foundational to discussions about aiding and abetting. When it comes to the drug and alcohol use, we are not only concerned with the addicted person themselves but with their *enablers*, any person who was in a position to intervene in—and thus should have stepped in to avert—the crisis. The meaning of the term enabler as we understand it now is relatively new. The present-day use of the term was not popularized until the early 1990s, at the same time as addiction was emerging as a social problem and a therapeutic field. In a 1991, "On Language," columnist William Safire identified *enabling* as a keyword, writing that "empowering" was out and "enabling" was in.[17] Safire described that thanks to the new therapeutic literature, the word had taken a turn from describing the promoting of positive goods to describing the facilitation of social ills.[18]

Today we tend to adopt a pessimistic view of enablers. Therapists and counselors provide advice about how to recognize and stop enabling behavior, and urge anyone who provides shelter for, loans money to, or cleans up after addicted friends or family members to take personal responsibility for aiding and abetting the problem of addiction. A psychologist describes typical characteristics of enablers: lacking self-worth, fearful of abandonment, and suffering from low self-esteem.[19] Calling someone an enabler is a hallmark of the shame culture; the accusation is less about what a person may have done, and more about their inherent identity, a presumed deficit of character that makes them a sucker who is too easily influenced by the persuasion of others. It is not just addicts themselves that are criminalized, but anyone that helped them along.

Given the multitude of issues competing for our attention on the world stage, unless we were directly affected by addiction, it is not likely that many of us paid rapt attention to news of the settlements by McKinsey, CVS, Walmart, or the Purdue Pharma bankruptcy. Yet, drug overdose deaths in the United States have continued to rise, hitting new records each year. This is the nature of the world. While we question our complicity in one crisis, in our inattention we may be facilitating another.

HUSH MONEY AND HONEYPOTS: COMPLICITY IN SEXUAL ASSAULT AND HARASSMENT

On May 25, 2018, having been accused of numerous incidents of sexual harassment and violence, film producer Harvey Weinstein was, at last, arrested. Weinstein's "perp walk" was carefully choreographed. Paraded from his apartment building in New York's Tribeca neighborhood by a female detective, the disgraced executive took wincing steps, wearing a cuddly baby blue sweater and carrying a biography of a more heroic Hollywood outcast, Elia Kazan.[20] That his arrest was such a carefully staged media event suggested that Weinstein's reckoning with the law was much bigger than the criminal case itself. The trial was a watershed moment not just for those directly involved in the case but for what had come to be called the global #MeToo movement, a groundswell of protests in 2017 that marked a rising awareness that sexual harassment and assault were endemic across industries and institutions.[21] An exposé on Weinstein in the *New York Times* describes how he conscripted others to enable his abuse, noting, "Harvey Weinstein built his *complicity machine* out of the witting, the unwitting and those in between. What's become clear is that there is a lot of 'in between.'"[22]

Examining the downfall of perpetrators like Weinstein, along with those who participated in their ascendancy, is a *tour de force* of the many incarnations of complicity.

As society confronts what seems to be an intractable problem of sexual assault and harassment, the ebb and flow of conversations are similar to those taking place in the context of racism and addiction. There are the people who clearly knew—in the commonly understood sense of the word—about predation or who acted like ostriches, hiding their heads in the sand to avoid the obvious. Adjacent to deliberate bad actors are those who covered up and concealed: the bishops in the Catholic church who ignored reports of abuse and repeatedly reassigned known abusers; military higher-ups who demoted complainants while promoting harassers; university administrators who deliberately ignored, minimized, or joked about repeated allegations of sexual abuse of students in their charge. Legal scholar Amos Guiora describes "armies of enablers" within institutions, who made deliberate choices to ignore, deny, or obscure claims of sexual misconduct that put others in peril.[23]

But there are also countless individuals whose implication is less clear and who are sorting through the different ways in which they personally might have enabled toxic cultures and behaviors. Writer Scott Rosenberg published an apology on Facebook that described his and others' entanglement in Harvey Weinstein's wrongdoing. He wrote,

> Everybody-fucking-knew . . . . .
>
> maybe we didn't know the degree.
> The magnitude of the awfulness . . . . .
> But we knew something.
> We knew something was bubbling under.
> Something odious.
> Something rotten . . . . .
>
> [but] we really, really, really, really LIKED them eggs.
> So we were willing to overlook what the Golden Goose was up to, in
>   the murky shadows behind the barn . . .

And for that, I am eternally sorry.
To all of the women that had to suffer this …
I am eternally sorry.[24]

Across institutions and industries, thought processes were taking place that considered how compliance with or deliberate ignorance of lesser offenses might have led to facilitation of much greater evils.

LAMBS TO THE SLAUGHTER

Particularly egregious examples of enabling sexual misconduct have emerged out of the entertainment industry, where employees describe participating in "honeypot" maneuvers, during which they initially joined Harvey Weinstein for meetings with targets then exited partway through, leaving the producer and unwitting victims alone.[25] Interviews reveal patterns of accusation and retaliation, where, repeatedly, claims of assault and harassment were dismissed, accusers demoted or fired, and hush money exchanged as a reward for silence. A former Miramax executive describes working with Weinstein as having made a "deal with the devil."[26] He describes himself and his co-workers as "all enablers, we were all complicit."[27] Members of the media, too, are questioning their roles in obscuring or failing to ask questions about sexual violence. Ta-Nehisi Coates, who wrote a lengthy article on convicted offender Bill Cosby in 2008, expresses regret at having been "in league with people who … looked away, or did not look hard enough."[28]

Even those who have themselves been victims are reckoning with the ways in which they might have been complicit. Actor Uma Thurman's February 2018 statement to the *New York Times* describing encounters with Weinstein sounds more like a confession than the narrative of a survivor. After disclosing having been harassed by the producer, the bulk of her statement is devoted to conveying regret that her choice to remain silent contributed to a "cloud cover" encouraging "lambs" to "walk into the slaughter."[29] Actor Salma Hayek similarly expresses remorse for "hid[ing] from the responsibility to speak out" based on "the excuse that enough people were already shining a light on [Weinstein]."[30]

Concerns about victims' own complicity infuse conversations about whisper networks, underground systems via which women allegedly shared information with one another warning of predatory male behavior. Some participants in these networks express regrets that in trying to help, they may unwittingly have bolstered oppressive systems; while the lists circulated among those in high-profile positions or with industry connections, it is unlikely they reached Hollywood newcomers or staff, who were the most vulnerable.[31] Those who profited from the culture of sexism and harassment were now questioning what their role might have been in the "complicity machine," how they might have, however unintentionally, encouraged serial predation.[32] These conversations challenge traditional victim/perpetrator dichotomies, highlighting the ways in which people can simultaneously be oppressed by a system and also be contributing to the harms that system is inflicting on others.

As with racism, many celebrities have clamored to distance themselves from allegations of sexual assault and harassment, offering convoluted apologies for not doing enough to stop a crisis they claim to have known nothing about. As allegations multiplied against Weinstein, stars like Matt Damon and George Clooney rushed to disclaim their complicity, mobilizing publicity machines to distance their projects from the producer's abuses.[33] Clooney described, heroically, that, had he known, he "would have done something about that," while Damon took the ostrich route, claiming that Weinstein's abuses were not "out in the open": "I never saw it. I never saw that . . . That darkness was his . . . he did that in private."[34]

The public's focus on potential facilitators and enablers of sexual harassment and assault is not always temperate. When actor Meryl Streep proffered that she was unaware of criminal or unethical conduct by Harvey Weinstein, artist Sabo placed posters around Los Angeles featuring Streep smiling next to the producer, her eyes covered by the words "she knew."[35] In October 2017, as the initial wave of allegations emerged against Harvey Weinstein, Gwyneth Paltrow, who worked closely with the producer, posted a benign pictorial landscape on Instagram.[36] Hundreds of comments flooded Paltrow's account, castigating the celebrity—who later revealed having experienced abuse by Weinstein herself—for a "shameful" failure to speak out.

The public censure of the complicit in the wake of #MeToo again brings up questions about the utility of shaming. Aside from a handful of highly publicized arrests, strikingly few alleged perpetrators have faced criminal legal prosecution. Rather, suspected rapists and harassers are much more likely to face callouts and cancellation in the court of public opinion, sometimes leading to extralegal penalties like job loss, or even suicide. The identification of suspected abusers on internet forums and in vehicles like the "shitty men list," a spreadsheet of men in the entertainment industry who allegedly engaged in sexual or gender misconduct, has led to concerns of scapegoating. While some of the behaviors described on the internet are clearly abusive, others are arguably just creepy or inappropriate. Accusations are often anonymous and unsubstantiated. People whose names have been circulated complain that they have been harassed or fired based on alleged behavior that would not meet any legal standard of harassment.

Arguments in defense of the quick and sure penalties faced by possible abusers resemble opinions that are offered in favor of imposing retributive penalties on alleged racists, even if the punishment may in some cases be disproportionate. A journalist writes that sexual assault and harassment constitute

> thousands of years of men taking whatever they wanted from women": "Does an abusive man lose his home, his family, his career, his community? Because these are the things that women often have to give up in order to get away from abuse. More often than not, the woman/victim loses everything and the ... abuser keeps it all and moves on to his next victim.[37]

Long-standing practices of victim-blaming mean that women overall have been precluded from obtaining justice in cases of sexual misconduct. If accusations always bear some risk of unfairness, some ask, why shouldn't it be alleged perpetrators instead of victims who bear that risk? Others vociferously argue that #MeToo has resulted in a rush to justice that demonstrates too little concern for due process, providing potentially harsh extralegal sanctions for individuals who do not have a fair opportunity to respond to complaints.[38]

In the post–#MeToo environment, it is not just individuals but institutions that are being called to account for their role in facilitating harms around sexual assault and harassment.

INSTITUTIONAL COMPLICITY, RELATIONAL CHANGE

At the same time as institutions have been under fire for their roles in facilitating racism, they have found themselves in the hot seat due to promoting practices and processes that undermine sexual assault accusers and insulate perpetrators from accountability. As survivors have come forward to voice experiences of sexual harassment and violence, investigations into long-revered organizations and industries reveal disturbingly similar patterns of mishandling allegations, concealing evidence, transferring known abusers, discounting victims' claims, and retaliating against accusers. As interesting as legal culpability is how we decide who is morally culpable. What should happen to the enablers who may or may not have known about specific incidents—and who might not meet the legal criteria for aiding and abetting—but who stood by silently as perpetrators preyed on the vulnerable?

In the case of sexual predators like Weinstein or Epstein, institutions and their representatives not only participate in direct concealment of sexual misconduct but serve the same reputation-laundering function that they do in regard to racism. JP Morgan Chase and Deutche Bank have agreed to high-dollar settlements with survivors of abuse by Jeffrey Epstein, acknowledging that, in continuing to manage Epstein's accounts and ignoring employees' repeated complaints about the financier, the banks facilitated Epstein's sex trafficking operation.[39] The banks, in turn, argue that responsibility does not end with them. They highlight the complicity of the government of the US Virgin Islands, which turned a blind eye to underage travelers and provided tax incentives to the financier.

The growing recognition of interconnectedness puts not only corporations but nonprofit organizations in increasingly complicated ethical situations. When allegations emerge against a serial sexual predator today— Weinstein, comedian Bill Cosby, or coaches Jerry Sandusky and Larry Nassar—it is all but certain that the good will be revisited along with the bad, and that there will be a massive groundswell calling for revocation of the many honors they received. In his lifetime, Harvey Weinstein has not only been a serial predator but a devoted humanitarian. The extensive list of awards stripped from the disgraced producer include suspension from the British Academy of Film and Television Arts, banishment for life from the Producer's Guild of America, expulsion from the Academy of Motion Picture Arts and Sciences, loss of Harvard University's W.E.B. Du Bois Medal for contribution to African American Culture, loss of the French Legion of Honor Award, and revocation of his title as a Commander of the Order of the British Empire, a disgraced status shared only by dictators Benito Mussolini and Robert Mugabe.[40]

Spelman College, a historically Black women's college, confronted a dilemma when Bill Cosby, who with his wife had donated $20 million to the institution, faced multiple allegations of sexual assault. The college ultimately returned the money, and terminated an endowed professorship titled in Cosby's name.[41] Other institutions encountered similar questions as to what to do with funding from Jeffrey Epstein. What to do with tainted funds is less than straightforward. On one hand, the effects of institutions serving a reputation-laundering function for racists, sexual abusers, and other perpetrators of all manner of harms are significant and far-reaching. Jelani Cobb describes, "charity doesn't contradict monstrosity. It enables it."[42] That Bill Cosby made his prodigious donation to a women's college seems extra terrible, a deliberate act "to certify

Cosby as a man whose credentials as a humanitarian were beyond impeachment."[43] It is impossible to measure the harm that has resulted from universities' acceptance of donations from racists, climate-change deniers, or sexual predators. How many vital ideas could have been on the table had diverse voices not been systematically discounted and devalued for centuries? Journalist Rhonda Lieberman describes museums as quite literally "painting over the dirty truth," articulating lofty ideals while funded by "blood money."[44]

On the other hand, while philosophically speaking money cannot be cleaned, there is the question of what good is being done by shuttering a museum or returning scholarship funds. As sexual misconduct allegations mounted against Bill Cosby in 2015, the Smithsonian made the decision to put on an exhibit showcasing Cosby's private collection of African American art and, quietly, to accept a $700,000 donation from the actor. When pressed, museum director Johnnetta Cole emphasized that the museum's duty was to share art with the public, not to make moral judgments about a donor's career or life. The Smithsonian, which ultimately placed a sign at the exhibit stating that they did not condone Cosby's behavior, advocated that closing the exhibition would do more harm than good, depriving visitors of the opportunity to view and engage with works by African American artists that were rarely displayed.[45] Other entities felt differently, with the Walt Disney Company opting to remove a bronze statue of Cosby from its theme park; Yale Notre Dame and other universities revoking honorary degrees; and the Kennedy Center rescinding two different honors that had been bestowed on the celebrity.

In 2023, the Brooklyn Museum came under fire after hosting "It's Pablo-Matic: Picasso According to Hannah Gadsby," an exhibition that was intended to showcase works by women artists while raising thought-provoking questions about misogyny.[46] Elizabeth Ann Sackler, a long-time social justice activist who advocates for repatriation of indigenous objects, sits on the museum's board of directors. Elizabeth's father, Arthur, was not part of Purdue Pharma and died long before Oxycontin came to market. Comedian Gadsby, who curated the exhibit, proclaimed she'd vetted Sackler's involvement, noting that it was not a "clean win-win" but that Elizabeth's family had "separated their earning streams from the problematic one."[47] Although it's true that Arthur Sackler had no involvement in Opioid sales, he almost certainly played a role in fueling the larger crisis of addiction. Over his wife and daughter's objections, critics point out that Arthur Sackler advised Hoffmann-La Roche in developing Valium and assisted in creating the types of marketing practices, such as providing lavish perks to doctors and consultants, that would turn the product into the first million-dollar drug. Psychiatrist Allen Frances describes, "Most of the questionable practices that propelled the pharmaceutical industry into the scourge it is today can be attributed to Arthur Sackler."[48] Gadsby reflected on the complex entanglement with a sense of resignation and pragmatism: "This is the world we've built, particularly in the US and it's like, how do you do anything here without corrupting yourself? I feel like it's impossible ... But also the exhibition is about Picasso and I really, really want to stick one up him."[49]

Over and over again, institutions that are dependent on donations are being asked to wrangle with the difficult questions of whether and how to separate bad money from good. Pressure to return contributions from a litany of donors—Cosby, Epstein, the Sackler family—is inspiring institutions increasingly to include morals clauses in donation agreements specifying that monies will be returned if donors are discovered to be ethically suspect.[50] What triggers the clauses is up for negotiation; institutions would prefer not to wait until a criminal conviction to sever ties, but ending a relationship with a problematic donor based on rumor is unfair, not to mention impractical in a field that is dependent on largesse.

Labeling donations as tainted raises an even thornier question: Is it possible someone like Cosby or Weinstein was *not only* a rapist but also an advocate for social justice, or even, ironically, a sincere proponent of women's rights? Human beings are complex. Ascribing a victim/perpetrator binary to behavior does not adequately account for this complexity.

These contradictions are on display as, on a regular basis, many of us wonder if we can still, in good conscience, continue to be viewers, listeners, employees, or constituents of those accused of sexual misconduct.

The complicity moment has led to important social changes. A pervasive corporate practice made visible by #MeToo was the signing of nondisclosure agreements (NDAs), contracts containing confidentiality clauses that prohibit parties from speaking about certain topics, events, or even potentially criminal incidents. The nature of these contracts means that there is almost always a power imbalance between parties, terms inuring to the benefit of corporations while silencing victims.[51] In the context of sexual harassment and assault, NDAs can be especially dangerous, undercutting public safety by hiding the actions of serial offenders.[52] As institutions rethink the roles they play in supporting systems of oppression, large companies like Microsoft and Salesforce have scaled back the use of NDAs and mandatory arbitration clauses in the context of sexual misconduct, recognizing that these contracts have contributed to systemic problems of sexual assault and harassment by fostering cultures of shame around victimization and failing to deter perpetrators from committing further harms.[53] Politicians are taking action, with several states passing laws that make NDA agreements unenforceable in the context of alleged sexual harassment or assault.[54] An amendment has been added to the IRS code disallowing corporate tax deductions for payments made relating to sexual misconduct when the payment is made subject to a nondisclosure agreement, a provision that is widely referred to as the Weinstein tax.[55]

Although institutional practices are undergoing some significant reforms, the road has not been straightforward. Despite an initial flurry of cancellations, the revelations prompted by the #MeToo movement seem to have had little impact on the careers of many of the accused. Comedian Louis C. K., who was briefly canceled after it came to light that he masturbated in front of numerous women in the workplace, is back touring in sold out venues. In 2022 actor Johnny Depp emerged victorious after a lengthy civil trial in which he sued his former spouse,

Amber Heard, for defamation after she accused Depp of physically and emotionally abusing her. The trial was infotainment, with videos bearing #JusticeForJohnnyDepp garnering 1.5 billion views on TikTok. Underlying the proceeding were serious allegations of intimate partner abuse and sexual assault, but observers treated the trial like a sporting match. Heard was not only widely disbelieved but was humiliated on social media via hundreds of thousands of memes, parodies, and reenactments. Depp's victory in the case was widely celebrated; at the 2023 Cannes film festival the actor received a seven-minute standing ovation.[56]

As rumors swirled about the misdeeds of Harvey Weinstein and other power players, attendees at the January 2018 Golden Globe ceremony dressed in black to show solidarity with the new Times Up campaign, a nonprofit organization launched by Hollywood power players, including Reese Witherspoon and Shonda Rimes, that was dedicated to combatting sexual harassment in the entertainment industry. An aura of complicity clouded attendees, who sported pins in support of Times Up yet continued to associate with and accept paychecks from suspected and known perpetrators.

The contradictions embodied by celebrities highlight a challenge we all confront: imagining a more just future often entails a painful recognition of our own contribution to problems in the past. Quick on the heels of spotting any issue comes the comprehension that we ourselves are, most likely, part of the problem. As the #MeToo movement gained steam, numerous politicians came under fire for alleged sexual misconduct. Minnesota senator Al Franken was an early target of the movement; in 2017 he resigned from office after having been accused of inappropriately touching women during a USO tour. Democrats hotly debated Franken's resignation, weighing the politician's prior abuses of power against his current commitment to progressive politics. In 2018, when allegations were brought against former New York governor Andrew Cuomo, whose gubernatorial run was backed by Planned Parenthood and the National Organization for Women, voters faced a similar conundrum. Was Cuomo, who during the confirmation hearings for Supreme Court Justice Brett Kavanaugh had tweeted, "#BelieveSurvivors," genuinely committed to gender equality, or had it all been an elaborate ruse to conceal abusive behavior?

Investigations revealed a complex pattern of power players enabling the governor's alleged misdeeds. Troublingly, however, these enablers were not an external threat but came from within Democratic and liberal sectors. The list of those who lost their jobs in the fallout of allegations against the former governor reads like a who's-who of social justice warriors: lawyer Alphonso David, former president of the Human Rights Campaign, and Tina Tchen and Roberta Kaplan, forced to resign from positions of leadership in the Times Up anti-harassment organization after having voiced support for the governor. The Cuomo scandal rang the death knell for Times Up, which already had been damaged by allegations that another founding member mishandled sexual harassment complaints.[57]

It turned out that deeply examining complicity revealed layers of hypocrisy, where individuals were not practicing what they preached. The downfall of progressive activists and legislators reveals a limitation of complicity—there is rarely an end to it. As theologian Christina Traina puts it, "[T]o fight against structural evil is to participate in it, to attempt to dismantle and rebuild the machine while it is still running in overdrive, while one is being either starved by its injustices or overfed by them. Not surprisingly, the consequence of any serious effort to dismantle it is often to be crushed by it."[58]

Individuals who crafted careers fighting for civil rights and equity now found themselves accused of having propped up the very systems they pledged to take down. Politicians worried that in attempting to rectify one set of injustices they might be weakening their political parties' ability to fight others. Organizations that were dedicated to promoting social justice fell apart at the seams; contemporary good intentions could not be easily disentangled from historical patterns of injustice.

GREENWASHING: COMPLICITY IN
CLIMATE CHANGE

Although many risks are discussed in this book, arguably the greatest danger posed to humanity today is climate change, long-term shifts in weather patterns and temperature largely brought about by human activities, such as the burning of fossil fuels. Psychologists Bethany Albertson and Shana Kushner Gadarian identify that we face two types of threats today. There are "unframed" threats, meaning hazards that average humans immediately comprehend as dangerous, such as an earthquake, volcanic eruption, or tidal wave.[59] There are also what the authors call "framed threats," hazards that "require more explanation ... [as to whether and] why the public should be worried."[60] Climate change is a prime example of a framed threat; the problem is often (although, increasingly, not always) invisible to the naked eye, and it is too deeply embedded and extensive to identify a single perpetrator. Debates over climate and environmental concerns illustrate the positive, pro-social, and negative distancing aspects of complicity.

The year 2022 was a landmark for beginning to think through complex issues of accountability for climate change. There were signs of hopefulness. The United Nations Climate Summit closed with an unprecedented agreement by the European Union and the United States to create a loss and damage fund to provide resources for poorer nations, where the impact of climate change is being exacerbated by Western polluters.[61] Although a few wealthy nations had been responsible for more than 50 percent of greenhouse gases since the 1850s, until 2022 they had stubbornly refused to accept responsibility for providing funding to poorer nations, who were disproportionately suffering the effects of a crisis that they played a comparatively miniscule role in creating. It was not only the pledge to be accountable that was significant but the rationale behind it. Nations were not accepting responsibility based on a liability theory, which would have looked backward from the harm to establish their proportional, direct roles in environmental pollution, but they agreed to be accountable based on a forward-looking recognition of the world's interconnection. As Pakistan's climate change minister put it, "This is not about ... charity.... This is a down payment on investment in our futures."[62] The Rockefeller Foundation, whose $6.3 billion endowment comes from the proceeds of Standard Oil, notorious for environmental pollution and monopoly control, announced that it would make climate change central to its future investment strategies.

As the public has become more aware of the threat posed by climate change, pressure is being put on nonprofit institutions to sever ties with climate abusers and polluters. *Greenwashing*, describing a cycle in which oil and gas companies donate profits from extracting and distributing fossil fuels to fund research institutes and museum exhibitions dedicated to sustainability and the development of clean energy, has become a new buzzword. Nonprofits find themselves in situations similar to Spelman, the historically Black women's college that decided to return Bill Cosby's tainted donation, when they are asked to decide whether it is right to accept funds from the fossil-fuel industry to fund new ventures visibly focused on sustainability. On one hand, there are billions of dollars on the table that could be used to fight climate change. On the other, to accept funds from a serial environmental polluter can act as a cover for ongoing harms. Stanford University in particular has come under fire for its new Doerr School of Sustainability, which is funded by big oil and gas companies in which the university continues to invest. Science historian Naomi Oreskes asks, "So consider this: Would you enlist unreformed drug dealers to help eliminate drug abuse? I know I wouldn't."[63]

This sounds cut and dried. Yet, we know from the Sackler debacle that in fact this is precisely what is happening. Many of the same institutions that are today making a show of rejecting donations from ExxonMobil and Shell were founded on money from the Rockefeller family, a century's worth of donations rooted in monopolization, labor exploitation, and climate destruction. Does it matter that the Rockefeller foundation now, in 2022, is shifting its priorities? The Rockefeller money, like the proceeds from enslavement, is like an invasive flower.

The plant looks beautiful to the casual observer, but underneath it is quietly eroding the soil, creating an environment in which it is impossible for other species to thrive.

Again, there is powerful pushback against the relational aspects of complicity. For decades the fossil fuel and chemical industries have strategically and effectively engaged in disinformation campaigns to make their products appear less toxic, funding teams of experts to refute claims that products cause long-lasting harm. In the late 1990s and early 2000s, activists and corporations sparred over how to frame the climate-change threat, some calling global warming an urgent crisis and others arguing that the problem simply did not exist. Corporate strategies capitalized on climate change denial. Publicity materials from ExxonMobil Corporation in the 1990s highlight the "scientific uncertainty" about the reality of global warming, noting only that it *"may* pose a legitimate long-term risk, and that more needs to be learned about it."[64] To support these claims, the fossil fuel industry hired the same scientists big tobacco had engaged to refute evidence that smoking was harmful, relying on paid experts, just like Johnson & Johnson had done in order to advocate for the safety of asbestos in baby powder, and like the precursors to Purdue Pharma used to defend the palliative properties of Valium.[65]

As a result of mounting factual information from scientists and efforts from activists, and due to unquestionably increasing weather events like floods and wildfires, by the 2010s, climate change was irrefutable.[66] We have shifted into a time when the strategies of corporations and states are based not in negation but displacement, acknowledging the risks, but attempting to shift responsibility for managing them onto individual shoulders.

In 2004, oil giant British Petroleum with the help of public relations firm Ogilvy and Mather released a new advertising campaign. The company released a series of ads asking individuals to take a hard look at their personal "carbon footprint," a term coined by ecologists in the 1990s to describe the amount of carbon compounds an individual emits. The ads were accompanied by an online calculator that still exists today, where individuals can go to weigh the harm they personally are doing to the environment. Calculating our carbon footprint has become another way in which individuals are tasked with evaluating and managing our personal responsibility for climate change on a day-to-day basis. Ironically, an important way we are told we can save the planet is by consuming—a barrage of advertisements encourage us to drive more fuel-efficient cars, purchase energy-conserving appliances, and buy new plant-based food options.

When the tobacco industry was faced with lawsuits from victims who developed cancer from smoking, a very successful strategy used by corporations was to situate smoking as not the result of insidious marketing practices or addiction, but as personal choice. Similarly, energy consumption is framed as a demand-side rather than a supply-side problem, with corporations arguing that, even if they had tried to curb production, whatever they did would have been powerless in the face of ever-growing consumer demand for fossil fuels.[67] In this narrative, individuals are posited as wrongdoers and corporations as leaders whose profits support research on sustainability and who are trying to convince consumers to purchase and consume less toxic products.

The promotion of the carbon footprint is part and parcel of a larger campaign of "climate shaming," placing moral responsibility for global warming on individual behaviors, as institutions and corporations seek to offload the management of risk.[68] In the summer of 2022 a new subcategory of climate shaming, flight shaming, emerged on social media. Memes and tweets called out celebrities for use of private jets. Businesswoman Kylie Jenner was labeled a "climate criminal" when news emerged that she had taken a seventeen-minute flight from one California town to another. Entertainer Taylor Swift was publicly chastised as being the celebrity with the worst record for CO_2 emissions.[69] Deeply committed climate activists like Greta Thunberg and Al Gore were criticized for their own, significant, carbon footprints.[70]

Identifying individual responsibility for climate change, like highlighting individual responsibility for other structural harms, can become an endless loop. No matter how closely we track our carbon emissions, it is unlikely that we can personally reduce our contribution to environmental pollution to zero.[71] We are implicated subjects who did not create the harm but, simply through existing, are contributing to it.

This is not to say that we should not reform individual behaviors—collectively, small changes can make a difference. But we should not focus on individuals at the expense of holding the real changemakers accountable.

"ENABLING TORTS": HOW COMPLICITY IS CHANGING LITIGATION

When a crisis or problem is identified today, we identify a web of accountability that extends well beyond a single perpetrator. The problems we are addressing are unwieldy; it is impossible to say that one person or entity caused racism, sexism, addiction, or climate change. Even when it is an interpersonal harm that has occurred, we recognize that there were probably larger forces at work—not solely individual, but societal—that fostered an environment that enabled the offender and allowed or encouraged the bad event to happen.

The thinking through of complicity is evident in new and inventive legal strategies emerging in the context of attempts to assign responsibility for climate change and other social harms. As our ideas about accountability are changing, civil and constitutional legal responses to harm are becoming more creative and expansive. Take, for example, the case of former USA gymnastics team doctor Larry Nassar, who in 2020 was found guilty of committing widespread sexual abuses against athletes under his care. Far from an ending, Nassar's conviction spawned more than 150 state and federal lawsuits seeking billions in recovery from fellow coaches, institutions like Michigan State University and USA Gymnastics (and their representatives), and state authorities, who along the way had ignored, dismissed, or covered up claims that Nassar was abusive. Tracing paths of complicity is clear in lawsuits against the varied parties who "turbocharged" the Oxy crisis. It is evident in actions against the city of Minneapolis, which awarded the family of George Floyd $27 million—by far the highest amount ever paid out by the city—and entered a consent decree with the Department of Justice after findings that the city engaged in a pattern and history of discriminatory behavior. Traditional legal approaches that were fallow are being reinvigorated and used to broaden spheres of accountability.

In the 1990s, law professor Robert Rabin identified a growing category of what he called "enabling torts," lawsuits that were attempting to hold defendants accountable not based on a direct action or specific duty of care but based on the allegation that a person or entity had increased the risk of harm, even if the link between the defendant's act and the plaintiff's injury was less than direct.[72] Today, more than sixteen hundred lawsuits are pending worldwide—twelve hundred in the United States alone—relating to climate change, and over four thousand suits have been filed related to injuries from "forever chemicals," such as perfluoroalkyl and polyfluoroalkyl substances (PFAS), which pervade global water supplies.[73] The theories underlying many of these cases are distinct from earlier waves of climate litigation, because they do not rely on claims of direct and proportional harm from pollution or emissions, but instead allege that corporate actor have polluted the environment and accelerated climate change through aggressive marketing of toxic products and by deliberately misleading the public about risks.[74] Rather than attempting to show a direct, causal link between perpetration and injury—for example, holding a single corporation responsible for polluting a local lake or stream—these new approaches argue that states and industry cannot be allowed to be ostriches, disclaiming knowledge of the abundant evidence of damage their activities and products have been doing to the world. In October 2019, the facade of the New York State Supreme Court was draped with a banner that resembled callouts of complicity in other contexts. It read simply, "#ExxonKnew."[75]

Enabling torts are increasingly common, not just in regard to climate change but other contexts. Gun manufacturers are being called to account for the marketing of firearms to troubled youths and drug cartels.[76] Manufacturers of diverse products from chocolate to athletic gear to cell phones and laptops are being taken to court at home and abroad for potential roles in sustaining dangerous and exploitative child labor practices.[77] Social media platforms are being sued for creating and using algorithms that, in promoting inflammatory content, may have fueled ethnic violence.[78] Hundreds of new lawsuits are being brought against hotel franchisers based on their failure to avert sex trafficking on their premises.

In 2023 the US Supreme Court heard a landmark case, *Gonzalez v. Google LLC*, in which the court considered if platforms like Google, Twitter, and Facebook were exempt under Section 230 of the Communications Decency Act from claims that content posted by users on their servers were promoting terrorism.[79] Although the court did not allow the plaintiffs' claims to go forward in *Gonzalez*, more and more questions are being asked about platforms' responsibility for facilitating misinformation and inciting violence.

In 2022, firearms manufacturer Remington entered into a $73 million settlement with the families of victims of a 2012 mass shooting at Sandy Hook Elementary. The suit, which resulted in the largest payout so far by a gun manufacturer, did not rely on typical arguments that the victims had been harmed by a faulty product. Rather, the families argued that Remington should be held accountable not just for the production of assault weapons, but for having disseminated hyper-masculine advertisements that encouraged troubled young men like the shooter to purchase and use those weapons. Like lawsuits that allege banks' facilitation of sex trafficking, consulting firms' enabling sales of addictive substances, or cities' failure to address longstanding racist policies and practices, the litigation against Remington defined harmdoing much more broadly than the direct perpetration of physical injury.[80] Although success in a lawsuit alone should not be understood as a proxy for justice, it can signal that we are making inroads toward social change and widening spheres of accountability to include parties who formerly evaded it.

The mass tort suits of the 1970s and '80s marked a period in which the public began to identify and hold corporations and institutions accountable for the harms for which they were *directly* responsible. Prior to that time, corporations had been able to raise an Act of God defense, distancing themselves from disasters that were in fact of their own making. Beginning in the 1970s, lawsuits resulted in recategorizing pollution, floods, explosions, birth defects, disease, and nuclear meltdowns not as inevitable but as the product of human negligence by institutions and the people who ran them.[81] As the public digested these events, they read account after account from whistleblowers who revealed long-standing institutional awareness—and in many cases deliberate concealment—of links between asbestos and mesothelioma, thalidomide and birth defects, tobacco and lung cancer. These revelations suggested an appalling lack of attention to potentially fatal problems, and a cost-benefit calculus that valued maximizing profits over human life. The impacts of these incidents are ongoing, changing topographies, altering communities, and affecting reproductive decisions for generations.

The legal claims being made against corporations, institutions, and governments today do not just work backward from the harm, portioning out accountability for a tragedy that already happened. Rather, many suits today are forward looking, seeking to attribute legal and moral responsibility for prevention of ongoing and future crises. President Biden described the Sandy Hook settlement as "a clear message to gun manufacturers and dealers: they must either change their business models to be part of the solution for the gun violence epidemic, or they will bear the financial cost of their complicity."[82]

Novel legal approaches, predictably, face challenges. One problem is standing, the rule that a person bringing a lawsuit must show that they, themselves, have an injury and that the injury is redressable, meaning the harm can be repaired. Another issue is causation. Morally speaking, it might seem obvious that actions by a corporation or its representatives are contributing to harm, but legal claims must fit into a relatively narrow range of causes of action, and plaintiffs must be able to show evidence of a connection between the defendant's action and injury they suffered.

The push back from entities that are being asked to account for long-standing marketing of toxic products or for practices of misinformation, obfuscation, or denial is strong. Defendants facing high-dollar judgments engage in behind-the-scenes litigation practices, declaring bankruptcy to shield subsidiaries or establishing "settlement trusts" that cap recovery and minimize the hit to the bottom line.[83] Bankruptcy courts commonly provide non-debtor releases which insulate executives board members from personal liabilities for injuries that occurred on their watch.[84] Litigation can take decades. Although settlements in the billions sound impressive, after the payment of lawyer's fees and creditors, individual victims may receive paltry compensation for the physical, economic, and emotional harms they and their families have suffered. There are often agreements—like those made in the Sacklers' case—that shield parties from ongoing liability or release them from an obligation to manage risks in the future.

In the courtroom, entities disclaim accountability by engaging powerful "freedom of choice arguments," which displace blame from harm creators onto individuals, blaming victims for the bad choices they make. While the recent settlement between gun manufacturer Remington and the families of victims of the Sandy Hook elementary school mass shooting was a significant step toward a broader corporate accountability for gun violence, at the same time, more Americans of diverse races and genders are buying guns than ever.[85] The rise in gun ownership continues to be influenced by the powerful narrative—promoted by manufacturers' $80 million per year advertising budget —that safety is a personal responsibility, and that the greatest threat to individuals comes not from the increasing production and distribution of weapons but from bad decision-making by other people.[86]

For organizations, disavowing complicity is a means of disclaiming responsibility for a range of issues and obligations. When in 2014 employees brought a suit against retailer Hobby Lobby on the grounds that the Affordable Care Act (ACA) required the corporation to subsidize employees' birth control costs, the company successfully argued that to do so would be to facilitate a moral wrong, financially supporting a practice that *might* lead to the destruction of embryos.[87] Management services company Braidwood Management used a similar argument to avoid a legal obligation to provide employees with prescription coverage for medication protecting against infection by AIDS, on the grounds that, in providing the coverage, the company's owner would be complicit in encouraging homosexual behavior and sex outside of marriage.[88] The potential that a behavior or practice could cause an organization to compromise its moral values undergirds recent court cases weighing diverse issues, such as whether an organization can use child labor or whether a business must conduct business with LGBTQ+ consumers or provide gender neutral bathrooms for employees.[89] The argument that engaging in a particular act might render a person or entity complicit is broader and less defined than a claim of religious liberty; it is based not in a specific tenet or doctrine but in the idea that serving an LGBTQ+ customer or providing a particular healthcare or medical benefit could cause someone to "facilitate" or "participate in" a behavior that is in opposition to "traditional" values.[90] Because complicity is both powerful and amorphous, the practice of seeking conscience-based exemptions to a host of activities is a boon to conservative groups, which are seeking to forge political alliances across different faiths and a range of social and economic concerns.

The concept of complicity as it is engaged by defendants is broad and undefined. There is no requirement that there be a causal link between the individual's or the corporation's action and the potential harm—it is certainly not clear that funding birth control actually leads to destruction of embryos, or that providing insurance coverage for a preventative medication would cause employees to engage in extramarital sex. These new uses of complicity eschew the traditional, backward-looking model of liability, where Individuals are held accountable for an act they actually did to cause harm and embrace a forward-looking model, questioning how an action today could impact the future. As in society, it is not clear whether legal claims of complicity have a logical end. Law professor Michael Dorf posits,

> Gluttony is one of the seven deadly sins. Can an employer now remove coverage for insulin from the health insurance provided employees on the ground that insulin facilitates survival with Type II diabetes, which in turn removes a disincentive to overeating and thus the sin of gluttony?
>
> Can employers who object to sloth—another deadly sin—escape their obligation to comply with the minimum wage and maximum hours provisions of the Fair Labor Standards Act on the ground that paying employees as little as possible and working them as long as possible keeps them busy?"[91]

Overshadowing any discussion of law is the possibility that decision-makers themselves may not be neutral, a concern that became apparent with the change in composition of the US Supreme Court during the Trump presidency. In 2022 the top, new legal term as voted by law professors was "complicit bias," a recognition that institutions like courts are not neutral but play a significant role in sustaining inequalities.[92] Alongside complicit bias, another key term in 2022 was "lawfare," the use of legal proceedings to damage an adversary.

CONCLUSION

The lawsuits being brought not only against direct perpetrators but distributors, consultants, and others who facilitate abuses, suggest a nascent but vital step toward beginning, collectively, to take apart and reimagine damaged structures with an eye toward rebuilding something new. Along with contemporary social movements and activism, they signal that, as a society, we are broadening our collective understanding of violence and injury, and a desire to move beyond individual accountability. Whether we emerge from this time as different or better depends on a lot of factors, not just how creatively and persistently we try to change the status quo—but how those in power resist.

Conversations about complicity in the context of addiction, sexual harassment, and climate change mark the acknowledgement of many of the challenges we face today as structural hazards, corruptions that threaten not just individual victims, but all of us. This newfound awareness of interconnection raises more questions than answers, something that becomes very clear when one examines criminal complicity.

THREE

Where There's Smoke, There's Fire

Criminal Accomplices

In May of 2020, the killing of George Floyd, who was unarmed, by
Minneapolis police office Derek Chauvin ignited a global wave of protests against state violence and racism. Chauvin, who forcibly restrained
the victim, did not act alone. He was accompanied by three other officers: J. Alexander Kueng, who knelt on Floyd's back as Chauvin pinned
the victim by the neck; Thomas Lane, who held his feet; and Tou Thao,
who stood by, restraining the crowd as Floyd grew unresponsive. After
the death, the Minneapolis chief of police opined, "Being silent or not
intervening, to me, you're complicit.... If there were one solitary voice
that would have intervened and acted, that's what I would have hoped
for. That did not occur."[1] The chief believed that the officers should be
held accountable not only for the harm they did directly to George
Floyd, but for what they did not do—their failure to intervene to stop
Derek Chauvin's crime.

Federal and state criminal charges were brought against not only
Chauvin but the three other officers who had been on the scene, helping to restrain Floyd and hold back the crowd. Although the charges
were filed against individuals, they were not only about individual
harms. Since 1980 more than thirty thousand people have died as a
result of police violence.[2] Black persons are at least three times more

likely to be killed by police than White individuals.[3] When deaths occur in police custody, prosecutors routinely fail to bring charges against the officers involved, and grand juries to refuse to indict.[4] Police are protected from claims of excessive force by a standard of objective reasonableness, which focuses not on the intent of specific officers but on how a reasonable officer would have acted in the same situation.[5] In the midst of a massive deficit in accountability, the charges against Lane, Thao, and Kueng were not only a statement about personal culpability but symbolized the desire for state agents to be held accountable for the infliction of harms against everyday persons, especially persons of color.

When in 2021 a jury found Thao, Lane, and Kueng guilty in federal court for willfully depriving Floyd of his constitutional rights, the verdicts were remarkable. The federal statute under which the charges were brought—18 U.S.C. §242—requires a high level of intent and is rarely used. Historically officers who use unlawful lethal force not only have escaped legal consequences but remained on the job. Qualified immunity, the judicially created doctrine that shields certain individuals from personal liability; the practice of closing ranks; and long-standing cultures of routinized violence make it exceedingly challenging to bring criminal charges against representatives of the state—let alone to obtain a conviction. After the protests of 2020, we were on the precipice of changing norms; it seemed like state actors at last would be held accountable for abuses of power.[6]

Over the course of 2022 and 2023, Kueng, Thao, and Lane were convicted in the state criminal court of aiding and abetting second-degree manslaughter.[7] Like the verdicts in federal court, the convictions of the officers for their complicity in Floyd's death were an indication that society had reached a tipping point. The convictions of not only the direct perpetrator but the other officers whose actions *and* failures to act contributed to George Floyd's death signaled a public moral reckoning. They also raised important questions about what it means to be legally complicit.

This chapter explores the legal elements of complicity and examines how the legal questions intersect with the moral ones we have been asking in everyday life. As the risks we face become more unwieldy and less predictable, society has been shifting from a liability-based model premised in attributing guilt after the fact to a more forward-looking approach that focuses on risk management. This is true not only in society, but in law. Accomplice liability is one of many areas where criminal courts assign culpability to defendants based not just on what they did, but on what they *could* have, *might* have, or *should* have done—for crises they should have averted.

This can be a good thing. Complicity can be used to broaden the parameters of accountability to include persons and entities who often are insulated from the reach of law—police and other state actors, governments, institutions, and corporations whose causal connection to harms is significant but indirect. When the death of George Floyd went viral in the summer of 2020, a process of connective witnessing occurred, in which White Americans—some for the first time—were confronting the brutal realities of state violence. The accomplice charges brought in connection with the killing of George Floyd demonstrated the connective, relational aspect of complicity, resulting in a demand that those in authority be held accountable for abuses of power.

Yet, calls to expand the net of legal accountability in order to achieve social justice goals too often assume the existence of a fair and equitable process, where culpability will be attributed to the most deserving parties. This may be true in some cases, but it is not true of accomplice cases in general, in which—not infrequently—harsh punishments are handed down to persons who had least involvement in the result.

LINGUISTIC TRICKERY? THE LEGAL ELEMENTS OF COMPLICITY

When we think about legal complicity, the word "accessory" might come to mind. The term reflects that, at the crime's inception in the

1700s, there were four categories of felony accomplice, each of which carried a different penalty depending on the extent to which a person was involved in the bad act. Current US state and federal criminal codes mostly do away with these distinctions and determine guilt based on one question: Did the defendant know about the crime before it happened? Accessories after the fact—those who were unaware the crime would happen but who help conceal evidence or mislead the police during an investigation—receive a lesser penalty. Anyone who provided assistance before or during a crime, no matter how minor, can be convicted as an accomplice. If found guilty, the helper is convicted of the same offense and can face the same punishment as the principal, in some states up to and including the death penalty.[8]

When complicity laws first were created, it was a rule that no other party could be convicted unless the principal was convicted first.[9] By the mid-1850s, however, the rule was changed so that accessories could be punished even if a principal fled, died, or otherwise evaded justice.[10] Today, it is not uncommon for principal actors to receive reduced sentences or even to be acquitted, while their accomplices get the maximum.[11] The combination of harsh sentences and separate trials means that complicity, like conspiracy, is a powerful negotiating tool for prosecutors, a means of convincing suspects to provide evidence against one another.[12]

To say that criminal legal scholars object to how complicity law is applied today would be an understatement.[13] Accomplice law has significant shortcomings in regard to every key element in criminal law: actus reus (voluntary act), mens rea (intent), and causation (that the defendant's action in fact caused the harm). Underpinning the contemporary criminal justice system is the theory of just deserts, that bad actors should be punished in keeping with their individual level of agency and culpability. Accomplice cases raise questions about whether a defendant has done enough to be held fully responsible for a harmful outcome, and whether it is fair to hold a person accountable for turns of events that may not have been foreseeable. Accomplice law's problems begin with the very first element, the requirement that, for a defendant to be guilty, they must have done a voluntary act.

Accomplice Law and Actus Reus

In general, US law does not impose many affirmative obligations; that is, individuals are much more often required to desist from doing something bad than to proactively do something good. Accomplice law is no exception. While it is possible to be an accomplice by omission—for example, by failing to intervene as a spouse violently beats a child—to be guilty of aiding and abetting, a person usually must have done something. Although many Americans, including the Minneapolis chief of police, might believe that silence is complicity, under state and federal laws a person cannot be a passive accomplice. To convict, a judge or jury needs to find beyond a reasonable doubt that the defendant *actively* encouraged or facilitated an outcome.

That said, a person doesn't have to do much to trigger the application of legal complicity. Contemporary interpretation of the doctrine is broad, giving rise to culpability not only for activities one might imagine—being a lookout or getaway driver—but for relatively minor actions, such as holding someone's child while they commit a crime, making food for a perpetrator, or lending the principal actor some clothes.[14] *Alexander v. State*, a Prohibition-era case, exemplifies complicity's broad range. In that case, the perpetrator's wife was convicted of aiding and abetting the interstate shipment of liquor based on the voluntary act of bringing her husband lunch while he was operating a moonshine still.[15]

The question of whether a lack of action is enough to trigger legal responsibility was at the heart of charges brought against Tou Thao, who performed the crowd control function as George Floyd was killed in police custody. The former officer refused to plead to second-degree manslaughter as his colleagues did, protesting that to plead to something he had not done would be "a lie and a sin." Thao argued that, in contrast to other officers who held Floyd down, he served merely as a "human traffic cone," single-mindedly focused on restraining bystanders, a person whose presence on the scene made no difference in the tragic outcome.[16] His attorneys argued that the defendant, if halfheartedly, had tried to intervene, retrieving a "hobble," a device which would have restrained Floyd differently and allowed him to breathe, although telling the other officers to hold off on using it.[17] In convicting Thao the presiding judge found that Tou's actions did in fact make a difference. He prevented bystanders, including an off-duty firefighter, from rendering aid, and failed to follow protocol in insisting on the hobble, an intervention that likely would have saved Floyd's life.[18]

Unlike Alexander Keung and Thomas Lane, who pled guilty, Tou Thao took the unusual step of requesting a stipulated evidence trial, a proceeding in which a judge rather than a jury decides if the defendant is guilty based on evidence submitted by each of the parties. The defendant does not put on a defense, no witnesses testify, and the judge considers no additional evidence besides what was submitted. This approach can be used when the biggest questions are questions of law: Was what Thao did enough to be guilty of aiding and abetting? Thao's conviction, like many accomplice cases, raises the question: If silence is not enough to establish legal responsibility, then what is? It also brings up a normative question: What should be?

Even more complexities arise as courts consider an accomplice's intent.

Ways of Knowing

Complicity is a specific intent crime, meaning that, to be convicted, a defendant must have intended two things: (1) that the outcome happen, and (2) to have helped bring that outcome about.

What does it mean that someone intended for an outcome to take place? A person, for example, might strongly encourage their spouse to commit a crime, believing that the crime will lead to a financial windfall. However, that same person might not know what the actual crime would be—and might be appalled to learn that the criminal endeavor their spouse undertook was not the financial fraud or pickpocketing they thought but a murder or an act of terrorism.

What does it mean that a person intended to help? A person who offers a friend a ski mask knowing that the mask will be used in an upcoming armed robbery should be treated differently, certainly, than a person who lent a fellow skier a ski mask to protect from the cold, only to find that the item was later used in a crime. The person knowingly offered the item, but they could not have known of its intended use.

The trend today is for courts to separate the analysis of the intents required for complicity, so that a defendant must have *known,* in the everyday sense, that they were rendering assistance to a perpetrator, but they need not have been certain, in practical terms, that a specific outcome would occur. Public policy does not favor ostriches who put their heads in the sand. While a person would not be guilty for—wholly innocently—lending a fellow skier a mask that is later used in a completely unforeseen holdup, a skier who lends a mask to a friend whom he knows to be a burglar could be held accountable. Does this seem confusing? It is.

Commonwealth v. Brown shows the complexities of intent in accomplice cases.[19] Timothy Brown, the defendant, hung out with an unsavory group of friends who sometimes engaged in armed robberies. Brown was not a robber himself, nor did he profit financially from his friends' criminal ventures. One evening Brown's friends committed a robbery and then came over to Brown's apartment, where they switched out their guns and clothing and chatted about their criminal plans. Brown lent his pals fresh hoodies and, reluctantly, a gun that he was pretty sure would be used in another robbery. The holdup went south, and two people were killed.

Brown was tried for felony murder, a doctrine still applied in most US states, that allows a jury to convict a defendant of murder if someone is killed in the course of a dangerous felony, even if the defendant is not the killer. To convict Brown, the state of Massachusetts had to prove beyond a reasonable doubt that he "knowingly" participated in the commission of the robbery.[20] To emphasize the significance of Brown's participation, the prosecutor used a sports analogy, describing that in "supplying a firearm and some clothing," the defendant had contributed to a "team effort."[21] Brown was convicted of first-degree murder and received a life sentence, the same punishment the primary shooter received.[22] The results for other codefendants were vastly different; two were found not guilty of all charges, and another served just seven years as a result of testifying against his friends.[23]

Another convicted accomplice is Rudolph Kessler. Kessler and his friends plotted together to commit an unarmed burglary of a local bar.[24] On the night in question, Kessler waited in the car as his friends entered the premises. Unfortunately, the friends encountered the bar's owner, who unexpectedly pulled out a gun. One of the friends managed to wrestle the weapon away from the owner, then used it to shoot the tavern keeper. As Kessler waited in the car, oblivious, the friend fled on foot and continued to fire the weapon, this time at a police officer who was giving chase. Based on his role as an accomplice, Kessler was convicted of attempted murder, and his conviction was upheld by the appellate court.[25]

There are two influential cases that address the intent required for complicity: the 1938 Second Circuit Court of Appeals case of *U.S. v. Peoni* and *Rosemond v. U.S.*, decided by the US Supreme Court in 2014.[26] *Peoni* involved a counterfeiter, Peoni, who sold fake bills to another person, Regno. When Regno tried to sell the bills to a third person, Dorsey, he was arrested, and prosecutors charged Peoni as an accomplice. The court held that Peoni was not guilty. Justice Learned Hand described that the highest level of *mens rea*—purposeful conduct—was required to be convicted as an accomplice. To convict, Hand explained, the result had to be something the accomplice "wishe[d] to bring about, that he seeks by his action to make ... succeed."[27]

In *Rosemond v. U.S.* the Supreme Court weighed in on the question of intent required for accomplice liability. The court considered the appeal of Justus Rosemond, who was part of a group who planned to engage in an unlawful marijuana sale. When the group drove together to the drop site, Rosemond was aware there was a gun in the car. After the sale went bad, the prospective buyers took the drugs and ran off. One of Rosemond's group grabbed the gun, chased the buyers down, and shot at them. Rosemond was convicted as an accomplice to drug trafficking.[28] His sentence was enhanced by another statute which added several years because he "actively participated" in the crime with "*advance knowledge* that a confederate would *use or carry a gun* during the crime's commission."[29]

In *Rosemond*, the court considered the meaning of "advance knowledge." What it means to *know* something in criminal law is different than what it means in an everyday sense. As a legal term of art, knowledge means having a *practical certainty* that a specific event will occur. Justus Rosemond's lawyers argued that this legal definition should apply; to be guilty, Rosemond had to have been practically certain that the gun in the car would be used against the victims.[30] The government argued, on the other hand, that, it wasn't necessary that Rosemond was practically certain the specific crime would occur. It was enough, the state opined, that Rosemond knew (in the legal sense of practical certainty) that there was a gun in the car, and that he was aware (in a general sense) that guns were commonly used in drug transactions.

The Supreme Court sided with the government. The court held that, to convict Rosemond as an accomplice, the state did not have to prove that Rosemond was practically certain that someone planned to use that particular weapon to shoot the buyers.[31] The government simply had to prove that the defendant was an active participant in the commission of the drug trafficking crime and "had prior knowledge" that somebody was armed. This was a big difference from what Learned Hand had to say in *Peoni*. Having a general awareness that something might happen is very different from *wishing* it would happen.[32]

The *Rosemond* decision is in keeping with numerous decisions that allow for "reckless" accomplices, where a defendant is guilty of being an accomplice to a crime as long as they intended to encourage or support the perpetrator—even if they did not know, precisely, what harm the perpetrator was about to do. A classic case of reckless accomplices are passengers who urge acquaintances to drive while intoxicated. If the driver injures a third party, not only the driver but the passenger can be held accountable for the harm.[33] Cases like this do not strictly apply the specific intent requirement; it is clear that neither party wanted the result to occur, although we might say that they *knew* (in the common-sense meaning of the word) that something bad might happen.

The idea that a person can be a reckless accomplice is foundational to aiding and abetting manslaughter, the crime former officers Keung, Thao, and Lane were convicted of after the death of George Floyd. The primary perpetrator, Derek Chauvin, was convicted on three counts of homicide: second-degree unintentional murder, third-degree murder, and second-degree manslaughter.[34] None of these crimes require that a perpetrator have acted with purpose or knowledge. For second-degree manslaughter, the state had to prove that Chauvin was negligent, having created an unreasonable risk of harm, and that he consciously took the chance of causing severe injury or death.[35] Third-degree murder required that the jury find Chauvin exhibited a reckless disregard for the loss of life.[36] Lastly, second-degree unintentional murder, Minnesota's felony murder statute, provides that a defendant may be guilty of a homicide that takes place while committing another felony. Minnesota's felony murder rule is one of the broadest in the nation. While most states that apply the felony murder rule provide that, to be guilty, the defendant must have been engaged in a predicate felony such as burglary, kidnapping, arson, or rape that is separate from—and does not merge into—homicide, Minnesota's felony murder rule does not follow the *no merger* rule but allows the intent to assault a victim to merge into an intent to kill.[37]

In convicting Chauvin's fellow officers as accomplices to felony murder and reckless homicide, the state was imposing culpability, not because the officers wished an outcome would happen but because of their conscious disregard of the risk posed to the victim—and to society.

Cause . . . and Effect

A third issue with accomplice law relates to causation. There are two causation requirements that must be met for a person to be convicted of a crime. First there must be "actual" or "but for" causation, meaning that a defendant's action must somehow be connected to the resulting harm. This is a very easy test. For example, if a person loudly sneezes, causing a passerby to step out into the street and be struck by a bus, the actual cause requirement would be met. More challenging—and more interesting—is figuring out whether a defendant's action was a proximate cause of harm, meaning that the bad outcome was foreseeable at the time the accomplice offered their assistance and that there is no other cause which intervened and superseded the defendant's action. The sneezing example fails, since the act is involuntary and the outcome unpredictable.

Philosopher Christopher Kutz offers two scenarios, adapted here, which illustrate the complexities of causation in accomplice cases.[38] In scenario one, a person, Sam, wants to murder their friend's spouse. Unbeknownst to his friend, Sam pours a cup of coffee and laces it with poison, knowing the friend will give the coffee to their spouse. Here, Sam clearly has intended to cause and has caused harm to the victim via their friend, who is a completely innocent agent. Not only should Sam be punished in full for the crime, but Sam is more responsible than the poison deliverer.[39]

In scenario two, assume that Sam still hates his friend's spouse. Sam purposefully talks with his friend about the spouse's nagging and other annoying habits. During one of these conversations, Sam suggests that rat poison is fast acting, that it is undetectable in coffee, and that they sell it at a local store. The friend buys the poison and poisons the spouse. The friend is clearly guilty of murder here—but has Sam aided and abetted the crime?[40] In this second scenario, where the friend is not an innocent agent but an independent actor, figuring out causation is more complicated. Morally speaking, Sam should not have hinted at murder, but does this moral shortcoming mean that Sam is legally guilty? What about a third scenario, where the friend heads out to get poison but decides to make a bomb instead?

The law proclaims that complicity is derivative, meaning that an accomplice's liability is derived from—or depends on—the guilt of the primary perpetrator. If this is true, one might think responsibility for causing harm should be parceled out proportionally by looking backward from the completed crime, with each defendant's guilt related to their piece of the criminal pie. In one scenario above, the friend might be one half guilty, and Sam the other half. In another, Sam might bear two-thirds responsibility. But this is not how accomplice law works. Instead, accomplices are punished for the entire completed crime, regardless of whether the primary perpetrator themselves were punished. Complicity law treats a bit player who held the door open for a bank robber the same as a computer genius who cracked the code to get into the vault. This lack of distinction causes Kutz to identify complicity as moving from derivative liability, where culpability is assessed based on the gravity of a completed harm, to inchoate liability, where the harm comes not from the act itself but from the actor's encouragement.[41]

Some courts deal with this causation problem by applying the doctrine of *natural and probable* consequences, which provides that, where two or more people have a joint plan to do something criminal—or profoundly stupid—and one of them commits a crime more serious than was intended, everyone should be held responsible. South Carolina accomplice law is called, poetically, the "hand of one, hand of all," reflecting that, by colluding, even a minor player can lead to major harms. In Texas, accomplices are convicted under the "law of parties." The rationale that groups can be more dangerous than individuals was embraced by the appeals court in upholding the conviction of Timothy Brown, whom the court described as a "coventurer."[42]

Despite attempts by courts to engage the idea of foreseeability, legal scholar Sanford Kadish argues that the causation element is never really met in cases of complicity.[43] He suggests complicity law should be revised to resemble vicarious liability, akin to how liability flows through a bad-acting employee to the employer who directed and supervised their actions. In that case, the level of culpability of the accomplice would depend not on whether the accomplice actually caused harm, but on how much free will was exercised by the primary perpetrator.[44] A person who held the door for a bank robber would receive a much lighter sentence than the tech genius who provided the code for the vault.

Joshua Dressler, on the other hand, advocates that the causation element of complicity law should be strengthened so that courts would evaluate not just foreseeability, but whether an accomplice's assistance actually contributed to the completed crime.[45] He argues that a commonsense definition of "causing" something should be applied to accomplice crimes, so that people who caused a crime (in commonsense terms) should be punished more harshly than people who provide only minor help.[46] In this scenario the code hacker, presumably, would face a penalty akin to that of the principal actor, while a person who merely held the door open would be looking at much less time.

The shortcomings of accomplice law in terms of action, intent, and causation put complicity in the category of what professor Paul Robinson refers to as an "inculpating" crime, a crime that allows for conviction of a defendant without the prosecution proving every element beyond a reasonable doubt.[47] Inculpating crimes are not unusual. Imposing criminal accountability can serve different functions. A society might criminalize behavior based on an individual's direct role in causing harm, or because of the danger a person poses to the collective, but we also might choose to make actions illegal based on less concrete goals, for example, because we perceive a behavior to be particularly hazardous, or because we fear that, by allowing one dubious incident to slide, we are opening the door to greater problems.[48]

We allow juries to overlook the requirement of intent—and sometimes of voluntary action—when a defendant commits a crime while drunk or high, when the defendant of their own free will has created a situation where they cannot form the mental state required by statute for the crime.[49] Strict liability crimes, such as speeding, require no proof of intent whatsoever. The felony murder doctrine, discussed earlier, assumes that a person who had the intent to complete a violent crime such as burglary, arson, or kidnapping also had the required intent for murder.

Inculpating crimes may not be problematic when a defendant's personal culpability is closely tied to their legal accountability. For example, the presumption that an extremely drunk driver could form criminal intent to commit vehicular homicide serves the traditional retributive and deterrent functions of criminal law. In other situations, however, there can be a disconnect between the severity of punishment and the defendant's actual role in the crime. There are many cases where accomplice defendants face sentences much longer than principal actors for doing less.[50] When we impose guilt on one person based on the actions of another, it is less than clear that the goals of punishment are being fulfilled.

Accomplice cases highlight the moral function served by US criminal law, a system that at its foundation was obsessed with identifying and reforming individual evil tendencies.[51] The carceral structures of the US criminal justice system, premised on removing "bad apples" from the community, reflect the idea that a person who commits a crime did not just do one bad act, but is a corrupt person who is in need of isolation, correction, and reform. Criminal charges may have less to do with whether a defendant has exhibited the required elements of intent, action, or causation and more to do with the defendant's moral character.

US law reflects a strong belief in autonomy, assuming that people freely make choices and should be held accountable for any bad choices they make. Underlying accomplice law is the idea that the defendant made a poor choice by helping out the wrong people. The accomplice is culpable based less on a direct role in causing a bad outcome and more due to morally blameworthy association.[52] As Supreme Court Justice Elena Kagan put it in upholding Justus Rosemond's conviction for drug trafficking: "[T]he player knew the heightened stakes when he decided to stay in the game."[53] Accomplice cases bring to mind the maxim *where there's smoke there's fire*, a phrase that might hold true in the everyday but makes for a troubling approach to legal reasoning.[54] To be clear, when one looks at the facts, most convicted accomplices have done something morally suspect; they have contributed at least some assistance to a perpetrator who has committed some kind of harm. However, convicting defendants without requiring proof beyond a reasonable doubt of every element of a criminal offense comes dangerously close to violating due process. Timothy Brown, jailed for lending his armed-robber friends a hoodie and freed in 2021 after having served twenty-nine years, describes complicity law as "linguistic trickery."[55]

THE MORAL ELEMENTS OF COMPLICITY

At the heart of the criminal law are the classical legal elements of action, intent, and causation, but behind the scenes are moral and ethical beliefs that inspire laws' creation, application, and enforcement. While on its face accomplice law may seem neutral, in reality scholars are only beginning to identify the disparate impact of accomplice laws in terms of race and ethnicity, particularly when these laws are combined with felony murder rules.

In 2023, legal researchers published the results of an experiment in which nearly six hundred mock jurors were randomly assigned to evaluate criminal responsibility in one of three fact patterns involving a potential accomplice to a felony murder scenario. The hypotheticals were nearly identical, except that in the first example suspects had White-sounding names; in the second, names that sounded Black; and in the third, names that were typically Hispanic or Latino.[56] The researchers found that mock jurors were statistically more likely to associate White defendants with individuality, using terms like "solo" or "single" to describe their crimes, while jurors were significantly more likely to group Black- or Latino-appearing defendants together, using terms like "group, pack, crew ... crowd ... [or] bunch."[57] When it comes to accomplice liability, where prosecutors advocate for conviction on team-player or law of parties theories, this tendency to see non-White defendants as more likely to act as part of a group or gang, can have significant consequences. The propensity to view non-White defendants as acting in concert can impact prosecutors' charging decisions and can influence a jury to convict.

There is no nationwide study on the racial consequences of accomplice liability, but what we know is stark. In Minnesota, the state in which George Floyd's was killed, Black men are sent to prison at a rate more than three times the national average; the state's twenty-five-to one imprisonment ratio of Black persons to White is the highest in the nation.[58] About 1 percent of the state's population is Native American, but Native Americans constitute about 10 percent of those incarcerated.[59] Minnesota is not an outlier. Twenty-five percent of people incarcerated for felony murder in Pennsylvania are persons of color, and eight of every ten defendants sentenced under Cook County's felony murder rule between 2010 and 2020 were Black.[60] While the killing of George Floyd brought to light systemic issues embedded in enforcement of the laws, much less attention has been paid to the inequities that are inflicted by the criminal law itself, which in both structure and application negatively impacts people of color.

Complicity law has disproportionate effects in terms of not only race but also gender. While overall there was a 500 percent growth in mass incarceration from 1980 to 2019, women's incarceration skyrocketed by 700 percent.[61] Complicity has played a significant role in the growing inclusion of women in the criminal justice system. Like conspiracy, complicity is a powerful negotiating tool, and parties can come under scrutiny—and fall into the net of liability—for minor actions, such as taking a message for a family member or purchasing household supplies that a roommate uses to manufacture drugs.[62] As sentences for drug-related crimes became harsher, prosecutors gained a powerful bargaining tool over women of circumstance—mothers, girlfriends, and sisters supporting loved ones engaged in the drug trade.[63] Of the women serving life sentences for murder in California, 72 percent were not the primary killers.[64] Although it is rare to see convictions of accomplices by omission, one place it is common to see them is in regard to child abuse, where nearly 100 percent of charges for failure to protect children from an abusive spouse or partner are brought against women.[65]

In addition to perpetuating racial and gender disparities, complicity law violates principles of proportionality, that the punishment should be proportional to the severity of the crime. Complicity law is replete with examples where accomplices receive dramatically different sentences from primary perpetrators. For example, there is Francisco Mojica, who committed burglaries along with his brother, Tomas. Tomas lived in the apartment next door to Francisco's.[66] Francisco was at home when he heard gunshots. When he rushed into the hall he saw a body on the floor and his brother's apartment door riddled with bullets. Tomas, injured and still inside the neighboring apartment, had shot through the closed door at the victim, who had come to seek revenge after being robbed. Mojica flagged down a police officer, who helped him transport his brother to the hospital.

Mojica's brother was sentenced to twelve to twenty-four years for third-degree unintentional murder based on recklessly firing shots at the victim through the door. Mojica, however, was convicted of the more serious crime of second-degree felony murder and sentenced to life, based on his knowing participation in the predicate offense of burglary. When Tomas learned about his brother's sentence, he was in disbelief and asked to trade, asking "How did they give you life? Who did you kill? I am the killer."[67]

Mojica's circumstances are not unusual. Lakeith Smith is serving a fifty-five-year sentence in Alabama for his role in a series of break-ins when he was just fifteen years old. Smith's friend was killed by a police officer during one of the robberies. Although the officer was not charged with any crime, Smith was convicted of felony murder.[68] Kenneth Robinson, sentenced under South Carolina's "hand of one, hand of all" law, is spending a half century in prison because he was a passenger during a shooting that took place when he was fifteen.[69] When she was nineteen, Pennsylvania resident Marie (Menchie) Scott was sentenced to natural life for her role as a lookout during the robbery of a gas station during which a worker was killed.[70] Her codefendant who pulled the trigger had his sentence vacated.[71] Scott writes that, shortly after her conviction, the presiding judge visited her in prison to apologize for having to hand down such a tough sentence.[72] He promised to help Scott advocate for parole but never followed through.

These cases are just the tip of the iceberg. There is Andrew James Cotto, who collaborated with two other men to stage an attack and was convicted of homicide while the primary perpetrator—who strangled the victim—was acquitted based on evidence that the victim actually died of an asthma attack.[73] And Brothers Reid and Wyatt Evans, who are serving life sentences as accomplices to felony murder for a crime committed in their teens. The brothers were incarcerated for a botched robbery after which the victim died of a heart attack, even though the principal actor was released.[74] Marion Hungerford received a 159-year sentence for driving her boyfriend to an armed robbery, while the boyfriend—who entered the premises while Hungerford waited in the car—received a sentence one-fourth as long.[75]

The data compiled around accomplice law is sparse, but stories compiled from defendants, activists, and attorneys suggest that, like conspiracy—nicknamed the "prosecutor's darling" due to its utility in convincing codefendants to provide state's evidence—complicity charges have a disproportionately negative impact on young, poor, and non-White persons. In 2012, the Supreme Court decided *Miller v. Alabama*, holding unconstitutional the mandatory sentencing of juveniles under eighteen to life without parole.[76] A quarter of those who were serving sentences of life without parole after having been convicted as juveniles were convicted of either complicity or felony murder.[77]

Broadening the Net

In criminal law there is a set of crimes called inchoate (meaning unformed) crimes, meaning that we punish people for their role in planning rather than their part in the result. Attempt, conspiracy, and solicitation are classic inchoate crimes. They hold a perpetrator accountable not because a bad act was done, but because society is safer if we intervene to avert something bad before it occurs. The more dangerous the crime, and the more skeptical we are of human nature, the sooner we want the state to intervene.

Accomplice liability can be distinguished from a similar crime, conspiracy, because unlike conspiracy, accomplice liability is supposed to be derivative. A person can be convicted of conspiracy or attempt even if the hoped-for crime never happens, but complicity is decided after the fact, by looking backward from the outcome. If the result is bad enough, we can not only hold the perpetrator accountable but also punish those who helped them along the way. Underlying contemporary applications of complicity, however, is the idea of punishing people for risk they created or the risk they failed to avert. Liability is derived less from a bad outcome than from the morally blameworthy association with bad people.

Accomplice liability is not the only area of criminal law to cast a widening net of accountability. The inchoate crime of attempt has been expanding to empower states to intervene earlier to avert possibly bad outcomes. In deciding whether a defendant was guilty of criminal attempt, a majority of jurisdictions used to apply the *last act test*, which assessed whether a defendant was guilty by measuring their nearness to the completed crime. Now, most jurisdictions ask whether a defendant took a *substantial step* toward completion of the offense.[78] The substantial step test permits the state to intervene sooner to interrupt the defendant's plans, leaving less room for a moral change of heart. Law professor Kimberly Ferzan describes attempt as shifting from a liability model to a forward looking approach where "the court is not focusing on ... what has been done—but on what the defendant might do. The court's goal is to set the act requirement at a point that will stop the defendant. It does not discuss the defendant's culpability and desert. It focuses instead of the state's preventive goals."[79] Similarly, conspiracy, an already popular charge among prosecutors, exploded during the wars on drugs, terrorism, and organized crime.[80]

Over the past few decades not only have the parameters of already existing inchoate offenses expanded, but more statutes are being created based on the belief that failure to intervene to avert bad conduct early on will lead to bigger problems in the future. Since the 1960s, the US criminal justice system has shifted its focus to prevention, penalizing minor offenses with the goal of protecting communities from worse, imagined crimes. Broken windows theory holds that serious, violent crimes can be deterred by penalizing minor infractions like graffiti or panhandling. In connection with terrorism "offenses of preparation," such as joining the mailing list of a potential terrorist group or accessing extremist websites, are criminalized even though the relationship between low-level radical behavior and involvement in acts of terrorism is speculative.[81] At the same time as we are punishing more nonviolent, preparatory or adjacent offenses, the category of "violent" crime also has been expanding. It is only in the last fifty years that a specific category of "violent" offenses was developed.[82] The violent label allows for enhanced sentences, like Justus Rosemond's sentence for engaging in a drug-related offense while carrying a weapon, that keep people behind bars for longer periods of time.

A different but equally notable expansion of liability has taken place in regard to gender-based violence, where there has been a push both to enact harsher penalties in terms of sexual assault and intimate partner violence and to criminalize adjacent crimes that might lead to or facilitate more severe harms. In recent years, statutes prohibiting stalking and sexting, have proliferated.[83] These statutes are enacted based on the belief that early intervention will avert potentially greater harms. It is not unusual today to see what Nick Zimmerman calls "double inchoate crimes," statutes that criminalize an inchoate offense where the objective is another inchoate offense.[84] For example, some states punish attempted stalking—punishing an unrealized effort to commit a crime that itself is premised on potential harm.[85]

Calls to expand the scope of accountability for harm creation can be seen as positive. Specific intent requirements can let too many bad actors off the hook for actions that are morally reprehensible, either too difficult to prove or not exactly illegal. Kutz points out that, while Lynndie England and seven fellow soldiers were convicted for torturing inmates at Abu Ghraib prison during the 2003 Iraq War, nothing happened to the authors of the "Torture Memos," the documents prepared by attorneys for the White House Office of Legal Counsel that justified the behavior.[86] Criminal law has limited success in reaching the most powerful, who may take pains to conceal their behind-the-scenes role in fostering harm or whose actions skate along the borders of illegality. Often, demands to expand legal accountability stem from the desire to expand the parameters of moral responsibility, and to hold more (and more powerful) people accountable for not only what they did but what they didn't do. As advocates rally for justice, however, it is vital to consider the ways in which the institution of law is itself complicit in doing harm, through both biased prosecutions and failure to prosecute, mass incarceration, and other means. The application of criminal law, like many discussions on social media, reflects a time in which we are increasingly distrustful of the intentions of others and dubious about the human capacity for reform.

CONCLUSION: THE DOUBLE-EDGED SWORD

Although the verb *complicare*, meaning to involve oneself, dates to the 1400s, and the noun complicity to the 1600s, use of the term *complicit* as an adjective—to describe a person—dates only to the 1800s, an era when agency and free choice were incorporated as core values in US society and in the criminal justice system.[87] We place a premium on personal choice and readily call others out for their bad decisions. In its operation today, complicity is inculpating crime, where punishment reflects moral judgment as much or more than the weight of the evidence.

Accomplice laws today serve an expressive function, reflecting changing societal norms of harm, responsibility, and culpability. The filing of criminal charges against the accomplice officers in connection with George Floyd's death, and the resulting convictions, marked a potential sea change during which state actors, at last, were being held to account for their roles in facilitating violence. The charges were about more than legal guilt. They signaled a shift in accountability for risk creation. For centuries, risk was understood as being a threat that flowed *from* individuals to society. But the American public was awakening to the fact that the criminal justice system long had posed an equal or greater risk *to* individuals, by routinizing policies and practices that have entrenched poverty, racism, and gender violence. The reassessment of risks shows the hopeful, relational effects of complicity, articulating a shift in the relationship between the person, the state, and the world.

At the same time, however, accomplice laws demonstrate the worst aspects of complicity. They illustrate that, as risks are growing and social ties are weakened by distance and polarization, we may be less likely to give fellow humans the legal or moral benefit of the doubt. The more distant we are from others, the more likely we are to ostracize, and the less likely we are to be empathetic.

FOUR

Accessories

White Women and Complicity

In 2017 HBO premiered a new miniseries. *Big Little Lies*, based on the novel of the same name by Liane Moriarty, followed five rich women, four of whom were White, as they plotted to cover up the group's connection to a homicide. As portrayed in the series, the primary perpetrator pushed the victim down a flight of stairs, after she rushed to help a friend who was being assaulted. The other women were accessories who were present at the scene and then helped the perpetrator cover up the incident.

Accomplice liability looked strikingly different on television than it did in reality. The circumstances of the wealthy Californians, nicknamed the Monterrey Five, who lunched, shopped, and attended catered benefits as they blithely evaded law enforcement, were about as far as one could get from those of defendants like Lakeith Smith and Marion Hungerford, who not only did not *get away with it*, but are serving Draconian sentences for their roles in offenses committed by others. Complicity was so glamorous that viewers rushed to purchase fashions inspired by the show and took virtual tours of homes owned by the suspects. They even could take a quiz to see which of the characters was most like them.[1]

Far from an outlier, *Big Little Lies* highlighted a notable feature of complicity: privileged White women seem to embody it. We are living at a time when anyone and everyone is at risk of being complicit in something—if not sexism or racism, then addiction, climate change, or economic inequality. Although anyone can be complicit, some suspects are more visible than others. In real life it is Black and indigenous persons who are overrepresented in the criminal justice system. But in conversations about complicity taking place in the news and on social media, it is White women who most visibly occupy the space between victim and perpetrator.

Liminality describes a period of transition from one stage to the next—a change or rite of passage that is uncertain and uncomfortable. US society is at a liminal moment, when many of us are renegotiating the relationship of the individual to the world. In the post-Holocaust period of the 1960s, social science research shifted focus from looking at obedience: asking how much pain ordinary citizens might inflict if told to do so by an authority figure; to examining accountability: questioning the harms everyday people might inflict in choosing not to speak up or out. With this shift came challenges to the assumption that average people, even people who themselves faced hardships, were powerless in the face of oppression. We are at a new tipping point, as the large-scale social crises and changes we have experienced cause many of us to reflect on our relationship to the larger world.

While this chapter focuses on White women's complicity, it is not just about White women. Anthropologists and sociologists observe that as an individual is undergoing a rite of passage or initiation into something else, they become—for a time—a liminal being, a person who embodies the contradictions of old and new.[2] At a time when social norms are rapidly changing, when society is on the edge of a transition, identifying and discussing liminal beings can provide a way to discuss the parameters of appropriateness on both individual and collective levels.

As a group, White women today are liminal figures who in the public discourse have come to embody the contradictions of our times. In the aftermath of recent social movements many people have been taking stock of the ways they not only may have been harmed by discriminatory structures and polices but how they might have benefited from them. Discussing White women's complicity provides a forum for debating questions about harm, accountability, and what it means to be an implicated subject.

This chapter examines complicity in the context of three public figures: politician Hillary Clinton, talk show host Ellen DeGeneres, and "Karen," the fictional or referential middle-aged subject of viral, pandemic-era memes. Public discussions about these women demonstrate complicity's capacity for connection, exposing networks that previously operated behind the scenes. For centuries, White women largely were viewed as passive beneficiaries of oppression, a group who profited from but were not direct agents of racist or sexist policies and practices. In the current era, society is reevaluating White women's roles in relation to discriminatory systems, and we are more likely to identify White women as active perpetrators of harm.[3] When a public figure like Hillary Clinton or Ellen DeGeneres is called out as complicit, or when we circulate a Karen meme, everyday people can chime in and participate in thinking through and defining the parameters of individual responsibility for inherited, present, and future problems.

Although the productive aspects of complicity are on display in conversations about public figures such as DeGeneres or Clinton, one can also see how easily women's actions can be conflated with their character. We are fascinated by misbehaving women. From notorious "bad mothers" like Susan Smith and Casey Anthony, who captured the public imagination after accusations of filicide, to soldier Lynndie England, described as the worst of the torturers at Abu Ghraib prison, women who commit acts of violence captivate the public, their cruelty seeming exceptional when juxtaposed against gendered norms of caring and compassion.[4] In crime narratives, women often gain notoriety not as primary perpetrators but for the roles they play behind the scenes, enabling or encouraging criminal behavior. There is Bonnie Parker, who joined her husband, Clyde in an epic Depression-era crime spree, and Ghislaine Maxwell, procuring young girls to be sexually abused by her boyfriend Jeffrey Epstein. Behind every gangster is a *moll,* a word originating in the term *molly,* or prostitute, a woman who has hitched her future to a male companion's criminal enterprise.

When asked to describe a "typical" criminal, most people list stereotypically male traits, like being physically large, tough, or aggressive.[5] In contrast to male violence, which is normalized, when women commit crimes we assume they are somehow deviant—sexual perverts, bad mothers, evil manipulators. It can seem almost natural to describe women as complicit because the term itself suggests deviousness and hints at a manipulative quality that is often ascribed to them. When it came to Hillary Clinton, this long-standing association of women and sneakiness made it easy for the Trump administration to convince adherents that they should "lock her up."

It is not surprising that women have emerged liminal figures today. In times of crisis and social change, women's bodies often become focal points for societies. Conversations about women's dress or behavior highlight that women's bodies are the site of reproduction of the national body, the locus of culture, and the battleground for struggles over tradition and morality.[6] But gender is not the only factor. Hillary, Ellen, and the fictional Karen are all women of a *certain age,* representing viewpoints and attitudes that might have been acceptable twenty years ago but are out of step with contemporary norms. A significant majority of people in the United States say there is no agreement on what constitutes racism or sexism in society today, and about half of people say it's hard to tell what other people might find offensive.[7] The struggles faced by Hillary, Ellen, and Karen in the midst of changing norms reflect the challenges many people confront as they consider how to navigate a new social terrain.

POLITICAL ACCESSORIES

In Fall 2016, an *Access Hollywood* tape surfaced showing presidential candidate Donald Trump making unsavory comments about sexual access to women. The candidate needed to rapidly deflect attention and did so by pointing the finger at his opponent, Hillary Clinton. His defense: "I've said some foolish things, but there's a big difference between the words and actions of other people. Bill Clinton has actually abused women and Hillary has bullied, attacked, shamed and intimidated his victims."[8] Trump's presidential campaign was notable for the promise to "Make America Great Again." In the background, however, the campaign was engaged in an equally effective initiative that defined the candidate by denigrating his competitors. Over the course of the campaign, a series of derogatory labels—*crooked, nasty, lying*—coalesced to shape opponent Hillary Clinton into someone endemically untrustworthy. Trump supporters chanted "lock her up," raising posters featuring Clinton behind bars or wearing a black-and-white jumpsuit.[9] The hashtag *crookedhillary* trended on Twitter.[10]

Susan Bordo and others identify the misogyny underlying the 2016 election, tracing how historical conceptions of women as inherently conniving were deployed by not just the Trump campaign but by Democratic primary opponents to demean and demonize Hillary Clinton.[11] Complicity was at the forefront as opponents emphasized that Hillary had enabled a range of interpersonal and structural harms, from sexual assault to terrorism to the mortgage foreclosure crisis. Other candidates accused her of being "in bed" with long-standing financial firms.[12] She was portrayed as an ostrich; the question of *what Hillary knew* was raised in connection with events ranging from an attack on the US embassy in Libya to a rebel coup in Honduras.[13] Rumors circulated that when she was a public defender in the 1970s, Hillary laughed about defending a man accused of sexually assaulting a child.[14] Male Democratic candidate Bernie Sanders was praised for his empathy and compassion; Clinton was portrayed as scheming and devious.[15]

Hillary Clinton was blamed for having played a direct role in numerous political and financial debacles, but, as importantly, she was shamed for having enabled her husband's abuses of power. As allegations emerged that Hillary had attempted to intimidate and malign Bill Clinton's accusers, Donald Trump invited several of them as guests to the third presidential debate.[16] The presence of the alleged victims, whom Trump attempted to seat in the VIP box, was a visible demonstration of the contradictory role Hillary herself embodied in regard to sexual assault reform, ardently advocating for women's rights while, behind the scenes, dismissing and deflecting accusations against her husband.[17] Criticism of Clinton was bipartisan. Conservative commentator Tomi Lahren observed that Hillary "ran for president on the whole women card, the whole female empowerment ... [but] Hillary is *just as responsible* as Bill was."[18] Feminist Naomi Klein followed up by articulating a question that haunted Hillary's campaign: *"[W]as it sexism to elect the grabber himself over an enabler?"*[19]

For many Republicans and no small number of Democrats, the flow of allegations of sneakiness, untruthfulness, and disingenuousness that emerged in regard to nearly every aspect of the candidate's career and personal life coalesced into a persona: Crooked Hillary. By late 2016, the idea that the candidate was—somehow—complicit had taken hold. A particularly incensed voter was driven to an act of mass violence out of his mistaken belief in a theory that Clinton was a conspirator in a criminal enterprise dubbed *pizzagate*, working with other high-profile Democrats to run a child sex trafficking ring out of a medium-sized Washington, DC, restaurant.[20] Another theory, #Clintonbodycount, drew attention to suspicious deaths surrounding the Clinton family. When accused sex trafficker Jeffrey Epstein hung himself in his jail cell in 2019, more than seventy thousand tweets circulated connecting Clinton to the crime via the hashtag.[21]

Hillary Clinton is not the only woman in politics whose career has been haunted by the specter of complicity. In spring 2017, at the beginning of the Trump presidency, *Saturday Night Live* (SNL) aired a skit in which first daughter Ivanka, played by actor Scarlett Johansson, was peddling a new perfume. The fragrance was called: "Complicit." It carried the tagline: "The fragrance for the woman who could stop all this, but won't."[22] The segment, a parody of the film *Titanic*, also featured actors playing First Lady Melania Trump and longtime Trump supporter Omarosa Manigault Newman, and showcased that the women in the Trump administration embodied contradictions. On one hand, the presence of women in high-level White House positions seemed to emphasize the president's support of gender equity. On the other, the physical appearance of most of the women in the Trump administration seemed to reflect a troubling male gaze, each one sporting "long glossy hair, high spiky heels, clingy outfits, sparkling teeth."[23] A journalist referred to Ivanka, senior counselor Kellyanne Conway, and communications director Hope Hicks as the president's "accessories," a double entendre which both highlighted and undervalued the women's impact on policymaking.[24]

For liberal voters, there was perhaps no greater accessory than Ivanka, described in the *Guardian* as an "attractive package," whose "peddling of kitten heels and suede tote bags and her saccharine-sweet Instagram account make her seem less like a woman complicit in the serious destruction of millions of people's rights and more like a girl just trying to have fun, as her dad tramples democracy."[25] In the fall of 2020, Ivanka and her husband, Jared Kushner, filed a defamation suit against the Republican, anti-Trump Lincoln Project after the project sponsored a billboard that appeared in New York City's Times Square featuring Ivanka standing in a white suit making a shrug-like hand gesture.[26] The gesture mirrored the positioning of Ivanka's hands when, earlier that year, she appeared in an advertisement for Goya beans, a product that was marketed to Hispanic and Latino families but whose CEO supported Trump administration policies of separating parents and children at the US-Mexico border.[27] Rather than a can of beans, next to Ivanka's hand were statistics showing the horrific COVID-19 death toll on New York City.[28]

The billboard highlighted that Ivanka's job as a Goya spokesperson seemed to reflect a dichotomy within the woman herself: a working mother, she seemed to be willfully blind to the struggles of detained mothers and children. Her stated support for reproductive freedoms stood in stark contrast to the administration's moves to curtail reproductive rights. Around the time of the billboard fiasco, Hillary and Bill

Clinton's daughter Chelsea announced that she was severing her friendship with Ivanka because Ivanka was "more than complicit.... And I
don't want to be friends with someone like that."[29]

Questions of complicity swirl around other political women. During
the vetting process for Supreme Court Justice Amy Coney Barrett, it
came to light that Coney Barrett, a devout Catholic, was a member of
People of Praise, a sect that subscribed to a belief that men should have
ultimate control over a family's decision-making.[30] Memes caught fire in
liberal circles, showing images of Coney Barrett cloaked in red robes rem-
iniscent of Offred in the popular series *The Handmaid's Tale*, a Hulu series
based on the novel of the same name by Margaret Atwood, which imag-
ines a dystopian future in which the state is ruled by a fundamentalist
regime that treats women as property.[31] Some quipped in response that
the Justice was no handmaid. Although, as a woman, Coney Barrett was
impacted by patriarchal structures, she was also an agent who was participating in the creation of harm. For *Handmaid's* fans, she was like the character of Serena Joy, the wife of a high-profile commander who readily
sacrifices the rights and liberties of other women in order to achieve
individual, selfish goals.[32] Conversations about Coney Barrett bore simi-
larity to those about Hillary Clinton, who in standing by her husband was
viewed as an enabler, as responsible as Bill was for abuses of power.

Accessories were abundant in the Trump administration. First lady
Melania Trump gained notoriety for being a woman of contradictions,
leading a campaign against cyberbullying while her husband was being
banned from Twitter for uncivil speech.[33] Melania's fashion choices
suggested an awareness of the juxtapositions she embodied. Appearing
in public for the first time after her husband's comments about grabbing
women by the genitals, she donned a "pussy bow" blouse.[34] Visiting a
detention site for children at the border, she wore a jacket bearing a
phrase that seemed to challenge members of the public to reflect on
their own connection to the world : "*I really don't care. Do you?*"[35]

Vice President Mike Pence was also a potential accomplice, referred
to in the media as the "enabler in chief" and "Mr. Complicit."[36] While

Pence is a cis-gender male, rhetoric used to describe him often feminized the politician.[37] As liberal critics took aim, the candidate was labeled with ineffectual terms like "lapdog," "sycophant," "bootlicker," and "wimp," labels that stood in contrast to the president's ardent displays of masculinity.[38] A prominent tactic of Pence's critics was to poke fun at what seemed like the vice president's constant checking in with his wife, whom it was rumored he called Mother.[39]

EMBODYING COMPLICITY

Refrains like *lock her up* are gold for political campaigns because they evoke emotions that are strikingly familiar. *Ad hominem* attacks against women candidates are particularly effective because they rely on the deeply embedded stereotypes that women are less trustworthy or sneakier than men. A long-standing characterization of women as instinctually and habitually untruthful is embedded in the law, where jurors in rape cases, for example, were provided with Hale instructions that cautioned them to weigh the testimony of women accusers with suspicion.[40] Leah Gilmore characterizes that in Clinton's case "[t]he words 'email,' 'lying' and 'woman' fell like a series of dominoes.... The deep emotion was tapped: You cannot trust women with power."[41]

It is significant that the product Ivanka is peddling in the SNL skit is perfume, suggesting that Ivanka not only is committing the *actus reus* of aiding and abetting, but that being complicit is part of her—it emanates. The video reflects that critiques of female politicians are often *ad hominem*—they are about the person.[42] The Trump campaign didn't merely attack Hillary's policies, they went after her very being, the refrain of *lock her up* providing a visceral image of her body in a cage. For liberal voters Ivanka was, quite literally, an *accessory,* a *package* of contradictions perched on kitten heels.

The SNL skit implies that even if Ivanka might have been a reckless accomplice—for several minutes the first daughter drifts around the party, oblivious that she is on a sinking ship—she was fully accountable for what transpired after 2016. The reflection in the mirror was not her but her president father, played by actor Alec Baldwin, highlighting that complicity is not a partial accountability. The aider and abettor is as culpable as the perpetrator.

Although gender makes political women more susceptible to personal attacks, conversations about the potential complicity of women in politics don't just malign the person. They provide important commentary on the person's role in upholding harmful structures and systems. In Clinton's case, discussions about complicity signaled that the policies the candidate supported were in tension with a more modern, inclusive vision of feminism. Hillary, whose campaign leaned heavily on themes like playing the *woman card* and breaking the *glass ceiling*, was criticized for ignoring and stepping over other women, especially women of color.[43] Her dismissiveness in regard to her husband's accusers—particularly her reaction to his extramarital affair with intern Monica Lewinsky, which it is a stretch to call consensual—were not in keeping with contemporary understandings about sexual assault and harassment. Clips of Clinton's support of the Defense of Marriage Act, which prevented same-sex couples from having marriages recognized under federal law, stood in contrast to the consistent support of LGBTQ+ rights from other Democratic frontrunners. Within the feminist movement, White women were facing criticism for centering their own experiences and oppressions while failing to fight for the rights of other women.[44] For voters, Clinton embodied these debates, representing the tensions between an old feminism and new, more inclusive and intersectional politics.

Discussions of women in politics show that complicity is a useful vehicle for raising complex moral questions, but it may not be the ideal means of moving forward toward the answers. Being accused of aiding and abetting upset Ivanka Trump so much that she made a special appearance on the evening news where she proclaimed, "I don't know what it means to be complicit!"[45] Although she was derided for the comment, Ivanka was echoing something much of the public also felt. Immediately after her appearance, there was a massive uptick in online searches for definitions of the term.[46]

Defenders argued not that Ivanka was innocent, but that we were all, in critical theorist Debarati Sanyal's words, *at the scene of the crime*—we were all complicit in *something*.[47] Complicity was a useful means of starting conversations about the liminal space between innocence and guilt, accountability and responsibility. But complicity also created a loop in which we were all, endlessly, victims and perpetrators.

In fairness, the conflicting roles that Hillary and Ivanka publicly played were, largely, ones they chose to take on. Ivanka wasn't forced to straddle the role of first daughter and administrative adviser. Clinton decided to be both the wife of a president and, independently, to hold political positions. But it is not only those who, arguably, have courted controversy that occupy this space of negotiation between victim and perpetrator. Sometimes it is those who try their hardest to avoid it.

THE KINDNESS CONUNDRUM

Just a few years ago, it seemed like talk show host Ellen DeGeneres could do no wrong. Having lived through significant life challenges, including the death of a longtime partner and the cancellation of her sitcom due to rampant homophobia, she had gone on to create an entertainment brand worth hundreds of millions, comprised of two television shows, a production company, digital media ventures, and numerous endorsements.[48] Her talk show earned more than thirty Daytime Emmy Awards.[49] The celebrity received the Presidential Medal of Freedom, awarded to Americans who "change the country for the better."[50]

Rather than being fueled by anger after her sitcom was canceled, Ellen reenergized her career by engaging a counter-intuitive strategy— she would be *relatable*, even to those people who had shunned her. In 2015, the words most commonly used to describe DeGeneres were "kind," "generous," "affable," and "nice."[51] The *Today Show* ran a spot declaring Ellen "the nicest celebrity," praising the star's "inner beauty," and lauding her promotion of "honesty, equality, kindness, compassion, treating people the way you want to be treated and helping those in need."[52] Her signature line of clothing urged people to "Be kind to one another."[53] The persona she had cultivated was perhaps best reflected in the animated character of Dory, a kindhearted fish who suffers from short-term memory loss, featured in the Disney movie *Finding Nemo.* Ellen described the character as having "not one speck of judgment or meanness ... just happy."[54]

Around 2020, rumors began to circulate that Ellen might not be as nice as she seemed on TV. Critiques arose regarding Ellen's treatment of guests on her show and her management practices. As Ellen built an outward-facing brand on generosity, under the radar were internal claims by staff of racism, sexual harassment, and under-compensation.[55] The problems were ones that existed in many large workplaces. For the public of 2020, however, they did not represent isolated disputes. Ellen was being revealed as an impostor, a person who had cultivated a veneer of kindness while fostering a culture of toxicity. These were moral transgressions, symptomatic not just of a lack of oversight or poor management but an intrinsic flaw in Ellen's character.

Underlying conversations about interpersonal disputes were concerns about the relational aspects of Ellen's behavior: How had her actions (or inaction) facilitated structural harms? Critiques of enabling surrounded Ellen's relationship with fellow comic Kevin Hart, whose Oscar hosting gig was cancelled in 2019 after he released a series of homophobic tweets.[56] Critics also questioned the comedian's friendship with Republican former President George W. Bush, whose values, such as opposing same-sex marriage, stood in contrast to Ellen's stated promotion of equality and respect.[57] Articles abounded asking, "What Ellen's kindness concealed?," and accusing the comedian of being an "apologist."[58]

The world was changing. Terms like *toxic nostalgia* were popping up on social media, describing how the warm fuzzy feelings evoked by the shows, songs, or books of one's youth might actually be contributing to an ongoing culture of racism, sexism, or homophobia. Psychologists coined *toxic positivity* to describe an insistence on positive thinking that ignored or obscured any negative emotions. In a post-#MeToo and Black Lives Matter world, Ellen's politics, once benign, began to look like appeasement.[59] The outsized lack of historical memory encompassed in a character like Dory was no longer an amusing idiosyncrasy but a tragic flaw. In the midst of criticisms that the star had created a toxic workplace, ratings for the *Ellen* show plummeted.[60] In a world of ever-growing dangers, the actor's admonition to "be kind" took on an insidious quality.

Ellen's cancellation exemplified the pitfalls inherent in the politics of respectability—when a representative of a particular group is held to a higher standard by the members of that group.[61] Ellen built her career on disclaiming an interest in politics, proclaiming all she wanted was "to be funny" and not to be "some gay activist."[62] For many LGBTQ+ people in 2020, this apolitical stance was unacceptable. Ellen was accused of passing, performing heteronormativity in a way that erased her sexuality and sexual orientation.[63] Contradictions inhered in her on set persona, which, radically, had introduced lesbian identity to a broad and unlikely audience but erased aspects of gayness that were uncomfortable for heterosexual viewers.

Upon close examination, Ellen's generosity started to seem inauthentic. She was not quietly selfless like singer Dolly Parton, who deflected praise for donating millions to vaccine development by situating herself as a "regular person" trying to do her best.[64] Rather, Ellen capitalized on kindness, selling shoes and dishes imprinted with positive phrases and a "kindness box" full of self-care paraphernalia bearing affirming phrases. Revelations of workplace toxicity in the midst of so much overt niceness caused commenters to wonder if despite all the humanitarian awards bestowed on her, Ellen's actions all along had been more saccharine than genuine. As critiques of Ellen multiplied, blame was laid at her feet for bullying, and even causing miscarriage and suicide.[65] Ellen herself described, "Being known as the 'be kind' lady is a tricky position to be in."[66]

Although some conversations about Ellen defaulted into binaries—good or evil, nice or mean—others suggested a more nuanced possibility: Ellen's brand was genuine, but nonetheless the celebrity should be held accountable for facilitating structural harms. Ellen found herself in a kindness conundrum. It was a space in which many nice people found themselves in the wake of social movements like Black Lives Matter and #MeToo.

In the television show *The Good Place,* there is a character named Doug Forcett, who is famous for being the one and only human being who figured out how to get into heaven.[67] The character's life is devoted to making the right choices: he grows his own food, consumes as few resources as possible, and adopts every stray animal (and person) that comes into his purview. Forcett is heaven bound for his good deeds, yet, in life he is miserable. Inevitably, his good choices come into conflict with one another, the attempt to make solely positive decisions leading to violent clashes and a paralyzing fear of doing something wrong. Ellen's nonjudgmental, bland niceness brought her into this realm of competing goods—a friendship with former president George W. Bush was *enabling,* reaching out to homophobes *appeasement,* helping animals suggested a deficit of empathy for fellow human beings. Even Ellen's positivity might be toxic.[68]

Ellen's rise as the "queen of nice" reflected the societal trends of the early 2000s. Fostered by a confluence of forces, including yoga culture, anti-bullying campaigns, and the hopefulness of the Obama presidency, the United States on the whole was increasingly treating kindness as a practice. By the time of the 2016 election cycle, though, society was questioning the trend of uncritical niceness. It was becoming clear that a person could be very nice to individuals and, at the same time, be contributing to massive structural harms like sexism, racism, or homophobia. In this time of social upheaval Ellen was a liminal figure, her persona situated on the threshold of changing expectations around race, gender, and sexual orientation. Many fans were asking themselves the same questions they had about the celebrity: What if doing good in one context is, unwittingly, contributing to harm in another?

The backlash Ellen faced was made possible by her gender. Kindness is not, traditionally, a macho characteristic. While all Americans are encouraged to be *good people* with *good values,* the theme of being kind—and raising kind children—particularly has been directed toward women, especially mothers. The COVID-19 pandemic made it clear that it is women who continue to occupy the center of the family, bearing primary responsibility for making consumer and health decisions, and for raising children who are moral, ethical, and *nice* people. Criticisms of Ellen demonstrated the pedestal problem: what seemed like ruthless actions in the workplace contradicted the belief that women as a category should behave morally and ethically *better* than male peers.

Importantly, though, critiques against the celebrity were not only gendered. Race, socioeconomic status, age, sexual orientation all played a role in the downfall of the self-appointed Queen of Nice. Unlike Clinton, who chose to embrace the "woman card" in her candidacy, Ellen took the opposite approach and elected to gloss over more political or controversial aspects of her persona. Shunned after coming out in the 1990s, in reentering the fold Ellen may have overcorrected, turning the other cheek too far.

As with discussions of Hillary Clinton and other female politicians, recent conversations have not only served as a public trial of Ellen, but a forum for debating anxieties shared by many Americans, who have been taking a hard look at themselves. This is also true in the case of another, rather surprising, character who emerged during the pandemic era.

ENTER, KAREN

During the COVID pandemic heroes and villains emerged—larger-than-life figures who became focal points for debates about a world in crisis. White House adviser Dr. Anthony Fauci was a hero, appearing nightly to advise Americans on whether to risk a visit with grandparents or if children should return to in-person school. Lauded too were the essential workers battling the virus on the front lines of hospitals, public transport, and delivery services.

While the persons who emerged as leaders might have been predictable, the pandemic spawned a surprising antihero. She was a middle-aged White lady with a painstakingly styled haircut who engaged in behaviors ranging from annoying (asking to speak to the manager) to racist (reporting non-White neighbors to law enforcement). Her name was Karen.

Throughout 2020 and 2021, social media was flooded with Karen memes. They sometimes angled for amusement, making fun of a tendency to hoard toilet paper or drink a little too much wine.[69] Other times they referenced more serious offenses—demeaning an essential worker, refusing to wear a mask in public, or objecting to vaccines.[70] As Americans worried over pandemic risks and searched for ways to alleviate boredom, these memes became hugely popular. One, featuring a group of blonde women, proclaimed, "A group of Karens in the wild is called a complaint!" Another asked, "What's a Karen's Favorite Drink?" Answer: "Whine!"[71]

While some memes were funny, others served a purpose that was dramatically different, drawing public attention to serious issues and behaviors. In summer 2020, a viral video circulated featuring Amy Cooper, a White woman, calling 911 to falsely report that she had been threatened by a Black man in Central Park.[72] Cooper was immortalized as the Central Park Karen, perhaps the most widely known of several racist "Karens," including a Yale University student who reported a fellow student for taking a nap in a common room and a woman who called the police on a Black neighbor who happened to be chalking *Black Lives Matter* on his own front walk.[73]

There are two incarnations of Karen—funny and serious—and both are products of this complicity moment. Although Karen memes sometimes originate from a specific incident, in time we remember less about the specifics of what a person did, and more about the harm her actions caused. In circulating Karen memes, people are—once again—thinking through the accountability of the person to the world.

KAREN AS CARICATURE

During the Second World War, the US military created a character, Private Snafu, to illustrate what not to do for new recruits.[74] In a series of short films Snafu bumbled through potential scenarios—falling into a booby trap, contracting malaria, and unwittingly providing information to an enemy spy. On social media, Karen was the Private Snafu for the pandemic, her lowest moments shared and exaggerated not only for amusement but for education. Karen wore her mask below her nose, she drank too much, and she complained loudly and obnoxiously to and about essential workers.

For online commenters, connections to other users are established via brief, sometimes coded messages. The easiest way to connect with others online is to use language that invokes visible, easily recognizable identities.[75] During a time of social distancing, Karen memes provided a way for online participants to connect to other people, to call out bad behavior, and at the same time to reinforce their own superior moral position.[76] While Private Snafu was gently amusing, portrayals of Karens had an edge. Recordings of public altercations were often made without consent, and jokes were undercut by a sense of schadenfreude. Karen was the collective punch line during a time that was distinctly unfunny.

Notably, Karens don't just make poor personal choices, but make choices that cause harm to the collective. They shop and eat at restaurants while demeaning the essential workers who provide those services. At the height of the pandemic, many Karens were castigated for refusing to wear masks, abetting the spread of COVID-19. Karen flaunts economic and racial privilege in a time of profound uncertainty, not only contributing to economic disparity, but embracing entitlement. One journalist described Karen as a person who, during the pandemic, thought that "social distancing should end because she need[ed] a haircut."[77]

The idea of privilege—that a person is receiving a reward from an unearned advantage—was popularized in the late 1980s by gender scholar Peggy MacIntosh.[78] Since that time, the idea of examining—and checking—our privilege has entered the vernacular. Karens flash their privilege but, significantly, they are by no means rich. Although criticized for conspicuous consumption, the Kardashians are not Karens. Rather than donning haute couture, Karen is firmly situated in the middle class, sporting an out-of-date haircut and, according to Reddit, usually wearing jeggings or capri pants and carrying a mid-priced Coach handbag.[79]

In terms of her actual power to effect structural changes, Karen might fall into a category social theorist Iris Marion Young identifies as privileged but not powerful, a person who is clearly a beneficiary of problematic systems, but not wielding direct control over the circumstances in which such systems are generated.[80] The Karens outed on social media for drinking too much wine or hoarding toilet paper during the COVID-19 pandemic were like many of us, if we were to make some very unfortunate public choices. Karen memes reflected the position many of us were in as implicated subjects, privileged enough to have some effect on systems but not sufficiently privileged to control those systems.

THE "CENTRAL PARK KAREN" AND STRUCTURAL COMPLICITY

In May 2020, Christian Cooper was birdwatching in Central Park and encountered an off-leash dog.[81] When he complained to the dog's owner, Amy Cooper, a heated exchange ensued. During the altercation, Amy Cooper, who was White, dialed 911 and told Christian Cooper, "I'm going to tell them there's an African-American man threatening my life."[82] In the 911 call Amy Cooper repeated the words "African American."[83]

On the same day Amy Cooper called 911, George Floyd was killed by officer Derek Chauvin. On the surface, Cooper's phone call might seem trivial compared to Chauvin's act of physical violence, but it was significant. Although she wasn't at the scene of Floyd's death, Amy Cooper's call activated and supported the same systems of power that emboldened Chauvin to place a knee on George Floyd's neck. In the eyes of many people, she was as complicit as the officers who failed to intervene as George Floyd died.

When the public called Amy Cooper the Central Park Karen, the term functioned differently than when it was used to describe a rude person at the grocery store. When asked about sharing the video of the encounter in Central Park, Melody Cooper, Christian's sister, connected Cooper's actions to those of Carolyn Bryant Dunham, the White woman who in 1955 accused fourteen-year-old Emmett Till, who was Black, of whistling and making "ugly remarks" to her, setting off a course of events that resulted in Till's murder.[84] Carolyn's testimony played a significant role in the trial of her husband, Roy Bryant, and his half-brother, J. W. Milam, for the crime. The pair were acquitted by an all-White jury but later confessed.[85]

As the public participated in connective witnessing of the actions of the Central Park Karen, conversations were about more than just the 911 call itself; social media consumers were questioning the role White women had played in the growth of the carceral state. Communication scholar Apryl Williams observes, "We as a culture have adopted this stance that white women are more virtuous and not complicit in upholding racism in particular.... The Karen meme says, no, they are conscious actors. These are deliberate actions. They are complicit."[86]

Gender-based violence is an area of law in which the parameters of accountability have been expanding. Over the past thirty years, criminal laws have been revised to encompass many behaviors that formerly might have been deemed immoral but not illegal. Since the 1990s, sexual assault has expanded as a crime category, with state statutes no longer penalizing just penetrative rape but degrees of criminal sexual conduct. Statutes in all fifty states penalize threats and surveillance behaviors. Thirty-eight states penalize nonconsensual distribution of pornography. As victims' rights activists call for broadening the reach of criminal law, there is concern that the expansion of the carceral state is coming at the expense of poor and non-White persons, and that those who call for strengthening penalties have paid too little attention to the potential impact this expanded net of laws may have on defendants, particularly non-White defendants.

Amy Cooper's actions on May 25, 2020, were much bigger than her 911 call itself. They inspired those who witnessed them on social media to consider the ways in which White women might not only have been victims but also agents of oppression. As columnist Charles Blow opined, Cooper's call revealed that white supremacy was "just as likely to wear heels as a hood."[87]

Conversations about Amy Cooper demonstrate how allegations of complicity can articulate interfoldedness, connecting a present-day action to centuries of discriminatory practices and processes. Discussions about the Central Park Karen show the connective function of complicity; they are an entry point for naming and beginning to reckon with structural racism. Interestingly, Christian Cooper described that it was a reflection on his own accountability to society that led him to film the incident in Central Park in the first place: "[W]e live in an age ... where Black men are gunned down because of assumptions people make about Black men, Black people, and *I'm just not going to participate in that.*"[88]

When one compares conversations about Amy Cooper with videos of blonde, carefully coiffed Karens popping up on sites like TikTok, it is clear that in 2020 being a Karen meant different things to different audiences. Karen originated within the Black community as a coded term that was shorthand to describe a particular way some White women behaved. Similar to the label Miss Ann, used in pre–Civil War times to describe White women who flaunted their entitlement, the term Karen signaled White women's capacity to wield power and privilege over

African Americans, encompassing the idea that White women not only benefited from but enthusiastically participated in racist systems.[89]

Like "woke," by 2023 the idea of the Karen was so pervasive it seemed to have lost all meaning. Clusters of White women sprang up complaining about Karens while engaging in suspiciously Karen-like complaining.[90] It was unclear whether the persistent popularity of Karen memes evidenced a long-awaited reckoning with White women's roles in perpetuating racism or was yet another misogynist trope being used to rhetorically discipline opinionated women.

CONCLUSION: THE CONTRADICTIONS OF COMPLICITY

Both Karen memes and conversations about Hillary Clinton and Ellen DeGeneres demonstrate the troubling ease with which *ad hominem* critiques can be used to confine and delimit women. They highlight how long-standing assumptions of women as inherently unreliable or untrustworthy continue to shape present day opinions. There are male Karens—sometimes called Chads—but, to steal a line from the film *Mean Girls,* people stopped making Chad happen. Rather, when men act in public in ways that are entitled, privileged, or selfish, they become Karens, portrayed in memes wearing the telltale fussy blonde wig. Anti-vaxxer quarterback Aaron Rodgers, became "Karen Rodgers." Entrepreneur Elon Musk, who laid off thousands of employees after the purchase of Twitter, is "space Karen." Not even Charles Dickens is immune; a reboot on Lifetime TV turns Ebeneezer Scrooge into an entitled middle-aged woman in the new classic, *A Christmas Karen.*

At the same time, conversations about the complicity of privileged, female public figures highlight an important—and, for many, new-found—recognition of White women's power and agency. Media portrayals of White women as complicit evoke the martini drinker, whose behavior is described in chapter 1. The martini drinker is not actively encouraging the boulder to fall, but they have done nothing to stop it.

With the public calling out of Hillary or Ellen or Karen comes a reimagination and reallocation of accountability for past and present problems. In examining these women's complicity, we peel back layers to expose what Corwin Aragon and Alison Jaggar call nested networks, how small actions, silences—and even kindnesses—can bolster structures like racism, homophobia, and economic exploitation.[91]

The question that remains is how to move beyond the isolating, stigmatizing function of complicity and more deeply engage this capacity for connection. We have become adept at identifying interconnection, but it is more difficult to put these discoveries into action.

FIVE

Assumptions of Risk

The tipping point is a sociological term, popularized by author Malcolm Gladwell in his 2002 book, that describes a "moment of critical mass, the threshold, the boiling point" when a new belief, practice, or behavior begins to spread and take hold in society.[1] We are at a tipping point—in a liminal space—in terms of numerous issues and crises—racism, sexual assault and harassment, climate change. Society is reckoning with inherited harms, and at the same time must figure out how to deal prospectively with risks that are continually emerging and rapidly growing. The unique coalescence of experiences of crisis and trauma, unprecedented new technologies, and changing beliefs has put us on the precipice of significant change. When we ask questions about complicity, we are attempting to figure out who is accountable for dealing with past harms, and who is tasked with managing and controlling risks—the scope of which we are just now starting to comprehend—on the horizon.

Americans tend to approach their lives as a choose your own adventure novel in which every person is an empowered entrepreneur responsible for their own decision-making.[2] The COVID-19 pandemic made clear the extent to which each of us is responsible for our own well-being; we regularly consulted online charts and graphs in order to decide whether to wear a mask, return to the office, or send children to in-person school. Corporations lean heavily on the rhetoric of personal accountability, attaching tag lines to all sorts of potentially hazardous products cautioning consumers to manage their own risks by drinking, smoking, or gambling responsibly. Ideas of personal responsibility are pervasive in discourse on climate change, as each of us is tasked to reduce our personal carbon footprint on the world.

When a person makes a bad choice in the face of a risk, we are often quick to shame them, calling out how their poor decision has made the world worse for all of us. The application of criminal accomplice laws reflects this idea that defendants should be held accountable not only for the harm they did, but for the poor decision they made in associating or "coventuring" with dangerous characters. It is for this reason that law professors describe complicity law as inchoate, or "risk-based," imposing culpability not for the harm a person actually caused but based on assumptions about their "antisocial or dangerous character."[3]

There are indications, however, that things are changing. After decades of treating risks to society as stemming *from* individual bad choices, systems are being called to account for the risks created through processes that adopted the veneer of objectivity while disenfranchising individuals and communities. Demands are being made of corporations, governments, and institutions like universities and religious organizations—and of those at work within those systems—to question how discriminatory policies and practices have contributed to creating a society that is unjust and unsafe. Complicity is at the forefront of these conversations, with the capacity to make visible the hidden, behind-the-scenes practices that are creating injustices, and as a means of holding persons and entities accountable for repair.

This chapter engages the Black Lives Matter and #MeToo social movements in order explore the potential, connective aspects of complicity. Sociologist Ulrich Beck described that there is a difference between a time of social change and a period of metamorphosis. Social change, Beck wrote, is "about the reproduction of the social and political order," acting better within existing systems that are themselves corrupt.[4] Metamorphosis, on the other hand, "is about the transfiguration of the social and political order."[5]

The chapter explores how in this time of what Beck might call metamorphosis—as society is emerging after one crisis and in the midst of others—our conversations about complicity are challenging our assumptions about risks, including how they are defined, who created them, and who is and should be accountable for managing them going forward.

CHALLENGING INDIVIDUAL COMPLICITY: THE BLACK LIVES MATTER AND #METOO SOCIAL MOVEMENTS

In 2020, the death of George Floyd was a catalyst for many individuals to reexamine their own biases and to question the ways in which, perhaps unconsciously, they might have been perpetuating usual cruelties, everyday actions and behaviors propping up racist systems or structures.[6] But Black Lives Matter was not just about personal awakening. In the wake of the killing of George Floyd society was questioning assumptions about risk, asking if perhaps the greatest danger to society might not have been emanating from individuals, as we had been told, but from the systems that proclaimed they were designed to protect us.

Since the inception of modern policing in the 1800s, the public had been told again and again that the risk of crime originated with individuals. The threat of violence is a framed threat; for most of us violent crime is not visible to the naked eye but defined for and conveyed to us via politicians and the media. Politicians characterize risk of crime as acute, a sharp cut that can be bandaged by the policies they promote. After the summer of 2020, however, the public was beginning to see the risk of violence not as acute but chronic, embedded in the criminal justice system itself. We began to look more critically at the net of laws that disadvantaged poor people and people of color and drew them unfairly into the carceral system, the redlining practices that impacted the ability of non-White persons to build equity, the school funding systems that were set up based on property values.

Black Lives Matter is not the only social movement to challenge assumptions of risk. In Fall 2017 in response to emerging, multiple accusations of sexual assault against film producer Harvey Weinstein, actor Alyssa Milano tweeted #MeToo, a hashtag adapted from activist Tarana Burke that has been shared tens of millions of times.[7] Preceding what came to be called the #MeToo social movement, perceptions about sexual assault and harassment were changing. Historically when rape allegations were made, rather than looking toward the perpetrator, scrutiny fell on the victim—what they did, where they went, what they wore. Claims of sexual assault, like allegations of state violence, were evaluated according to a standard akin to contributory negligence, the tort law doctrine that barred plaintiffs from recovery if they were at all at fault for the injury they suffered.

By 2020, however, society's views were transforming. Throughout the early 2000s, the public was confronted by revelations that mass sexual abuses had been taking place inside the walls of almost every trusted US institution—the Catholic Church, esteemed colleges and universities, the Boy Scouts, the military. The financial costs of lawsuits against these entities were astronomical, reaching tens of billions. But it was not just the economic costs that were staggering. Many of us were expanding our conception of violence, and realizing that harms were not just perpetrated by individuals, but by the toxic institutional cultures that enabled them, and that engaged in cycles of gaslighting, denial, and betrayal. Rather than providing a sense of closure, the arrest of a perpetrator became a starting point for discussions about who else was responsible, culpable, or blameworthy. Discussions of complicity provide a vehicle for reassessing and redistributing risk, tracing maps of accountability through individuals, implicating the entities, systems, and structures that enable harm.

UNREASONABLE SUSPICION

Patterns and practices of racism and discrimination were being identified across many sectors of society in 2020, but they were most apparent in the context of the criminal justice system. The assessment of risk is foundational to that system. Since the 1970s, police, corrections, and courts increasingly have turned to complex algorithms to predict and prevent crime and to measure the threat that might inhere in potential criminals.[8] These systems rely on complex instruments that promise to predict the probability of danger—what we think a person *might do* based on data about them.[9] Scientists claim that they can identify potential criminal traits even before a child is conceived.[10]

While risk assessments purport to be value neutral, evaluative instruments are created and interpreted by human beings. As such, systems can bake in biases that are more likely to identify poor people or people of color to be at "high risk" of reoffending or as having a genetic predisposition for crime, and data can be interpreted in ways that reinforce this bias.[11] When we identify a person or group as "at risk" of committing crime, there is an elision, when being "at risk" is transformed into the idea that a person is, themselves, a "risky" individual.[12] Epidemiologist Laura Eichelberger identifies how this phenomenon occurs in the context of contagious disease.[13] When a population is identified as likely to carry infection, it can lead to stigmatization and othering, where the population is then blamed for their own illness and is expected to bear the burden of managing and controlling the problem.

The designation of being *at risk* can signal that a group is receiving attention and resources. Statistics showing children, for example, as at risk of falling behind academically can be the basis for providing interventions or additional state or federal funding. More often, though, being *at risk* from a crisis leads to the identification that a person or group is *at fault* for that crisis. In the US criminal justice system, categorizations of people as risk bearers often intersect with specific characteristics: being non-White, or economically disadvantaged. It is a small step from identifying a risk of danger to identifying the *risky* persons who embody the threat.[14] When a person or group is identified as risky, it impacts self-identity, heightening the sense of responsibility and shame.[15]

The increasing reliance on risk-based approaches in the criminal justice system has gone hand in hand with the growth of preventative approaches in law and policing. As judicial interpretations legal doctrines like accomplice liability, conspiracy, and attempt allow for earlier state intervention to avert potential harm, law enforcement—also—is encouraged to step in as soon as possible. Broken windows ordinances encourage law enforcement to intervene to address small issues of disorderly conduct so that more violent issues, hopefully, will not occur; hotspot technologies increase police presence in areas anticipated to be more dangerous; registries collect names of previous sex and violent offenders to guard against potential reoffending. The idea is that serious crime can be thwarted if the government acts soon enough.

A prominent example of proactive process is stop and frisk, when police engage in a supposedly low-stakes encounter in order to avert a potentially greater threat. The constitutional standards for stop and frisk were articulated by the Supreme Court in 1964 in *Terry v. Ohio*.[16] For a *Terry* stop to be legitimate, an officer must be able to show they had a reasonable suspicion that a crime was about to occur.[17] Until recently, stop and frisk was a go-to law enforcement tactic—in 2013 alone, New York City police briefly detained residents about half a million times.[18]

In *Terry* the court tried to strike a balance, providing police with a mechanism to intervene to prevent potential harm, and to protect individuals from undue interference with their daily lives. In practice, however, stop and frisk resulted in rampant racial profiling, abuses of power, and widespread community distrust. In New York City, Black and Hispanic persons were stopped about twice as often as White persons.[19] Only about 2 percent of frisk searches turned up actual weapons or contraband.[20] Data showed that stop and frisk negatively impacted individuals who were detained; Black youths who were regularly stopped by police performed lower on standardized tests, were less likely to go to college, and were less likely to vote.[21] In neighborhoods where the practice was active, there was sometimes an adversarial environment between residents and police, leading to an underreporting of criminal activity.[22] In 2014 a District Court found New York City's stop and frisk practices unconstitutional.[23]

By 2020, stop and frisk was not the only criminal justice practice being cast into question. Debates were happening around so-called quality of life offenses—vagrancy, vandalism, prostitution. Punishing these types of offenses was part and parcel of a broken windows approach, on the theory that punishing low-level offenses would head off potentially greater crimes. With officer-involved deaths of persons like Michael Brown, shot by a police officer in Ferguson, Missouri, after having been told to use the sidewalk, and Eric Garner in Brooklyn, New York, suffocated by law enforcement officers after being accused of unlawfully selling cigarettes, many members of the public began to question whether policies of treating poor people as potentially violent criminals was the right way to go. Many wondered if, rather than averting future harm, the criminalization of infractions like driving without a license or policies like *pay or stay,* mandating jail time for persons who could not pay outstanding fines, might in fact be creating the potentially dangerous populations the state claimed to want to protect us from.

In traditional criminal justice narratives, it is individuals who are accountable for managing the risk of crime and who are expected to adjust their behavior to minimize that risk. Recent social movements were challenging this narrative, highlighting how the criminal justice system itself was complicit in furthering racism and discrimination. In the midst of what was called, inaccurately and ill-advisedly, the *defund the police* movement, nearly three hundred bills to reform law enforcement were approved by state legislatures after summer 2020.[24] Localities did away with cash bail for non-felony offenses, decriminalized misdemeanors, placed restrictions on chokeholds and use of force, and created databases recording officer misconduct.[25] Referenda proposed to divert funding from police to social services, shift oversight of police departments to civilian boards, and send teams of social workers into the field with law enforcement.[26] Proposals for reform extended well beyond the criminal justice system, prompting corporations and nonprofit organizations to question the ways in which their practices or products might have functioned as "accessories" to state violence.

After a notable downward trend, however, from 2020 to 2022, violent crime rates rose dramatically across the United States.[27] Conservatives were quick to blame the jump on the defund movement, arguing that policies like eliminating cash bail for minor offenses, failing to prosecute quality of life crimes, and ending stop and frisk were leading to more criminals on the streets. Liberal activists countered that the reasons for rising crime rates were more complex, linked to the availability of firearms and deeply entrenched histories of poverty and discrimination.[28]

By 2023 very few jurisdictions had decided to defund police departments in a meaningful way; and federal funding for police had risen by $1 billion.[29] The movement toward reducing qualified immunity insulating officers from civil and criminal claims stalled in the legislature and courts.[30] Corporations that had promised to bring jobs and services to high-crime areas shuttered new locations, voicing concerns about employees' well-being.[31] In the 2021 elections, a solid majority of Minneapolis residents voted down a measure that would have replaced the Minneapolis police department with a reenvisioned Department of Public Safety.[32]

Disagreements over rising crime rates were not just political but resulted from some very practical problems. After the killing of George Floyd, residents in the area pledged that they would no longer be complicit in state violence by calling 911 to report minor offenses.[33] Tent cities popped up, and drug dealers flooded the area, making it unsafe for children to play outside.[34] Residents described that when they did call the police with urgent matters, law enforcement failed to respond.[35] Some people who resided in localities plagued by gun violence called for expanded police presence and the revival of stop and frisk practices, raising the concern that activists once again had spoken *for* the communities they ostensibly sought to protect rather than creating space for members of those communities to speak for themselves.[36]

Localities that did want to enact defunding measures sometimes found themselves hamstrung by more conservative state legislatures that constrained what individual voters and localities could accomplish. When the city council in Austin voted to reallocate a third of its police budget to social services Texas's conservative Governor Greg Abbott signed bills into law that would reduce or freeze tax revenue to cities that reallocated funds originally earmarked for the police.[37] Legislatures in Florida and Georgia approved similar measures.

Concerns arose as to whether reforms that were enacted would be lasting or whether changes were market driven. Steps taken by police departments and governments might be performative, masking more insidious practices behind the scenes. A visible decline in US mass incarceration over the past few years has been accompanied by a boom in e-carceration, the expansion of alternatives to imprisonment, such as electronic monitoring systems, including tethers and facial recognition programs, that at the outset may appear less invasive of individual privacy but in reality are a means for the state, quietly, to expand and deepen its surveillance power over a growing number of individuals. This demonstrates, again, the challenge of institutional complicity—while entities might publicly take accountability for the risks they created in one context, they could behind the scenes be creating new risks in another.

COMPLICITY, RISK, AND THE #METOO MOVEMENT

Like Black Lives Matter, the #MeToo social movement ushered in a massive transformation in how, as a society, we understand ideas about complicity and risk. Historically, sexual assault laws in the United

States were replete with victim-blaming. When misconduct occurred, the focus was rarely on what an alleged perpetrator did or why they did it, but the behavior of the victim: What were they wearing? Were they drinking? Did they say "no" or fight back? A notable exception was when the alleged victim was White and the alleged perpetrator was not, when racist assumptions tended to eclipse sexist ones.

In recent years, however, a significant change has been taking place. Over the past thirty years, society has been shaken by revelations of mass instances of sexual misconduct that have taken place across the spectrum of revered institutions—universities, military, churches, social organizations. For centuries parents entrusted the care of their children to colleges, coaches, scouting organizations, and religious establishments in order to foster their moral growth and protect them from the risk of harm. All the while, it turned out, risks were emanating from something rotten at the core of those institutions. In the wake of #MeToo society was coming to understand that sexual assault was not the fault of victims—or even, perhaps, wholly the fault of individual perpetrators—but a product of rape culture, the set of ideas, policies, and practices all around us that encouraged, enabled, or facilitated sexual assault. Like racism, sexual misconduct was coming to be understood as not a series of isolated events but a public health crisis that institutions were complicit in spreading.

This shift in understanding is visible in comparing the two criminal trials of comedian Bill Cosby. Cosby was first tried for the sexual assault of Andrea Constand in 2017, months before Alyssa Milano would tweet #MeToo. In 2002, during a visit to Cosby's home, Constand complained of a headache. In response, Cosby gave her some pills, which she reported made her lose consciousness. She recalled waking up "with her sweater bunched up around her and her bra undone."[38] Constand said she'd been assaulted; Cosby claimed they'd had a consensual encounter. Constand reported the incident to the police, but the state declined to prosecute. In 2015, however, the investigation into Constand's allegations was reopened. The state determined there was probable cause to proceed with a criminal trial.

During the first trial, a key procedural argument concerned whether accusers besides Constand should be permitted to testify. The state wanted to introduce testimony from other accusers to show Cosby had a "signature"—a unique pattern of behavior that involved using his fame to secure women's trust, then incapacitating and assaulting them. The defense countered that, in Hollywood, using fame to manipulate victims was not a calling card but a cliché. The state was describing behavior *so common,* the defense argued, that even if Cosby had done all of these things, they were not unique enough to be a signature.[39]

The judge excluded testimony from other accusers, accepting the defense's argument that the banality of coercive sexual encounters between powerful older men and young women weighed against a suggestion of serial predation. In other words, the casting couch was so pervasive that what took place could not be used as evidence against the accused. When the state argued that the presence of multiple accusations reinforced the celebrity's guilt, Cosby's attorneys countered that a "spate" of angry women coming forward saying "me too" merely suggested his status as a "wealthy target."[40] It was enough to prompt two jurors to find reasonable doubt and to cause a mistrial.

Eleven months later in the spring of 2018, the state of Pennsylvania again tried Bill Cosby. This time, prosecutors tried a different strategy. They argued that the prohibition against introducing prejudicial evidence of prior acts should be overcome by the "doctrine of chances," the mathematical probability that, had Cosby engaged in bad behaviors with others, he also would have done so with Andrea Constand. For the argument to work, other accusers' claims did not have to be proven in court but they needed to be credible. The judge found that they were. Five accusers besides Constand were permitted to testify at the second trial, and Cosby was convicted.[41]

Factually, nothing had changed between the first Cosby trial and the second. For alleged victims and perpetrators, however, 2018 was a different world. The #MeToo movement marked a tipping point in terms of who bore the risk of sexual assault and harassment. The first Cosby trial was clouded by contributory negligence, the idea that victims were accountable for their own abuse. In the first trial, the idea of the "casting couch" weighed in favor of the defense: *If so many young women were offering sexual favors to Hollywood power players*, the reasoning went, *then taking advantage could not be the imprimatur of a serial predator.* Just one year later, however, in the public imagination the casting couch had become a strikingly different place. What we had taken for granted as a harmless transaction in fact had been a crime.

The term "casting couch" is just one of a seemingly endless array of terms—seductress, temptress, Delilah, Lolita, jailbait, jezebel, gold digger—that serve one purpose: to excuse abuses by implying that a victim was somehow complicit in their abuse.[42] These terms justify abhorrent behavior not because that behavior is morally ok, but because the victim bears the risk of harm. Women traditionally have been expected to minimize this risk by taking preventative measures, such as not drinking alcohol, dressing modestly, or not walking alone at night.

Criminal law is replete with examples of how assumptions about complicity have operated to further harm victims and to insulate perpetrators from accountability. In 1910, the Mann Act, problematically referred to as the "white slave traffic act," was passed by Congress allegedly to prevent the interstate trafficking of women.[43] Supported by the progressive lobby, the Act was premised on the assumptions that to engage in sex work, women must have been coerced, abused, or exploited.[44] The first Mann Act cases held that, because they were the intended victims, women could not be convicted as accomplices to prostitution. However, in 1915, the US Supreme Court held that in fact a transported woman could be a co-conspirator if it was shown that the woman was as "able to look out for herself as was the man."[45] Although the stated intention of the law was to protect women, over a ten-year period more than 150 women were sentenced to prison for Mann Act violations.[46] Almost all of those convicted had low IQ scores, and 80 percent had not gone to school beyond the eighth grade.[47] Rather than its original intent of breaking up interstate trafficking rings, the

Mann Act served a moral function, punishing women who engaged in sex work.

A particularly egregious example of treating victims as complicit is accomplice-witness rules. For a century across the American South, prosecutions for the crime of father-daughter incest were hampered by rules which provided that the complaining witness in any incest case needed to present corroborating testimony from a third party.[48] Of course, finding corroboration usually was impossible; not only did alleged acts take place in private, but another rule prohibited mothers— the most likely witnesses—from testifying against their husbands in criminal cases.[49] The application of the accomplice-witness rule meant that defendants could not be convicted of incest even if it was abundantly clear that sexual acts between an adult and minor had occurred.[50]

These rules are not distant history. In 2017, in *Phelps v. State*, the Texas Court of Criminal Appeals was still debating the legitimacy of accomplice-witness rules in incest cases.[51] John Robert Phelps was convicted of prohibited sexual conduct with his biological daughter, who was nineteen at the time of the incident in question. Citing a 1974 case, Phelps challenged his conviction on the grounds that his daughter, who alleged that she had been sexually abused by the defendant starting at six years old, was an accomplice, and therefore needed to provide third-party corroboration for her testimony.[52] The court explained the rationale: "Incest is an offense against society in which both parties ordinarily engage with the same intent and purpose; hence *both parties* to the offense are principals and equally guilty."[53]

Although the majority in Phelps denied the defendant's appeal, emphasizing that the daughter was a victim and not an accomplice, there was—disturbingly—a dissent in the case that squarely placed responsibility on the victim. Justice Bailey C. Moseley wrote that, while the evidence clearly showed that there had been an ongoing and "brutal" abusive relationship between Phelps and his daughter throughout Ashley's childhood, "there was no evidence of that brutality when … Phelps was trying to get her to engage in sex acts with him on the night in question.... It appear[ed] ... from the record that Ashley was not totally unable to place any limits on Phelps' sexual conduct toward her."[54] In other words, the burden was not on Phelps, the longtime abuser, but on Ashley, the victim, to manage the risk of harm.

Prohibitions against statutory rape, a term describing a non-forcible sexual encounter between an adult and a child, also historically have treated young victims as complicit. Like laws against incest, statutory rape laws originated in the idea that women were property, and that a young women's value to the family declined if she was unchaste.[55] Traditionally there were three possible defenses to a charge of statutory rape. The first, mistake of fact as to the victim's age, rarely worked, because most jurisdictions made statutory rape a strict liability offense, meaning that no proof of criminal intent was required.[56] More commonly accepted was the defense was that the victim was promiscuous. British jurist Glanville Williams explained that, despite a victim's age: "Sometimes the girl may be an *active temptress* who is more experienced than the youth whom she herself seduces."[57] In other words, the more abuse a girl child suffered, the less credible she became. Some states allowed a third defense, consent. The consent defense was closely related to promiscuity, premised on the assumption that an underage victim of her own free will could decide to engage in a sexual relationship with an older man.

Until the 1970s, the state of Florida allowed the consent defense to statutory rape as long as a child victim was over twelve, provided that the victim was determined to have been previously unchaste.[58] Other states mandated that a victim had to prove her virginity for a statutory rape case to be brought at all.[59] One might be tempted to view these defenses as relics of a distant, less evolved past, but this is not the case. It was not until 2013 that Tennessee did away with its rule that classified statutory rape victims over age thirteen as accomplices, meaning that a case never could be brought on a victim's word alone.[60]

Today, definitions of injury and violence are changing, expanding to include not only physical, but emotional, psychological, and systemic harms. As Michelle Oberman describes, we are recognizing that "the fact that some girls might consent to sex which is inherently exploitive ... [is] not evidence of their competence to consent, nor of their 'womanliness,' but rather, of their immaturity and vulnerability to exploitation."[61] Further, rather than identifying incidents as the result of negligence by a victim, or the malintent of a perpetrator, we are more likely today to identify sexual assault and harassment as the result of failure by corporations, governments, or institutions, such as law, education, the military, or religious organizations, to protect the vulnerable. The #MeToo movement fueled this recognition, as more than 20 million people worldwide disclosed incidents of sexual assault and harassment in posts and tweets. As impactful as the sheer numbers of victims who disclosed personal experiences was their proximity—Facebook and Twitter feeds were flooded by posts from neighbors, teachers, friends, emphasizing the extent to which sexual assault and harassment had been normalized.

With the recognition of jaw-dropping institutional failures has come a reckoning with complicity. Once we identify the risk of sexual assault and harassment as not just emanating from individual perpetrators but as something systemic, we are faced with coming to terms with the way in which we ourselves might have been enablers—maybe laughing at a sexist joke, or failing to speak up after we experienced harassment—our inaction failing to protecting future victims.

It isn't just individuals that have been forced to reckon with their own complicity after #MeToo. There are noticeable, systemic reforms. In 2022 the military, plagued by issues of sexual assault and harassment for decades, strengthened criminal sanctions around sexual misconduct and, after years of pressure, Congress at last acted to move handling of cases out of the chain of command.[62] Companies reevaluated the use of nondisclosure agreements and mandatory arbitration practices in the context of sexual harassment and violence, moving to put an end to using *hush money* to silence accusers and protect powerful perpetrators.[63] A wave of firings has taken place across institutions and industries as network executives, college presidents, and CEOs have departed from the ranks having been outed as suspected abusers or enablers of abuse.

Compelled to acknowledge their role in—if not facilitating, then turning a blind eye to—sexual violence, institutions make spectacular displays of attempting to control and manage the risks of gender-based misconduct. Anti-harassment trainings proliferate with mixed results. While it is easier to identify blatantly illegal behaviors, it has been particularly tough for institutions to address the gray-area of harassment— subtle comments on appearance, or sexist comments or jokes. Women, non-White persons, and LGBTQ+ persons are more likely to experience micro aggressions and incidences of more blatant harassment. Problematically, those not directly impacted by harassment may not even see it, as evidenced by the array of anti-harassment trainings rolled out at institutions like the University of Southern California and University of Michigan after university leaders themselves were accused.

Structural changes also have taken place in law. In 2016 online site *Buzzfeed* published a victim impact statement by Chanel Miller (then known as Emily Doe) criticizing the jail sentence received by her attacker, Stanford student Brock Turner, after Turner sexually assaulted her while she was unconscious.[64] The best way to describe the public reaction to Turner's sentence was outrage, not just at the arguably light sentence the perpetrator received but at the systems that enabled and then failed to punish his behavior. More than a million people signed a petition to recall Judge Aaron Persky, who presided over the Turner case, resulting in Persky becoming the first California judge in eighty-six years to be recalled before finishing his term.[65] As the public gained an understanding of the uphill battles faced by survivors, they lobbied for stiffer penalties for perpetrators and expansion of statutes of limitation for sexual assault.[66] The force behind the #MeToo movement had been gathering since the 1970s. The sharing of #MeToo on social media was the spark it took to bring it all down.

Institutional efforts to deal with the risk of sexual misconduct bring up yet again the question of performativity—whether entities are making a good faith effort to manage risks or are searching for ways to deflect and displace accountability. Like racism, gender-based misconduct is a broad and ongoing problem. Even if it happens to us, we cannot really know its scope and significance until the issue is framed by the news media, by activists on social media, or by politicians.

There is an abundant focus on personal responsibility. The final chapter of this book talks about bystanders. In recent years, bystander intervention has emerged as a primary means of addressing workplace sexual harassment. These programs can be important in interrupting harassing behaviors in the day-to-day, where they may not be visible to management. However, bystander interventions are not effective unless they are embedded in a larger cultural context that is also committed to ending harassment.[67] Bystander programs have been part of the anti-harassment strategies used by the military for more than twenty years, yet rates of sexual assault and harassment in the institution remain high.[68] The power of individuals stepping up can only go so far if sexual assault and harassment are manifestations of a larger workplace disorder.

Part of #MeToo culture is praising survivors for speaking up. We laud the "silence breakers," brave individuals who speak out after having experienced assault or harassment.[69] A success of the movement is that reporting rates have gone up dramatically, not only in the United States but globally.[70] While creating more robust processes of reporting are important, placing accountability for speaking up primarily on the shoulders of individuals can mean the displacement of institutional accountability. Genevieve Guenther notes, in discussing climate change, that politicians tend to adopt "we" language, which initially seems to make sense in talking through a global problem. However, she argues, the "*we* responsible for climate change is a fictional construct, one that's distorting and dangerous. By hiding who's really responsible for our current, terrifying predicament, *we* provides political cover for the people who are happy to let hundreds of millions of other people die for their own profit and pleasure."[71]

In the context of sexual misconduct, speaking out is framed as healing, but there are questions as to whether the exercise benefits all victims. NDAs, for example, may hurt society at large by hiding acts of perpetrators, but in some cases they have benefited individual victims by allowing them to maintain personal privacy and settle claims efficiently, sometimes with significant compensation.[72] Historically, the idea of victimhood is connected to martyrdom and rooted in ideals of self-sacrifice.[73] When they fail to speak up to warn others of harms, victims can face criticism for not fulfilling the martyr stereotype. The specter of complicity looms large in the use of terms like hush money and whisper networks.

There is the question of whose stories we are inclined to believe. In both criminal courtrooms and in the court of public opinion, we gravitate toward stories about the weak and blameless who are targeted by evil, unknown offenders.[74] As Justice Thurgood Marshall articulated, being a legitimate victim can depend on "the eloquence with which family members express their grief and the status of the victim in the community."[75] White victims are twice as likely as Black victims to make victim-impact statements in criminal cases.[76] Media stories about non-White victims tend to be less sympathetic and more likely to focus on victims as risk-takers versus innocent parties.[77]

There is a call to expand "bad Samaritan" laws that incentivize bystanders to report crimes, sometimes with penalties attached for inaction.[78] In a society where personal choice is highly valued, penalizing people for choosing not to intervene to avert a bad situation seems logical—it is a visible accounting of the responsibility each of us bears for the fate of the collective. As we focus on individuals as the locus for interventions, however, it becomes individuals who bear the risk of misidentification and mistake; allegations that seem dubious or unsupported are often quickly labeled false claims and can subject claimants to if not criminal prosecution then public disdain.

In the wake of revelations of bad behavior, it is easy to become preoccupied with the *evilness* of direct perpetrators and their collaborators, something that can make us lose sight of larger and more complex goals for systemic reform. When serial predation comes to light, members of the public rush to call for harsh punishments to be levied on offenders, calling for perpetrators to receive a life sentence, to be raped in prison, or even to be executed.[79] On a positive note, comments like these suggest movement away from interrogating victims and toward situating responsibility on harmdoers. However, as discussed in earlier chapters, calls for increasing punishments, expanding crime categories, or expanding statutes of limitation may themselves be complicit in growing the criminal justice system, a system that is overwhelmingly more likely to negatively impact non-White and non-wealthy defendants than it is to punish or deter a future Nassar, Weinstein, or Epstein.

THE TUG-OF-WAR

As the Black Lives Matter and #MeToo movements gained steam, activists called out the complicity of legislatures, institutions, and corporations in fostering systems of inequality. Reflecting on the protests and litigation that took place in the 1970s through the '90s, anthropologist Mary Douglas characterized the battle between institutions and individuals over accountability for risks as a tug of war.[80] Faced with allegations of complicity, industries and institutions push back forcefully, sometimes in unexpected ways. As movements waxed and waned, tensions sprang up around the previously obscure concept of critical race theory, a theoretical lens used by legal scholars to help identify how historical systems and structures continue to contribute to contemporary social inequality.

In 2020, President Trump issued an Executive Order "to combat offensive and anti-American race and sex stereotyping and scapegoating," prohibiting federal offices from promoting the belief that "an individual, by virtue of his or her race or sex, bears responsibility for actions committed in the past by other members of the same race or sex."[81] On the heels of Trump's executive order, later repealed by President

Biden, STOP W.O.K.E. bills and referenda banning teaching CRT in public schools were passed by legislatures in more than twenty states.[82] In Oklahoma, House Bill 1772, signed into law in 2021, prohibits public school K-12 teachers from teaching that "[a]ny individual should feel discomfort, guilt, anguish or any other form of psychological distress on account of his or her race or sex."[83] A similar bill, voted down by the Michigan senate, proposed to ban "race of gender stereotyping," defined as promoting the belief "[t]hat individuals bear collective guilt for historical wrongs committed by their race or gender."[84]

Complicity is at the heart of the debates about CRT taking place throughout the United States. In multiple contexts—racism, sexism, climate change, LGBTQ+ rights—Americans are being asked to reassess their own behaviors, and to take accountability not only for actions they knew in a factual sense were wrong but for the times when they— and their ancestors—were ostriches, deliberately ignoring things they *should have known* were unjust. Although the majority of Americans proclaim that they don't know exactly what CRT is, descriptions by conservative activists and legislators are strikingly accurate. Applying critical race theory involves tracing pathways of complicity, forging connections between individuals and larger structures of oppression, and identifying how problems such as racism, sexism, ableism, or homophobia comprise not only intentional acts by individuals but unconscious ones, actions we took based on assumptions that were so embedded in the fabric of society we failed to notice them.

At a time in which, across issues, people are being held accountable not only for what they knew, but what they should have known, anti-CRT and Stop-W.O.K.E. bills attempt to limit the expansion of accountability by narrowing the definition of knowledge. Anti-W.O.K.E. laws don't argue that racism does not exist, or that systems of enslavement, Jim Crow, and redlining did not result in exclusion and disenfranchisement. Rather, they proclaim that Americans do not need to be informed about such systems and are not required to think through their own connection to unjust structures. The language of these laws is paternalistic—couched in parents' responsibility to protect young people from emotional harm and guilt. But, just as objections to desegregation after *Brown v. Board of Education* were not about states' rights, protests to CRT are not about parental autonomy. Anti-CRT bills and mandates against policies of diversity, equity, and inclusion are intended to ensure that all of us remain ostriches; we will be incapable of challenging discriminatory systems and structures because we are, very simply, prohibited from seeing them.

The rush to promote anti-CRT bills and Stop W.O.K.E. legislation is an indication that society is at a conjuncture where new beliefs and ideas are beginning to take hold. Once settled norms are disrupted, and existing definitions and categories are, suddenly, open to debate. Protests against anti-racism are identified as *backlash*, but they are better described as the last salvos of once-powerful customs and norms, a response to efforts to revisit accepted truths and renegotiate the parameters of responsibility for past harms. As society excavates its foundations, there is fear as to what will be uncovered and concern as to who will be empowered to interpret and give meaning to the artifacts.

While some willingly engage in the process of reckoning with personal accountability for past harms, others react to broadening categorizations of racism and injury with skepticism or resistance. In the wake of contemporary social movements, many people have been undergoing a transformation, in which they are both taking on accountability for past harms, and—sometimes for the first time—seeing themselves and loved ones as capable of inflicting future harm. Faced with this daunting task, it is tempting to resist the notion that racism can result from anything but personal choice. When resistance is supported by a politics of fear, taking the easy way out is tempting, rather than doing the hard work of taking account of our own implication in the world's problems. The discourse of personal responsibility is a powerful one; it can be used to great effect by institutions to make sure that, rather than holding entities accountable, we shame and blame one another.

CONCLUSION

We are at a liminal moment in which assumptions about risks—who bears them, and who is accountable for dealing with them going forward—are changing. For the first time, we are approaching issues like racism and sexual misconduct not as interpersonal harms but as public health crises. Society is questioning long-standing practices that served to insulate the powerful by placing blame on victims for the harms they experienced.

There is tangible change. Institutions have revised long-standing policies, corporations are renaming products, redesigning logos, and instituting chief diversity officer positions. Museums are returning tainted donations, and universities are revisiting legacy admissions. Since the Civil Rights era of the 1960s and the first wave of the women's movement in the 1970s, the forces of change were amassing at the top of the mountain. The pandemic, along with the inspiration provided by the #MeToo and Black Lives Matter movements, was the catalyst to set them loose. We are not just thoughtlessly or carelessly toppling once-revered monuments, but dismantling them, then gradually excavating troubled histories and attempting to envision more inclusive practices and policies that might take their place.

At the same time, resistance is strong. In 2022, voters in cities across the United States overwhelmingly failed to support movements to defund the police. Supporters of reform complained that the wording was the problem—"defund" sounded too radical, when the intention was to make more subtle changes, such as the addition of line items for education and social services, or the hiring of behavioral evaluation teams. But the problem was not just in the name. The pressure being exerted against institutions and corporations to change long-standing, discriminatory policies and practices signaled a larger, societal shift in assumptions about risk. Americans across race, gender, and economic status together were trying to shift accountability for harm creation off of individual shoulders and onto the systems, institutions, and corporations.

At certain historical moments we can identify a time of metamorphosis, when a change can take place in the way we view the relationship of the individual to the world. But instituting lasting change is not an easy task. Ananda Abeysekara, who studies the contentious world of politics and religion in Sri Lanka, refers to certain moments in time as "contingent conjunctures."[85] A conjuncture is a crisis juncture—a time when society is on the threshold and uniquely open to transformation and change. The changes that will result from a given conjuncture, however, are not predetermined, but "contingent"; in a world of competing claims for authority and power, it is less than clear which voices will prevail.

The roadblocks encountered in the wake of the Black Lives Matter and #MeToo movements highlight that, even when one sees the risks inherent in a system, it is exhaustingly complicated to reimagine that system. We are in a place where we are tasked with choosing between continuing hugely imperfect, yet concrete, practices or going all in on an imaginary future. Complicity may be a useful means of excavating the past, but it is less clear that complicity is equal to the task of rebuilding something new.

SIX

Beyond Complicity

On March 13, 1964, around 3 a.m., twenty-eight-year-old Kitty Genovese was murdered in the quiet New York City borough of Kew Gardens, Queens. The young woman's death came to characterize the viciousness of indifference. Her killer, Winston Moseley, stalked the victim, was frightened off, and returned to commit a fatal attack. All the while, the *New York Times* reported at the time, thirty-eight of Genovese's neighbors watched the scene unfold but failed to intervene.[1] Reporter Loudon Wainwright wrote for *Life* magazine that "the witnesses, crouching in darkened windows" were "like watchers of a Late Show, look[ing] on until the play had passed from their view."[2] We were becoming "a callous, chickenhearted and immoral people," Wainwright lamented.[3]

Genovese's death captured public attention not only for its brutality but for what seemed to be a particularly vicious apathy among witnesses to the crime. Dissected by numerous psychologists, the murder contributed to the recognition of the bystander effect, a widely accepted theory that people in groups are less likely to intervene to avert harm than when they are alone.[4] Shortly after Genovese's death, psychologists Bibb Latané and John Darley performed an experiment in which college students were set up to witness a person pretending to have an epileptic seizure. The researchers found that, when by themselves, 85 percent of observers stepped up to help the victim; when those same people were in a group, only around 30 percent tried to help.[5] Latané and Darley came to two conclusions. First, there was a free rider effect—people in groups were less likely to step in because they assumed somebody else would do the hard work. Second, and significantly, people in groups were less likely to intervene because they would not face any consequences if they did not act.[6] "However much we wish to think that an individual's moral behavior is divorced from considerations of personal punishment or reward," the psychologists noted, "there is both theory and evidence to the contrary. It is perfectly reasonable to assume that, under circumstances of group responsibility for a punishable act, the punishment or blame that accrues to any one individual is often slight or nonexistent."[7] Latané and Darley's conclusion rested on an extremely important (and flawed) assumption: The fear of being shamed for silence will incentivize individuals to act better.

The story of the Genovese killing appeared in the news when the United States was experiencing a moment of plasticity; having been witness to unimaginable suffering during the Second World War, Americans were primed to consider new ideas and theories about human responsibility to the world. The story of the heartless bystanders in the Genovese case captivated not only academics like Darley and Latané but ordinary people, many of whom read and watched accounts of the Nuremberg proceedings, the first international prosecution of crimes against humanity, and who were reeling from the collective shock of the recent assassination of beloved President John F. Kennedy. Civil rights protests were erupting throughout New York City and the nation.

In a confusing time of rapid social change, journalists' skepticism about human nature seemed to be supported by academic research. Months prior to Kitty Genovese's death, psychologist Stanley Milgram published the results of an experiment demonstrating that it was not just Nazi leaders but the average person who would be willing to administer deadly shocks to other humans if told to do so by an authority figure.[8] The common understanding from research by Milgram and

later studies by Philip Zimbardo, in which Stanford students enthusiastically leaned in to assigned roles as prison guards, was that "[a]ll
human beings are Nazis in waiting. Under the right circumstances,
they will cheerfully administer lethal shocks to strangers, or watch as
their neighbors are murdered, or organize genocides. If they have not
committed acts of depravity, it is because they live in a society that
keeps their baser instincts under control, not because they lack the
instincts themselves."[9] In the immediate aftermath of the Second World
War, researchers generally assumed average citizens were simply following state orders, but by the mid-1960s, scholars were beginning to
question how everyday acts—or even passivity—by ordinary persons
might have contributed to inconceivable tragedy.[10]

Since the 1960s, we have been preoccupied by questions of human
nature, leading to the massive growth of subfields of social science and
psychological research on bystanders. All of the most popular social
psychology textbooks mention the bystander effect.[11] Most of them
engage the Genovese story, taking for granted that being callous, apathetic, or even cruel are inherent human traits and that public shaming
can be a powerful motivator for people to step up to intervene.[12] The
takeaway from bystander research is at the same time disheartening
and hopeful. We think the worst of people, but we believe that, through
the right interventions, we can train them to act better.

In this historical moment, the sense that our fellow humans may be
"Nazis in waiting" again is pervasive. In 1976, 86 percent of Americans
expressed confidence in others' judgment; in 2021 this number plummeted to 55 percent.[13] After the 2020 election, nonprofit organization
More in Common surveyed Biden and Trump voters about their opinions
about one another. A significant percentage of Americans across the
political aisle expressed that they were not merely angry but "disgusted"
with those who held opposing political points of view.[14] Disgust is an
emotion that is deeper and more troubling than anger. It reflects moral
outrage; it is a precursor to dehumanization.[15] In a world filled with people we assume have dubious motives, writer Jackson Arn describes the

comfort we take in focusing on prevention: "We might be murderers, and we might not, but isn't it safer to assume we are and be proven wrong than to assume we are not and hope to be proven right? As with cancer, so with evil: A false positive is safer than a false negative."[16]

The heartless bystander narrative draws on confirmation bias. It is likely to ring true for many of us who in the past few years have discovered that once-beloved celebrities and politicians acted in ways that facilitated discrimination and inequality, or that neighbors, friends, and colleagues secretly harbored sexist or racist views. Returning to the hypothetical at the start of chapter 1, in this liminal moment each of us is standing on a ledge, witnessing multiple boulders that are rolling toward unsuspecting hikers in a crevasse below. Faced with the imminent disasters of global polycrisis—climate change, racism, sexism, addiction—we understand that each of us must do something. The bigger, nearer, or more fast-moving the risk, the less tolerance we have for complacency, and the greater disgust we have for the complacent.

The examples in this book give us reasons to believe, however, that human beings are not as callous or chickenhearted as we have been conditioned to think. We are trained to focus on the negative— political polarization, disinformation, and discrimination. But while we have been confronted by a multitude of large-scale and immensely complex problems, synapses have been firing at all levels of society— individual, social, and systemic—marking a transition in the relationship of human beings to the larger world. We are connective witnesses, who have not only been watching events unfold but bearing witness to them in an almost Biblical sense, dissecting their meanings and questioning the ways in which human action (and silence) might be impacting distant geographies and people very different from ourselves.

Out of significant experiences of trauma can come personal and collective growth and increased abilities for cognitive and emotional empathy.[17] In the aftermath of tragedy, humans can emerge with a newfound resilience, an optimism that results not from rose-colored glasses but from a newly realistic assessment of human capacity for gratitude, empathy, and personal and social change. Surviving a traumatic experience makes people more likely to ask existential questions: *What is my relationship to the larger world?* After a seismic event, such as war, a mass shooting, a pandemic, it becomes natural to challenge previously sedimented ways of thinking, and to formulate a new concept of what it really means to live a meaningful life. We are more able to imagine ourselves walking the paths of others, and to examine situations from new points of view.

Rather than focusing on human shortcomings, it is productive to acknowledge how, as individuals and as a society, we have been becoming *better*—something that is demonstrated by our capacity to notice—and to learn—more and different lessons from the Genovese narrative, sixty years later, that we simply couldn't see before. This is not a straightforward narrative of progress but is replete with fits and starts, recognizing that while human beings are, perhaps, not as inherently inclined toward brutishness as we might have thought, we are also inherently imperfect, likely to do many wrong things even if our intention is to do the right one.

AT SCENE OF THE CRIME

It is popular in criminal justice narratives to observe that perpetrators often return to the scene of the crime, to take pride in their misdeeds, to clean up evidence, or—perhaps—from a sense of remorse or regret. Returning to the scene, and closely examining the death of Kitty Genovese and the assumptions it spawned, can reveal the shortcomings of complicity as a strategy for holding individuals accountable, and suggest the importance of identifying the often unacknowledged operation of systems and structures that influence human behavior and decision-making.

Reflecting on the March night when Kitty Genovese was killed sixty years later, it turns out that, like most folk narratives, the real story is more complicated than we usually assume. First and foremost, upon interrogation, the idea of a mass of disengaged bystanders as portrayed in the *Times* does not hold up. In journalists' accounts neighbors are described as watching an attack on Genovese unfold as though they were spectators at a Broadway play. However, as chronicled by historian Joseph De May, who did extensive research into Genovese's life and death, the victim actually experienced two distinct attacks on the night of her murder. The first was a brief assault that was thwarted when a neighbor yelled out. The second, more sustained attack took place indoors at the back of the apartment building, a location outside most residents' line of vision.[18] A second factual error is in regard to the number of witnesses; far from thirty-eight, there were just six people who were deemed to have enough information to testify at Moseley's trial.[19] Of the six, none saw the entire incident unfold.[20]

The most significant factual error the in *Times*' story is the insistence that *no one intervened*. In fact, several people who saw the attack probably did something, and at least two people called the police. Fifteen year-old Michael Hoffman saw the first attack and promptly told his father, who waited on hold with a dispatcher for more than five minutes to report that "a lady was 'beat up, but got up and was staggering around.'"[21] Assuming Genovese had gone home, Hoffman senior nonetheless stayed awake until the police arrived, and when they did, he immediately went downstairs to speak with them. Having seen the victim walk away, the Hoffmans were later dismayed to find out what they'd witnessed was an attempted murder.[22] Hoffman was not the only neighbor to run downstairs. Two women also heard Kitty's screams and rushed to the scene immediately after Moseley left. One of them, Sophia Farrar, cradled Genovese in her arms in the dark hallway until the police arrived.[23]

The story of how police came to identify Winston Moseley as Genovese's killer also weighs against the assumption that, if left to our own devices, human beings will be apathetic in the face of harm. Moseley was apprehended not due to a police investigation, but by chance, after being caught by two bystanders while committing a burglary.[24] A man spotted Moseley taking a television out of a neighbor's home and loading it into his car and stopped to question him. Doubting Moseley's excuse that he was helping a neighbor move, the good Samaritan called a friend. Together, the two took action, disabling Moseley's car and calling the police.[25]

Although some recent accounts have sought to debunk the factual errors and omissions in the Genovese narrative, the overall theme of the heartless bystander is deeply embedded in the public imagination. All ten of the leading undergraduate psychology textbooks include a reference to the Genovese case, and eight of those describe neighbors having watched an attack from their windows.[26] None of the textbooks mention the heroic story of Moseley's capture. The American Psychological Association describes the myth of the heartless bystanders to Genovese murder as a "tall tale," making it sound like harmless amusement.[27] But the narrative is far from harmless; the myth of the apathetic bystander is foundational to our self-identity. Imagine if, rather than a story of uncaring onlookers, the narrative we told about Kitty Genovese related the heroic acts by the neighbors who stepped in to avert a burglary and captured a serial killer, or those of Sophia Farrar, who cradled Kitty Genovese in her arms in the dark at great personal risk. There are lessons to be learned from unfolding and reimagining the narrative of Kitty Genovese.

OBSERVATION ONE: WE ARE BETTER THAN WE THINK

A first, key takeaway from unfolding the Genovese narrative is that human beings might be better than we think. Historian Rutger Bregman listened to hundreds of hours of tapes and interviewed research participants from the Milgram and Zimbardo studies and discovered something important. Rather than having been "cheerfully" willing to inflict violence, as many thought, it turns out that many participants in these research studies were reluctant to abuse others, even in a pretend scenario.[28] Students assigned to play guards in Zimbardo's experiment had to be convinced to use aggressive tactics; one third of participants assigned to the guard roles treated prisoner participants with kindness.[29] Some who did act aggressively later expressed having known that they were playing a role and confessed they'd acted out for the money—the fifteen dollars per day they received was equal to about one hundred dollars today.[30] Similarly, more than 40 percent of participants who administered shocks in Milgram's study described having been aware that, rather than real-life, they were engaged in a an experiment where another person was not in fact being harmed.[31]

Some of Milgram's research participants who did believe they were mistreating human victims expressed having been motivated to continue with the studies not to inflict pain but because they thought they were contributing to a greater good.[32] For example, one participant described signing up for every scientific research study he could because his daughter suffered from cerebral palsy, and he hoped scientific research would eventually lead to a cure.[33] Psychologist Don Mixon, who replicated Milgram's experiment in the 1970s, came to a dramatically different conclusion than Milgram himself: "In fact, people go to great lengths, will suffer great distress, to be good. People got caught up in trying to be good."[34]

When asked whether society's morals are declining, a significant majority of people across the globe respond in the affirmative, agreeing that the state of moral values is becoming worse over time.[35] Business professor Adam Mastroianni and psychologist Daniel Gilbert argue, however, that the widespread perception of society as becoming less moral or ethical is mistaken.[36] Analyzing responses from more than 12 million people who participated in surveys around the world from 1940 through today, the researchers show that, while we tend to view past generations in a positive light, we are much less likely to give our contemporaries the benefit of the doubt.[37] When asked questions like, "Would you say most of the time people try to be helpful?" or "During the past 12 months, have you let a stranger go ahead of you in line?" responses from past decades are no different from those today.[38] Some people are generous, and some aren't. When questioned about specific issues, such as treatment of African Americans, the LGBTQ+ community, or disabled persons, at least half of respondents today describe things as getting better.[39] Nonetheless, most people are inclined to say that people are becoming less generous, and the world less safe. Mastroianni and Gilbert hypothesize that two things are going on: we tend to misremember negative events from the past, and we are drawn to negative stories about other people in the present, something readily exploited by the media.[40]

Scholars are only beginning to question how negative assumptions about human nature may have impacted researchers' conclusions about the bystander effect. In 2020, a research team viewed surveillance videos from more than two hundred violent, public encounters that took place in numerous cities around the world.[41] They found that, far from being apathetic, when witnessing a conflict, nine out of ten bystanders were likely to intervene, taking steps such as pulling the aggressor away, attempting to placate the parties, or consoling the victim. In contrast to Latané and Darley's studies, these researchers found that the presence of other bystanders in fact increased the likelihood of intervention.[42] They conclude, much more hopefully than Darley and Latané, that "[p]eople have a natural propensity to help others in distress."[43]

Over the years, Kitty Genovese's neighbors have offered many, sometimes conflicting, answers as to why they did not step in to avert the crime. Some, like the Hoffmans, said they didn't understand the extent of the violence they had witnessed. Other people—often women or the elderly—said they sensed a crime was happening but failed to step in because they feared becoming victims themselves.[44] In the end, the most common reaction among Genovese's neighbors was frustration— they did not know what they could do to help.[45] Individuals can be paralyzed by anxiety, the fear that even the smallest of our individual decisions might do harm causing us to fail to act at all. Yet, the Genovese case and recent research studies show that many of us can and do act.

How might society be radically different if, rather than starting from the assumption that bystanders will be uncaring, the focus was on humans' ability to make small, but positive interventions, or that even bad choices might be the result of misguided efforts to do the right thing?

OBSERVATION TWO: WE ARE A PRODUCT
OF OUR TIMES

To be a legal accomplice (at least technically) requires having acted knowingly, having an awareness that a crime will be committed, and providing intentional assistance toward the commission of the offense. Allegations of complicity, however, have a knowledge problem. Human beings only have the capacity to *know* that a problem exists when they have the moral and ethical positioning to see it, the vocabulary to name it, and the social supports to do something about it.

To say that the criminal justice system of the early 1960s was hostile to women victims would be an understatement. When harms were done to women—particularly women like Kitty Genovese who worked in bars or returned home unescorted late at night—assumptions about the victim cast doubt on their veracity and insulated perpetrators from blame and accountability. Many more neighbors saw or heard Moseley's first attack than the second one that occurred behind the building. What they imagined they'd witnessed was a violent encounter, possibly a rape, after which the woman got to her feet and walked unsteadily away.[46] Some reported that they heard a woman yelling, but assumed it was a lover's quarrel.[47] Most did not interpret the event as an attempted murder by a stranger.[48] Statements from neighbors who did identify the event as serious are peppered with victim-blaming justifications for failing to intervene: "What was she doing out so late, anyway?" and "If that girl had been where she belongs, this would never have happened."[49] The killer was so confident neighbors would not follow up that, after the first attack, he decided to return to his car, repark it in a less visible location, and return to the building to finish the homicide.[50]

The statements by Genovese's neighbors reflect the world of 1964, a time in which rape was significantly underreported and under-prosecuted, marital rape was legal, and the attitude of law enforcement toward domestic disputes was, generally, to turn a blind eye. It was not until the mid-1970s that rape shield laws, courtroom rules protecting victims from attacks on their credibility based on evidence of sexual histories, were introduced. The terminology of victim-blaming would not be widely used until the early 1970s, when activists and researchers began to highlight the ways in which those who experienced injuries as a result of racism or sexual misconduct routinely were being held responsible for harms that befell them. Statements by many neighbors reflect something that remains true about the bystander effect today: people are much more likely to step up to help when they share a sense of identity with the person in distress.[51]

The witnesses to Kitty Genovese's murder did not have the capacity we have today to identify that a crime was happening, nor—if some did comprehend that a crime was taking place—did they have the social supports to intervene. The responses by many of Genovese's neighbors demonstrate that humans' capacity for effecting social transformation is a product of the historical moment we inhabit. The neighbors' justifications for nonintervention are appalling to read in contemporary context. But rather than callous or chickenhearted, it is more accurate to say that the observers that night were human, their ability to interpret and respond to a crisis delimited by the technologies, systems, and structures of the time.

OBSERVATION THREE: WE ARE ALL IMPLICATED SUBJECTS

A third lesson one might take from the Genovese story is that, although it is tempting to see human behavior in stark terms, adhering to a victim/perpetrator dichotomy, in reality people are much more complex. A major driver of the heartless bystander myth was a quote from Karl Ross, a friend and neighbor of Kitty Genovese's who heard her screams during the second attack but failed to open his apartment door. Ross infamously justified his failure to intervene with a pointed statement: "I didn't want to get involved."[52] While the statement was widely quoted, the context in which it was made is mostly absent from discussion.

Something not reported at the time was that Kitty Genovese was a lesbian, living with her partner, Mary Ann Zielonko.[53] Karl Ross was also gay, and on the night of the murder was very drunk. When he heard Kitty's screams he called a friend, who counseled Ross against getting involved. Unsatisfied with the response, Ross called a different neighbor, who told him to call the police.[54] Fearful of being identified if he used his own phone, Ross crawled across the roof to the neighbor's apartment, where he called the police anonymously.[55]

To the contemporary reader, Ross's tortured reasoning in the face of an ongoing attack can seem illogical, but it is less so when one considers the relationship between individuals and law enforcement in 1964. There was no 911 emergency system at that time; the implementation of that system would be inspired by the Genovese case.[56] Wait times for police responses were very long, particularly in the hours when bars were closing, and it was a fifty-fifty proposition whether police would arrive on the scene at all.

According to Mary Ann Zielonko, Ross was a fearful man who rarely left his apartment.[57] Complicating Ross's decision-making on March 13 was that in pre-Stonewall 1960s New York City, the relationship between law enforcement and the LGBTQ+ community was extremely hostile. LGBTQ+ persons were frequent targets of police raids, animosity, and violence. Journalist Peter C. Baker reflects, "[I]t's easy to hear 'I didn't want to get involved' as 'I didn't want to help my suffering neighbor.' But the more one learns about Ross, the easier it becomes to hear another translation: "I didn't want to get involved with the police, who ... view homosexuality as a menace to society."[58]

Ross's wariness seems to have been warranted based on what transpired once officers arrived. Rather than searching for a stranger, officers focused their attention on Mary Ann Zielonko, interrogating her for more than six hours with their questions focusing primarily on the couple's sex life.[59] Ross, whose drunkenness was identified as an impediment to the investigation, was arrested for disorderly conduct. Exhausted, Mary Ann was unable to work the next day and was fired.[60] Although the couple had been living together for more than a year, Mary Ann was banned from attending Kitty's funeral because Kitty's family disapproved of the women's relationship.[61]

In revisiting the horrific crime against Kitty Genovese one can see how human actions are constrained and delimited by social systems that surround us. A problem with focusing on individual complicity is that, while accusations might identify some direct perpetrators—criminal masterminds and evil doers—it is just as likely to stigmatize what Rothberg calls implicated subjects, persons who bear some responsibility for an event but are far from the ultimate decision-maker, and whose actions are themselves constrained by systems of oppression or discrimination.

BEYOND COMPLICITY

We find ourselves at a threshold, when questions of blameworthiness and accountability are front and center. When it comes to a historical event like the Genovese murder, none of us are disinterested third parties. We were not direct perpetrators but we nonetheless must reckon with the assumptions and biases of the past in order to construct a more just future.

Moving beyond complicity and toward something new is not an easy task. We have a capacity to know, in both a legal and moral sense, much more than we did before. But this enhanced ability brings up concerns about what we might discover, and debates as to what we are obligated to do with newfound information. Identifying that society is at a liminal moment is one thing, ensuring that positive changes take hold is another thing entirely.

One of the most significant shortcomings of complicity is that there is no logical end to it. When World War II ended, millions of Germans were mandated to enroll in denazification programs; residents in Allied zones filled out questionnaires detailing their activities in order to be placed in one of five categories ranging from exonerated to "major offender."[62] To a large extent, these programs were not successful. There was an issue of corruption, where decisions were thwarted by uncooperative witnesses and unenthusiastic judges, and a robust pardon process, nicknamed *Persilschein* after a popular laundry detergent.[63]

As big a problem as corruption was the fact that so many people seemed to have been, somehow, complicit. While about twenty-five thousand people were categorized as direct collaborators, the vast majority of German citizens—more than 8 million people who had been members of the National Socialist German Workers Party—fell into the lowest category of participation, the Mitläufer, meaning "those who followed the current."[64] Ethicist Victoria Barnett describes the process of holding persons to account immediately after the Holocaust as plagued by a question that we continue to confront today: "Where is the line that differentiates a bystander from a perpetrator?"[65] Ultimately, the formal denazification process was abandoned. With so many layers of acts and actors, there was no way to impose formal accountability without risking the stability of the nation itself.

The challenges to reckoning with widespread complicity in the Holocaust continue to plague contemporary crises. In 1994, Rwanda's Hutu government exterminated nearly all people from the nation's Tutsi ethnic group. Decades later, only seventy individuals have been convicted out of the thousands who participated in the massacre.[66] Religious and national leaders who acted far too slowly to respond, and the media, which provided platforms that amplified dehumanizing discourse, have faced few if any consequences.[67] Thirty years after the Bosnian War, more than four thousand people still await trial for their participation in hundreds of thousands of war crimes; human rights groups describe these trials as a "race against time," as with each passing day, evidence becomes staler, witnesses grow less reliable, and suspects die and disappear.[68] Victims of incidents of horrific violence taking place across geographies—Afghanistan, Bangladesh, Syria, Ethiopia, Chechnya, Bosnia, Ukraine—face similar deficits of legal accountability. As

Martha Minow writes, the failure to hold bad actors accountable while the oppressive structures that benefit them remain in place risks "institutionaliz[ing] forgetfulness," creating an environment in which bad behavior can continue without consequences.[69]

The ever-expanding borders of complicity are apparent in contemporary discussions around issues like racism, sexual misconduct, and climate change, where the extent and breadth of accusations has led to an overwrought culture, in which apology is both expected and meaningless. Some individuals face disproportionate shaming and ostracism, while others are too easily welcomed back into the fold.

On an individual level, just when we are satisfied that we are doing good in one context, we may realize that we have been connected to harmdoing in another. As millions of people took to the streets to protest in connection with the MeToo and Black Lives Matter social movements, some wore what has become known as fast fashion, low-cost garments produced by workers from Bangladesh, Vietnam, and other developing nations. The fast fashion industry is notorious for its reliance on forced labor and is a massive environmental polluter, creating 1.7 billion cubic tons of carbon dioxide per year.[70] Protesters might have snacked on products produced by Nestle, sued for its role in facilitating child labor practices in Africa's Ivory Coast; sipped coffee from Starbucks, under fire for union busting, or used an iPhone as manufacturer Apple disavowed accountability for reliance on forced labor from China's Uyghur minority.

Reflecting on her family's experiences as German citizens during the Holocaust, author Geraldine Schwarz describes a personal coming to terms with the idea that complicity could occur not only through bad acts or indifference, but through attempts to do good. She describes a realization that small acts of kindness might have contributed to worsening the situation for Jews in the 1930s, creating a false sense of security and normalcy among neighbors that obscured the larger, horrific intentions of the state. In hindsight it can be impossible to separate out innocent acts from guilty.[71]

Any deep dive into complicity necessarily reveals troubling truths. It might turn out that politicians we supported based on their social justice platforms behind the scenes were enabling or obscuring sexual harassment, that once-favorite authors used racist tropes and stereotypes, or the celebrities whose music we adore casually are using private jets in the face of climate change. As we assess our position in regard to the risks we confront today, many of us may come to see ourselves and others as, if not agents of harm, then implicated subjects who "contribute to, inhabit, inherit, or benefit from regimes of domination."[72] This awareness can feel overwhelming.

Interrogating complicity is a political task. Since the 1990s European nations have been engaged in processes of unfolding layers of interactions that contributed to Nazi atrocities. After a painstaking investigatory process, Switzerland was found guilty of accomplice liability by an international commission, as a result of the nation's "declin[ing] to help people in mortal danger."[73] France has paid out more than $6 billion in restitution to Holocaust survivors and their families in an acknowledgment that "the criminal folly of the (Nazi) occupiers was assisted by the French people."[74]

As other European nations have been questioning the roles of not only states but ordinary citizens in the Holocaust, Poland adamantly resists any suggestion that the nation or its people were complicit. In 2019, the Polish government passed a law providing a fine (the bill initially provided jail time) for any person claiming that Poland was "responsible or co-responsible" for Nazi atrocities. In 2021, a court decision that was later overturned mandated that two Polish historians apologize for having implied that ordinary Polish citizens played any role in Nazi crimes.

Poland's adamancy in disclaiming complicity in the Holocaust highlights that unfolding complicity will necessarily unearth unsettling truths. In the United States, the arrival of the American troops at Normandy is widely treated as a triumph of good over evil. While we celebrate the historic landing, however, less commonly interrogated is its aftermath, which involved the deaths of thousands of civilians, the scapegoating of non-White soldiers, and the serial humiliation of the defeated. Researchers estimate that after D-Day at least fourteen thousand French women were raped by American troops, who had been encouraged by the state to see civilians as having enabled German advancement.[75] Reflecting the biases inherent in the American criminal justice system at the time, only 152 American soldiers were tried for rape.[76] Appallingly, 139 of those tried were African American.[77] While most executions in France were carried out by guillotine, a significant proportion of these military executions were carried out by hanging, based on the idea that fear of the noose would be a particularly effective deterrent to rape among Black soldiers.[78] There is a private cemetery at Normandy, Plot E, that houses the bodies of eighty Black soldiers who were executed for rape in France.[79] One of those graves belongs to Louis Till, the father of Emmett Till.

The vast majority of US narratives about World War II focus on the complicity of German soldiers and citizens in Nazi atrocities. To interrogate the silence of the Greatest Generation in the face of systemic gender-based violence and racism is to question the collective US historical imagination, the very foundations on which society is built. Like unfolding an intricate piece of origami, tracing complicity can reveal unexpected and seemingly endless paths and intersections. There is a fear that in unfolding a fragile structure with too much force, we risk tearing the structure itself.

Fears about the excavation, revision, and control of historical memory are driving contentious and divisive political initiatives, such as book bans, anti-W.O.K.E. legislation, and debates over the teaching of critical race theory. There are concerns about what we will find when we excavate the past, and who will control the narrative in the future. Political stratagems like anti-W.O.K.E. campaigns are the most visible objections to accountability. More insidious resistance is happening behind the scenes—policymaking on addiction funded by big pharma, sustainability centers supported by fossil fuels, strategies that insulate bad actors from accountability, like qualified immunity and bankruptcy proofing.

The challenges to holding the most egregious actors accountable for large-scale crises cause some to press for the expansion of criminal legal complicity. Some argue that standards of intent should be relaxed, so that behind-the-scenes actors can be punished for not only knowingly but recklessly—or even negligently—facilitating mass atrocities. Others advocate that causal requirements could be amended, so that the legal net encompasses not only those who directly committed violence but entities whose policies and practices encouraged or facilitated actions behind the scenes.

As debates about the power of international law and courts persist, a focus has been on bringing individual bad actors to justice. In 2022, what is likely to be the last Nazi war criminal trial was held in Germany as Irmgard Furchner, a typist, was convicted in juvenile court (Furchner was eighteen at the time of her crimes) of more than 10,000 counts of accessory to murder for having assisted the "systematic killing" of persons detained at the Stutthof Camp.[80] Furchner's prosecution was one of several recent trials of elderly Germans who were low-level actors—secretaries, custodians, and guards—in the Nazi party, for their roles in facilitating the machinery of death. The prosecution of these individuals, whose contribution to harm was overlooked for years, has come as a result of expanding conceptions of what it means to be an accomplice under German law.[81]

For the public, prosecutions of minor players who have facilitated mass instances of state violence can provide an important way to exercise connective witnessing by bearing witness to—not only documenting but making present-day sense of—a crisis or tragedy. Criminal trials like that of Irmgard Furchner, or the officers involved in the killing of George Floyd, come to represent a collective "legal memory"; they are less about the specific people involved and more about the shared acknowledgment of state violence and movement toward social change.[82] The charges against Furchner, who received a suspended sentence due to her advanced age, were less about effecting goals of individual deterrence or retribution, and instead provided a clear statement from and to German society that even a minor act, such as typing a memo, could be a cause of significant harm. For some, these long-delayed convictions of ordinary Germans whose everyday actions contributed to genocide is seen as, at last, affirming connections between individual actions and global harm.

While in some cases criminal convictions may mark a step toward progress, however, convictions or punishment of individual or even organizational actors alone will not result in collective healing and social change. The core purpose of criminal law is to punish bad actors who do not conform to social norms, to bring wayward persons in line with society's ethics and morals through the imposition of guilt or shame. In making an example of individual bad actors, we risk treating the bad behavior in which they engaged as abnormal or isolated, rather than acknowledging that bad behavior as ongoing, embedded in the very fabric of revered social and political systems.

We tend to view the complicit as having made one bad decision to collaborate; however, as Geraldine Schwarz describes, this is not the case. The millions of ordinary Germans who were members of the Nationalist Socialist Party were not at all like the students in Stanley Milgram's laboratory who were immediately and directly ordered to inflict harm on other humans.[83] Rather, the behavior of Nazi party members was shaped within the society in which they lived, through a years-long process in which the state tested thresholds for tolerance of worse and worse acts.[84] We are quick to stigmatize individuals and slow to question how corrupt systems of power are operating behind the scenes, creating conditions in which persons may feel they have no choice but to comply. Activist adrienne maree brown advises approaching systemic violence as one would approach a patch of mushrooms, where what we see above ground belies countless paths of interconnection below the surface. She writes, "We won't end systemic patterns of harm by picking off individuals, just as we can't limit the communicative power of mycelium by plucking a single mushroom from the dirt."[85]

Wrestling with complicity reveals how much faith we put in the liability-based legal model and the limitations of that model in effecting lasting social change. In the US criminal justice system, accomplice charges can implicate the least responsible parties, and fail to reach the persons in power behind the scenes. This is true in international law as well. Although there have been notable successes, overall, the imposition of accountability on the most powerful for contributions to mass atrocities continues to fall short.

As social theorist Iris Marion Young contended, a "fault" model may not be the most productive way to approach implication in systemic harms, where large numbers of actors contribute to problematic processes but may not have full understanding of how their actions are harmful.[86] In some cases, imposing guilt or shame on individuals for their part in past harms may be unfair, since people did not intentionally engage in a "collective project to make ... [others] vulnerable to deprivation or domination."[87] In other cases, imposition of individual liability may seem just but is clearly radically inadequate—eradicating the most visible problem while ignoring the rotting networks of interconnection below the surface. It is also not clear that punishment leads to reform. Traditional means of punishment like incarceration are passive, requiring little more than a perpetrator pay their fine or do their time.[88]

When we push for expanding criminal laws, particularly laws like accomplice liability which contribute to the growth of mass incarceration and surveillance, we risk ourselves being complicit in growing a system that is at best, ineffective, and at worst, can cause significant harm. It is important to think through ways we can assume responsibility for repair without being mired in cycles of guilt or shame.

METAMORPHOSIS

Physicist Rosalyn Yalow is credited with the statement that "new truths become evident when new tools become available." This is true not only in scientific studies, but in life. We see things differently now than many people did in 1964. Since the time of Kitty Genovese's death our factual knowledge of what transpired that spring night has grown, but, more importantly, our capacity to *know* that something bad was happening—to understand the harm within the social context in which the crime took place—radically has expanded. In order to intervene, a bystander must both notice that a bad event is happening and interpret the event as a crisis in which one person's intervention can make a difference. Today, we have an improved capacity for both.

We inhabit a vastly different world from that in which Kitty Genovese and her neighbors lived. Our world has changed, even, from the one inhabited by Corey Menafee in 2016 when he broke a Yale dining hall window depicting enslavement. The coalescence of experiences of crises such as the COVID-19 pandemic, addiction, and climate change, rising awareness of injustices inspired by social movements, and the rapid advancement of technologies and platforms connecting social identities and geographies has given us the ability to see things in new ways.

In certain historical moments, humans have a unique ability to expand their moral circles, and to apply newfound knowledge to change the course of society for the better. The chaotic period of the early to mid-1960s was one of those moments. The Genovese case drew national attention because it spoke to the people of the time, who were starting to comprehend that not only action, but indifference or inaction, could be a form of violence.

It is important that we build on the ways that today we are seeing more and better than we did more than sixty years ago. After a report of a sexual assault or incidence of police violence, we are much less likely to engage in victim-blaming, and more likely to ask tough questions about the institutions that might have enabled bad acts and actors. We are pushing back against individual accountability for climate change by claiming the right to clean air and a livable planet. States and private entities are being held accountable for fostering what has become a crisis of addiction and for helping cope with that crisis going forward.

The changes that have occurred in the very recent past suggest an expansion of society's capacity for moral witnessing, questioning what ethical obligation each of us bears in relation to inherited harms. As a society we are beginning to acknowledge the injury that can result from not only blatant abuse or prejudice but also less visible unconscious or implicit biases or aggressions. Problems like sexual assault or addiction that were identified as the result of individual failings or isolated perpetrators are now widely identified as societal hazards. Racism is understood not as an overt action resulting from an individual act but as a set of behaviors, tacit and overt, that are enabled by long-standing and deeply embedded policies, practices, systems, and structures. We are examining the celebrities and the politicians we revere and the media we consume with fresh eyes, newly aware that what appeared to be benign could be toxic. With expanding conceptions of violence and injury, our moral circles also can expand, increasing our capacity for empathy, growing feelings of connection, and leading to engagement in more prosocial activities—activism, donations, volunteering.

These are not just local conversations. On a global level, institutional and governmental actors are being held to account not only for directly causing harm but for facilitating and enabling cultures and environments that allowed crimes to occur. Recent verdicts and settlements, such as the $73 million paid by Remington firearms to the Sandy Hook families, the historic $27 million paid by the city of Minneapolis to the family of George Floyd, and increasingly creative claims being brought against social media platforms alleging they have fueled viral violence and hatred, suggest that inventive legal theories are broadening spheres of accountability and, gradually, driving social change.

There remain differences in what we are able to *know*, in the harms we are capable of seeing. Women are more likely to identify a broader range of behaviors than men as sexual harassment.[89] It is much more likely for those in the nondominant group to identify instances of discrimination than for those in the majority.[90] Implicit biases can cloud individuals' capacity to recognize microaggressive—or even overtly aggressive—behaviors, particularly when they happen to people differ-ent from themselves.[91] Nonetheless, as a whole, we are becoming better bystanders—meaning that, even if we ourselves don't immediately rec-ognize it, we are willing to try to understand that other people have been harmed, even if it didn't happen directly to us.

To move away from shaming and punishing individuals is hard. We have spent centuries living within a victim/perpetrator dichotomy that convinces us to view the world in terms of good and evil. Many people are not only angry with but *disgusted by* persons across the political aisle. While a slim majority of Americans say we "need to heal as a nation," a nearly equal number argue that it is more important to "defeat the evil within."[92] Deeper and more insidious than anger, disgust is a dehuman-izing emotion that can lead to violence. When we dehumanize other people, our own capacity for empathy declines and our own moral cir-cles become smaller.

In detective novels and movies there is an a-ha moment at the end, when the protagonist identifies the perpetrator and the various plot lines in the book comes to a tidy conclusion. The investigation into complicity provides no such moment. The identification of one responsible party is not the end but reveals a trail of countless others who are culpable.

In the art of origami, unfolding complex structures exposes crease pat-terns, reminders of paths taken and not taken that cannot easily be repli-cated. A catch is that, to discover these patterns, one has to take apart an existing structure, making a commitment to dismantle something func-tional in order to create something new. If the object is fragile—as we understand society to be—there are risks involved. The paper can tear. We can lose our way as we travel along the myriad paths that are revealed.

The media highlight how political polarization is growing in the United States, fueled by contentious politics and rampant misinforma-tion. Focusing on social and political division, however, does not acknowledge the radical ways in which our moral circles have been growing in a very short period of time. Less than ten years ago, Corey

Menefee was fired for breaking a window depicting the slavery system. Today, his act is widely seen as one of civil disobedience. Since 2020, more than two hundred monuments to the confederacy have been dismantled around the United States. The US Senate recently passed a landmark bill that stops employers from using NDAs and mandating arbitration of workplace sexual harassment or assault claims. Industries are redesigning products that idealized racist and sexist stereotypes. Institutions and governments are reevaluating the ways in which their actions contributed to harm through reputation laundering and greenwashing. It is tempting to become preoccupied with the ways we, as individuals, might be causing harm and to fail to appreciate the significant steps forward we have taken in holding systems to account.

The 1960s and '70s were a period of significant transformation, when, in the post–World War II period and at the height of the US civil rights era, large swaths of society were starting to identify that harm could be caused not only by active participants but by the silence and apathy of bystanders. On the whole, however, society was not yet capable of identifying, let alone articulating, how the structures and systems of the present were built upon the discriminatory practices and policies of the past. Largely unaware, we continued to build on contaminated sites. Today, we can start to excavate them.

There are white nationalists, of course. There are despots. There are those who deliberately enable hate via acts of racism or gender-based violence. But we have shifted from arguments over whether racism, sexism, or climate change exist, to debating how to come to terms with inherited problems and who is accountable for managing risks going forward. We are collectively pushing for change as we participate in recent, diverse, and large-scale social movements, and we are exploring new opportunities for civil and criminal legal accountability. In identifying complicity we have taken an essential first step in beginning to unfold complicated structures. The task now is to learn from the patterns that are being revealed, to reimagine and rebuild, and to move beyond complicity to something better and new.

NOTES

INTRODUCTION

1. Bill Chappell, "'Complicit' Is the Word of the Year in 2017, Dictionary. com Says," NPR, November 27, 2017, https://www.npr.org/sections/thetwo -way/2017/11/27/566763885/complicit-is-the-word-of-the-year-in-2017-dictionary-com-says#:~:text=Race-,%27Complicit%27%20Is%20The%20Word%20Of %20The%20Year%20In%202017%2C,with%20others%3B%20having%20 complicity.%22.

2. Lindy West, "Trump's First Year in One Word," New York Times, November 29, 2017, https://www.nytimes.com/2017/11/29/opinion/complicity-word-of-the-year.html; Carina Chocano, "Behind Every Villain Stands Someone 'Complicit,'" New York Times, January 17, 2018, https://www.nytimes.com/2018/01/17 /magazine/behind-every-villain-stands-someone-complicit.html.

3. Max H. Bazerman, *Complicit: How We Enable the Unethical and How to Stop* (Princeton University Press, 2022), 35, 50–51.

4. Corwin Aragon and Alison M. Jaggar, "Agency, Complicity, and the Responsibility to Resist Structural Injustice," *Journal of Structural Philosophy* 49, no. 3 (2018): 439–60, 451.

5. Gregory Mellema, *Complicity and Moral Accountability* (University of Notre Dame Press, 2016).

6. Thomas Blount, "To the Reader," in *Glossographia: Or a Dictionary, Interpreting All Such Hard Words of Whatsoever Language, Now Used in Our Refined English Tongue; with Etymologies, Definitions, and Historical Observations on the Same* (*Tho. Newcomb* for *George Sawbridge* at the Bible on *Ludgate hill.* 1661).

7. Elizabeth Papp Kamali, "*Felonia felonice facta:* Felony and Intentionality in Medieval England," *Criminal Law and Philosophy* 9, 397–421, 414–15 (2015); S.E. Thorne (ed.), *Bracton on the Laws and Customs of England*, Vol. II (Cambridge, 1968).

8. *Blackstone Commentaries* 4, 1–40.

9. Ruth Leys, *From Guilt to Shame: Auschwitz and After* (Princeton University Press, 2007); David Brooks, "The Shame Culture" (opinion), *New York Times*, March 15, 2016, https://www.nytimes.com/2016/03/15/opinion/the-shame-culture.html.

10. Brooks, "The Shame Culture."

11. Eliza Aaltola, "Defensive over Climate Change? Climate Shame as a Method of Moral Cultivation," *Journal of Agricultural and Environmental Ethics* 34, no. 6 (2021); John Wilson, "Shame, Guilt and Moral Education," *Journal of Moral Education* 30: 71–81 (2001); Tressie McMillan Cottom, "What's Shame Got to Do with It" (opinion), *New York Times*, April 12, 2022, https://www.nytimes.com/2022/04/12/opinion/whats-shame-got-to-do-with-it.html.

12. "I Never Thought Leopards Would Eat My Face," Reddit, https://www.reddit.com/r/LeopardsAteMyFace/; Tressie McMillan Cottom, "The Limits of My Empathy for Covid Deniers," *New York Times*, September 10, 2021, https://www.nytimes.com/2021/09/10/opinion/covid-empathy-grief.html; Elizabeth Breunig, "Stop Death Shaming," *The Atlantic*, September 2, 2021, https://www.theatlantic.com/ideas/archive/2021/09/stop-death-shaming/619939/.

13. "Bye Bye Job," Reddit, https://www.reddit.com/r/byebyejob/.

14. Kristy Hess and Lisa Waller, "The Digital Pillory: Media Shaming of 'Ordinary' People for Minor Crimes," *Continuum* 28, no. 1 (2014): 101–11; Mona Kasra, "Vigilantism, Public Shaming, and Social Media Hegemony: The Role of Digital-Networked Images in Humiliation and Sociopolitical Control," *Communication Review* 20, no. 3 (2017): 172–88.

15. Borwin Bandelow and Sophie Michaelis, "Epidemiology of Anxiety Disorders in the 21st Century," *Dialogues in Clinical Neuroscience* 17, no. 3 (2015).

16. Iris Marion Young, *Responsibility for Justice* (Oxford University Press, 2011), 60.

17. Young, *Responsibility for Justice*.

18. Adam Tooze, *Shutdown: How Covid Shook the World's Economy* (Viking, 2021).

19. See, for example, Adam Kelly and Will Norman, "Complicity Then and Now," *Comparative Literature Studies* 56 (2019): 673; Ulrich Beck, *The Metamorphosis of the World*, 80–81(Polity Press, 2016); Ulrich Beck, "Emancipatory

Catastrophism: What Does It Mean to Climate Change and the Risk Society?" *Current Sociology* 63, no. 1 (2015): 75–88, 77; William MacAskill, *What We Owe the Future* (Basic Books, 2022), 40; Charlie R. Crimston et al., "Toward a Psychology of Moral Expansiveness," *Current Directions in Psychological Science* 27, no. 1 (2018): 14–19, 17–18; Tooze, *Shutdown*.

20. Gabe Mythen and Sandra Walklate, "Not Knowing, Emancipatory Catastrophism, and Metamorphosis: Embracing the Spirit of Ulrich Beck," *Security Dialogue* 47 (2016): 403, 412; Beck, *The Metamorphosis of the World*, 80–81; Beck, *Emancipatory Catastrophism*, 75, 77, 80

21. MacAskill, *What We Owe the Future*, 10.

22. Kelly and Norman, "Complicity Then and Now," citing Thomas Haskell, "Capitalism and the Origins of Humanitarian Sentiment," pts. 1 and 2, *American Historical Review* 90, no. 2 (1985): 339–361, 547.

23. Malcolm Gladwell, *The Tipping Point: How Little Things Can Make a Big Difference* (Back Bay Books, 2002), 12.

24. Abeysekara, *Colors of the Robe*, 4n10.

25. MacAskill, *What We Owe the Future*, 40.

26. Adam Kelly and Will Norman, "Complicity Then and Now," *Comparative Literature Studies* 56 (2019): 673; Aragon and Jaggar, "Agency, Complicity, and the Responsibility," 446; Paul Reynolds, "Complicity as Political Rhetoric: Some Ethical and Political Reflections," in *Exploring Complicity: Concepts, Cases and Critique*, edited by M. Neu, R. Dunford, and A. Afexentis (Rowman and Littlefield, 2017), 35–36.

27. Crimston et al., *Toward a Psychology of Moral Expansiveness*, 14, 17–18.

28. Michael Rothberg, *The Implicated Subject: Beyond Victims and Perpetrators* (Stanford University Press, 2019), 8; Victoria J. Barnett, "The Changing View of the 'Bystander' in Holocaust Scholarship: Historical, Ethical, and Political Implications," *Utah Law Review* 4 (2017): 633, 639

29. Literary theorist Raymond Williams identifies that in every society there are "keywords," terms that mark "a crucial area of social and cultural discussion." Raymond Williams, *Keywords: A Vocabulary of Culture and Society* (Oxford University Press, 1985), 9.

30. The ways in which we choose to write about persons and communities are continuously evolving, reflecting a process of learning and growth. I have chosen to capitalize the names of racial and ethnic groups in this manuscript to highlight the significance of racial and ethnic identities to lived experience and to make explicit that these identities are not neutral but have meaning in social and political life.

ONE. BLOOD ON OUR HANDS

1. Hugh Breakey, "Acting Selfishly Has Consequences Right Now—Why Ethical Decision Making Is Imperative in the Coronavirus Crisis," *The Conversation*, March 23, 2020, https://theconversation.com/acting-selfishly-has-consequences-right-now-why-ethical-decision-making-is-imperative-in-the-coronavirus-crisis-134350.

2. Scott T. Allison, "COVID-19 Pandemic Turns Heroism Upside Down," *Heroes: What They Do & Why We Need Them* (blog), April 3, 2020, https://blog.richmond.edu/heroes/2020/04/03/covid-19-pandemic-turns-heroism-upside-down/; Amanda Hess, *The Pandemic Ad Salutes You*, New York Times, May 22, 2020, https://www.nytimes.com/2020/05/22/arts/pandemic-ads-salute-you.html.

3. Allison, "COVID-19 Pandemic Turns Heroism Upside Down."

4. Alyson Krueger, "Summer's Here, and America's Ready to Quarancheat," *New York Times*, June 25, 2020, https://www.nytimes.com/2020/06/25/style/coroanvirus-america-summer.html.

5. BBC News, "George Floyd: What Happened in the Final Moments of His Life," July 16, 2020, https://www.bbc.com/news/world-us-canada-52861726.

6. Dana R. Fisher and Stella M. Rouse, "Intersectionality within the Racial Justice Movement in the Summer of 2020," *PNAS* 119, no. 30 (July 12, 2022).

7. John McWhorter, "Racist Is a Tough Little Word," *The Atlantic*, July 24, 2019, https://www.theatlantic.com/ideas/archive/2019/07/racism-concept-change/594526/.

8. Charlie R. Crimston et al., "Toward a Psychology of Moral Expansiveness," *Current Directions in Psychological Science* 27 (2018): 17–18; adrienne maree brown, *We Will Not Cancel Us and Other Dreams of Transformative Justice* (AK Press, 2020), 26, 41.

9. Sean O'Kane, "Ford Employees Ask the Company to Stop Making Police Cars," *The Verge*, July 8, 2020, https://www.theverge.com/2020/7/8/21317894/ford-employees-black-police-vehicles-law-enforcement-george-floyd.

10. O'Kane, "Ford Employees Ask."

11. Martha C. White, Stephanie Rhule, and Charlie Herman, "Corporate America Faces Reckoning on Cost of Silence, Pauses Political Donations," NBC News, January 11, 2011, https://www.nbcnews.com/business/business-news/corporate-america-faces-reckoning-cost-silence-pauses-political-donations-n1253813; Rebecca Heilweil, "Target's History of Working with Police is Not a Good Look Right Now," *Vox*, June 5, 2020, https://www.vox.com/recode/2020

/6/1/21277192/target-looting-police-george-floyd-protests; Farah Stockman, Kate Kelly, and Jennifer Medina, "How Buying Beans Became A Political Statement," *New York Times*, July 19, 2020, https://www.nytimes.com/2020/07/19/us/goya-trump-hispanic-vote.html; Carlton Reid, "Trek Urged to Divest from Police Business after Bicycles Used against Black Lives Matter Protestors," *Forbes*, June 8, 2020, https://www.forbes.com/sites/carltonreid/2020/06/08/trek-urged-to-divest-from-police-business-after-bicycles-used-against-black-lives-matter-protestors/?sh = 22d057135ec8; Greg Bensinger, "Now Social Media Grows a Conscience?" (opinion), *New York Times*, January 13, 2021, https://www.nytimes.com/2021/01/13/opinion/capitol-attack-twitter-facebook.html.

12. Julianne Cuba, "Trek Bicycles Declines to Divest From NYPD Despite 'Abhorrent' Use of Bikes Against Protesters," *StreetsBlogNYC*, June 10, 2020, https://nyc.streetsblog.org/2020/06/10/trek-bicycles-declines-to-divest-from-nypd-despite-abhorrent-use-of-bikes-against-protesters/.

13. Jacob Silverman, "Workers of the Facebook, Unite!," *New Republic*, December 29, 2020, https://newrepublic.com/article/160687/facebook-workers-union-labor-organizing; Colin Lecher, "Microsoft Employees Are Protesting 'Complicity in the Climate Crisis,'" *The Verge*, September 19, 2019, https://www.theverge.com/2019/9/19/20874081/microsoft-employees-climate-change-letter-protest; Stan Schroeder, "'Silence is Complicity': Facebook Workers Speak Out after Zuckerberg Refuses to Take Action on Trump," *Mashable*, June 1, 2020, https://mashable.com/article/facebook-employees-speak-out-zuckerberg-trump/.

14. Alec Karakatsanis, *Usual Cruelty: The Complicity of Lawyers in the Criminal Injustice System* (New Press, 2019).

15. Ron Carucci and Ludmila Praslova, "Employees Are Sick of Being Asked to Make Moral Compromises," *Harvard Business Review*, February 21, 2021, https://hbr.org/2022/02/employees-are-sick-of-being-asked-to-make-moral-compromises.

16. American Psychological Association, "APA Apologizes for Longstanding Contributions to Systemic Racism," October 29, 2021, https://www.apa.org/news/press/releases/2021/10/apology-systemic-racism.

17. Ananya Roy, "Serious About Racial Justice? Then Divest from Policing," *KnockLA*, June 22, 2020, https://knock-la.com/ucla-racial-justice-divest-policing-lapd-72b274924111 (emphasis mine).

18. Chandelis R. Duster, "Yale Janitor's Act of Civil Disobedience, A Stand against Racism," NBC News, July 19, 2018, https://www.nbcnews.com/news/nbcblk/yale-janitor-s-act-civil-disobedience-stand-against-racism-n610416.

19. Duster, "Yale Janitor's Act of Civil Disobedience."

20. Daniela Brighenti and David Yaffe-Belany, "Crowd Cries 'Free Corey'; Case Continued," *New Haven Independent*, July 12, 2016, https://www.newhavenindependent.org/index.php/article/menafee_court/.

21. "Yale Gags Rehired Cafeteria Worker," *New Haven Independent*, July 16, 2016, https://www.newhavenindependent.org/article/menafee.

22. "Yale Gags Rehired Cafeteria Worker."

23. David Mislin, "How a 1905 Debate about 'Tainted' Rockefeller Money Is a Reminder of Ethical Dilemmas Today," Associated Press, October 2, 2019, https://apnews.com/article/972b8e37aef3df0a17751bd4fa42f308.

24. White House, "FACT SHEET: President Biden's Safer America Plan," August 1, 2022, https://www.whitehouse.gov/briefing-room/statements-releases/2022/08/01/fact-sheet-president-bidens-safer-america-plan-2/.

25. Executive Order No. 13950, "Executive Order on Combating Race and Sex Stereotyping," September 22, 2020, revoked by E.O. 13985, January 20, 2021, https://www.federalregister.gov/documents/2021/01/25/2021-01753/advancing-racial-equity-and-support-for-underserved-communities-through-the-federal-government.

26. CRT Forward, https://crtforward.law.ucla.edu/about/.

27. CRT Forward.

28. CRT Forward.

29. Taylor Rogers, "Companies Urged to Honour Racial Justice Pledges," *Financial Times*, January 18, 2022, https://www.ft.com/content/f29449c1-aa80-40b3-9794-5b02bb557019.

30. James Reinl, "Goodbye Anti-Bias Training! Amazon, Applebee's and Twitter Are Among Companies DITCHING Woke Diversity Teams as They Cut Costs," *Daily Mail*, February 17, 2023, https://www.dailymail.co.uk/news/article-11724079/Goodbye-anti-bias-training-DEI-teams-axed-diversity-RECKONING.html.

31. Rather than safety reasons, critics accused the corporation of using safety concerns as a proxy to avoid unionization. WBZ News, "Starbucks CEO Says 'There Are Going to be Many More Store Closings,'" July 20, 2022, https://www.cbsnews.com/boston/news/starbucks-store-closings-safety/; Nathaniel Meyersohn, "Why Walmart Is Closing Half Its Stores in Chicago," CNN, April 13, 2023, https://www.cnn.com/2023/04/12/business/walmart-chicago-stores-closing/index.html.

32. Mette Mortensen, "Connective Witnessing: Reconfiguring the Relationship Between the Individual and the Collective," *Information, Communication and*

Society 18 (2015): 1393; Apryl Williams, "Black Memes Matter: #LivingWhileBlack With Becky and Karen," *Social Media + Society* 6, no. 4 (2020); Pamela Aronson and Islam Jaffal, Zoom Memes for Self-Quaranteens: Generational Humor, Identity, and Conflict during the Pandemic," *Emerging Adulthood* 10, no. 2 (December 2021), https://journals.sagepub.com/doi/full/10.1177/21676968211058513.

33. Mortensen, "Connective Witnessing," 1393.

34. Zack Block, "When We Do Nothing in the Face of Racism and Brutality, We Represent Amy Cooper and Derek Chauvin. We are Complicit," *PublicSource,* June 3, 2020, https://www.publicsource.org/when-we-do-nothing-in-the-face-of-racism-and-brutality-we-represent-amy-cooper-and-derek-chauvin-we-are-complicit/.

35. Ashlee Banks, "Amy Cooper Proves Once Again that White Privilege Prevails," *Essence*, February 17, 2021, https://www.essence.com/op-ed/amy-cooper-proves-once-again-that-white-privilege-prevails/; Eli Davis, "Central Park Karen (Amy Cooper) Should Be Charged with Assault with a Deadly Weapon—Her Whiteness," *Medium,* May 27, 2020, https://medium.com/@ancestors400/central-park-karen-amy-cooper-should-be-charged-assault-with-a-deadly-weapon-whiteness-63f246fdba67.

36. Jan Ransom, "Case Against Amy Cooper Lacks Key Element: Victim's Cooperation," *New York Times*, July 7, 2020, https://www.nytimes.com/2020/07/07/nyregion/amy-cooper-central-park-false-report-charge.html.

37. Touré, "Condoleeza Rice's CRT Stance Proves She's a Footsoldier for White Supremacy," *The Grio*, October 22, 2021, https://thegrio.com/2021/10/22/condoleezza-rice-foot-solider-for-white-supremacy/.

38. Eliza Aaltola, "Defensive over Climate Change? Climate Shame as a Method of Moral Cultivation," *Journal of Agricultural and Environmental Ethics* 34, no. 6 (2021), 12, citing John Wilson, "Shame, Guilt and Moral Education," *Journal of Moral Education* 30: 71–81.

39. Maya Rajamani, "Black Birdwatcher's Sister Supports Charging 'Central Park Karen,' Even Though He Doesn't," 1010 Wins, July 13, 2020, https://www.radio.com/1010wins/articles/christian-coopers-sister-supports-amy-cooper-charge; BET, "Christian Cooper's Sister Speaks Out on Him Refusing to Cooperate with Prosecuting Amy Cooper," July 13, 2020, https://www.bet.com/article/4zc62l/christian-cooper-s-sister-speaks-out-on-amy-cooper.

40. Alisha Ebrahimji, "San Francisco Official Proposes 'CAREN Act' Making Racially Biased 911 Calls Illegal," CNN, July 8, 2020, https://www.cnn.com/2020/07/08/us/caren-act-911-san-francisco-trnd/index.html/; Jessica Campisi et al., "After Internet Mockery, 'Permit Patty' Resigns as CEO of

Cannabis-Products Company," CNN, June 26, 2018, https://www.cnn.com/2018/06/25/us/permit-patty-san-francisco-trnd/index.html.

41. brown, We Will Not Cancel Us, 41, 47.

42. Kat Tenbarge, "People Are Urging Influencers and Celebrities to Support Black Lives Matter Online or Stop Posting Entirely," *Insider*, June 1, 2020, https://www.insider.com/celebrities-influencers-support-black-lives-matter-stop-posting-instagram-2020-6.

43. Tenbarge, "People Are Urging."

44. Tenbarge, "People Are Urging."

45. Hecate, "Blake Lively and Ryan Reynolds Donate $200K to NAACP, Acknowledge Their Complicity,'" *Celebitchy*, June 2, 2020, https://www.celebitchy.com/666037/blake_lively_ryan_reynolds_donate_200k_to_naacp_acknowledge_their_complicity/.

46. Stephen LaConte, "16 Actors Who Have Admitted They Regret Their Past Problematic Roles," *Buzzfeed*, April 2, 2021, https://www.buzzfeed.com/stephenlaconte/problematic-castings-actors-apologize.

47. Jennifer Freyd and Pamela Birrell, *Blind to Betrayal: Why We Fool Ourselves We Aren't Being Fooled* 115 (John Wiley & Sons, 2013).

48. Max H. Bazerman and Ann E. Tenbrunsel, *Blind Spots: Why We Fail to Do What's Right and What to Do About It* (Princeton University Press, 2011).

49. Tyler G. Okimoto, Michael Wenzel, and Matthew J. Hornsey, "Apologies Demanded Yet Devalued: Normative Dilution in the Age of Apology," *Journal of Experimental Social Psychology* 60 (2015): 133–36.

50. Celebrity Apology Generator, https://apologygenerator.com.

51. Dan Levin, "Colleges Rescinding Admissions Offers as Racist Social Media Posts Emerge," *New York Times*, July 2, 2020. https://www.nytimes.com/2020/07/02/us/racism-social-media-college-admissions.html?searchResultPosition=1; Scott Jaschik, "Harvard Latest Revoked Admissions Offer," *Inside Higher Ed*, June 23, 2019, https://www.insidehighered.com/admissions/article/2019/06/24/harvard-rescinds-admissions-offer-over-applicants-past-racist-writings.

52. Alyssa Schukar, "A Racial Slur, A Viral Video, and a Reckoning," *New York Times*, December 26, 2020, https://www.nytimes.com/2020/12/26/us/mimi-groves-jimmy-galligan-racial-slurs.html.

53. Jaschik, "Harvard Latest Revoked Admissions."

54. Avram Finkelstein, "SILENCE = DEATH: How an Iconic Poster Came Into Being," *LitHub* December 1, 2017, https://lithub.com/silence-death-how-an-iconic-protest-poster-came-into-being/.

55. Finkelstein, "SILENCE = DEATH."

56. Victoria J. Barnett, "The Changing View of the 'Bystander' in Holocaust Scholarship: Historical, Ethical, and Political Implications," *Utah Law Review* 4 (2017): 634, 635.

57. Alana Wise, "Biden Calls George Floyd Killing 'An Act of Brutality,'" NPR, May 29, 2020, https://www.npr.org/2020/05/29/865511082/biden-calls-george-floyd-killing-an-act-of-brutality; Charles Davis, "Biden Condemns 'Russian State' for Poisoning of Alexei Navalny, Says Trump's 'Silence Is Complicity,'" *Business Insider*, September 3, 2020, https://www.businessinsider.com/biden-condemns-russian-state-for-poisoning-of-alexey-navalny-2020-9; Nick Clegg, "Joe Biden on America under Trump: 'Silence Is Complicity—Our Children Are Listening,'" *Anger Management with Nick Clegg*, July 13, 2018, https://www.youtube.com/watch?v=qZlHiO9lUi8; Jarrett Renshaw, "Biden, Saying 'Silence Is Complicity,' Signs COVID Hate Crimes Bill into Law," Reuters, May 20, 2021, https://www.reuters.com/world/us/biden-saying-silence-is-complicity-signs-covid-hate-crimes-bill-into-law-2021-05-20/.

58. Ari Shapiro, "There Is No Neutral: 'Nice White People' Can Still Be Complicit in a Racist Society," National Public Radio, June 9, 2020, https://www.npr.org/2020/06/09/873375416/there-is-no-neutral-nice-white-people-can-still-be-complicit-in-a-racist-society; Robin DiAngelo, *White Fragility: Why It's So Hard for White People to Talk About Racism* (2018).

59. Shapiro, "There Is No Neutral"; DiAngelo, *White Fragility*.

60. James Vincent, "Blackout Tuesday Posts Are Drowning Out Vital Information Shared under the BLM Hashtag," *The Verge*, June 2, 2020, https://www.theverge.com/2020/6/2/21277852/blackout-tuesday-posts-hiding-information-blm-black-lives-matter-hashtag.

61. Aja Romano, A History of "Wokeness," *Vox*, October 9, 2020, https://www.vox.com/culture/21437879/stay-woke-wokeness-history-origin-evolution-controversy.

62. Bijan C. Bayne, "How 'Woke' Became the Least Woke Word in U.S. English" (opinion), *Washington Post*, February 2, 2022, https://www.washingtonpost.com/opinions/2022/02/02/black-history-woke-appropriation-misuse/.

TWO. ENABLING, LAUNDERING, GREENWASHING

1. Art Van Zee, "The Promotion and Marketing of OxyContin: Commercial Triumph, Public Health Tragedy," *American Journal of Public Health* 99, no. 2 (2009): 221, 222.

2. Van Zee, "The Promotion and Marketing of OxyContin," 223; Joanna Walters, "Sackler Family Members Face Mass Litigation and Criminal Investigations Over Opioid Crisis," *The Guardian*, November 19, 2018, https://www .theguardian.com/us-news/2018/nov/19/sackler-family-members-face-mass-litigation-criminal-investigations-over-opioids-crisis; David Armstrong, "Sealed Testimony Reveals Extent of Sackler's Complicity in Opioid Crisis," TruthDig, February 22, 2019, https://www.truthdig.com/articles/sealed-testimony-reveals-extent-of-sacklers-complicity-in-opioid-crisis/; S.P. Sullivan, "N.J. Sues Billionaire Sackler Family for 'Fueling' Opioid Crisis," NJ. com, May 30, 2019, https://www.nj.com/news/2019/05/nj-sues-billionaire-sackler-family-for-fueling-opioid-crisis.html.

3. Van Zee, "The Promotion and Marketing of OxyContin," 224.

4. Josh Katz and Margot Sanger-Katz, "'It's Huge, It's Historic, It's Unheard-of': Drug Overdose Deaths Spike," *New York Times,* July 14, 2021, https://www .nytimes.com/interactive/2021/07/14/upshot/drug-overdose-deaths.html.

5. Department of Justice, "Opioid Manufacturer Purdue Pharma Pleads Guilty to Fraud and Kickback Conspiracies," November 24, 2020, https:// www.justice.gov/opa/pr/opioid-manufacturer-purdue-pharma-pleads-guilty-fraud-and-kickback-conspiracies.

6. Samantha Delouya, "Court Grants Sackler Family Immunity in Exchange for $6 Billion Opioid Settlement," *CNN*, May 30, 2023, https://www .cnn.com/2023/05/30/business/sackler-purdue-opioid-liability/index.html.

7. Delouya, "Court Grants Sackler Family Immunity."

8. Delouya, "Court Grants Sackler Family Immunity."

9. Walters, "Sackler Family Members Face;" Pain," https://www.sackler-pain.org.

10. "How Did the Opioid Epidemic Overtake America? The Prevailing Narrative Offered Too Easy a Scapegoat … If Not Purdue, Who Drove the Epidemic?" Judge for Yourselves, May 2020, https://www.judgeforyourselves.info.

11. Ibid.

12. "McKinsey Settles with US Local Governments Over Opioid Consulting Work," Consulting.us, October 28, 2022, https://www.consulting.us /news/8330/mckinsey-settles-with-us-local-governments-over-opioid-consulting-work.

13. Steve Dubb and Amy Costello, "The Sackler Family Made Billions from OxyContin. Why Do Top US Colleges Take Money Tainted by the Opioid Crisis?," *The Guardian*, January 27, 2018, https://www.theguardian .com/us-news/2018/jan/27/universities-sackler-family-purdue-pharma-oxy-

contin-opioids; Alex Marshall, "Museums Cut Ties with Sacklers as Outrage over Opioid Crisis Grows," *New York Times*, March 25, 2019, https://www .nytimes.com/2019/03/25/arts/design/sackler-museums-donations-oxycontin .html; Raag Agrawal, "Columbia's Crisis of Complicity," *Columbia Spectator*, October 1, 2019, https://www.columbiaspectator.com/opinion/2019/10/02 /columbias-crisis-of-complicity/.

14. Dearbail Jordan, "Is This America's Most Hated Family?," BBC News, March 22, 2018, https://www.bbc.com/news/business-47660040.

15. Lev Golinkin, "Why Do Stanford, Harvard, and NASA Continue to Still Honor a Nazi Past?," *New York Times*, December 13, 2022, https:// www.nytimes.com/2022/12/13/opinion/stanford-harvard-nasa-nazi-scientists .html.

16. Katherine Clark, "Clark, Rogers Release Report Exposing Purdue Pharma's Corrupting Influence at the World Health Organization," Katherine Clark, 5th District of Massachusetts, May 22, 2019, https://katherineclark .house.gov/2019/5/clark-rogers-release-report-exposing-purdue-pharma-s-corrupting-influence-at-the-world-health-organization.

17. William Safire, "On Language; Empowering Out, Enabling In," *New York Times*, June 21, 1998, https://www.nytimes.com/1998/06/21/magazine/on -language-empowering-out-enabling-in.html.

18. Safire, "On Language."

19. R. Skip Johnson, "Codependency and Codependent Relationships," BPD Family, https://www.bpdfamily.com/content/codependency-codependent-relationships.

20. Doreen St. Felix, "The Rush of Seeing Harvey Weinstein's Perp Walk," *New Yorker*, May 25, 2018, https://www.newyorker.com/culture/annals-of-appearances/the-rush-of-feeling-seeing-harvey-weinsteins-perp-walk-arrest; Jessica Bennett and Maya Salam, "Harvey Weinstein 'Perp Walked' into the Future of #MeToo," *New York Times*, May 25, 2018), https://www.nytimes .com/2018/05/25/us/harvey-weinstein-perp-walk.html; Jeet Heer, "Was Harvey Weinstein Sending a Message with the Books He Carried to His Arrest?," *New Republic*, May 25, 2018, https://newrepublic.com/article/148552/harvey-weinstein-sending-message-books-carried-arrest.

21. The #MeToo movement was founded in 1996 by activist Tarana Burke as an effort to address systemic issues impacting Black women and girls. The movement became a global phenomenon in 2017, after a tweet by actor Alyssa Milano went viral. MeToo, accessed December 30, 2022, https://metoomvmt .org/get-to-know-us/tarana-burke-founder/.

22. Carina Chocano, "Behind Every Villain Stands Someone 'Complicit,'" *New York Times*, January 17, 2018, https://www.nytimes.com/2018/01/17/magazine/behind-every-villain-stands-someone-complicit.html (emphasis mine).

23. Amos N. Guiora, *Armies of Enablers: Survivor Stories of Complicity and Betrayal in Sexual Assaults* (ABA Publishing, 2020).

24. Mike Fleming Jr., "'Beautiful Girls' Scribe Scott Rosenberg on a Complicated Legacy with Harvey Weinstein," *Deadline*, October 16, 2017, https://deadline.com/2017/10/scott-rosenberg-harvey-weinstein-miramax-beautiful-girls-guilt-over-sexual-assault-allegations-1202189525/.

25. Ronan Farrow, "From Aggressive Overtures to Sexual Assault: Harvey Weinstein's Accusers Tell Their Stories," *New Yorker*, October 23, 2017, https://www.newyorker.com/news/news-desk/from-aggressive-overtures-to-sexual-assault-harvey-weinsteins-accusers-tell-their-stories; Jodi Kantor and Megan Twohey, *She Said: Breaking the Sexual Harassment Story That Helped Ignite A Movement* (Penguin Press, 2019).

26. Matt Donnelly, "'We Were All Complicit': Three Bombshells from the Harvey Weinstein 'Frontline' Special," The Wrap, March 2, 2018, https://www.thewrap.com/harvey-weinstein-frontline-pbs-bombshells-complicit/.

27. Donnelly, "'We Were All Complicit.'"

28. David Carr, "Calling Out Bill Cosby's Media Enablers, Including Myself," *New York Times*, November 24, 2014, https://www.nytimes.com/2014/11/25/business/media/calling-out-bill-cosbys-media-enablers-including-myself.html; Ta-Nehisi Coates, "The Cosby Show," *The Atlantic*, November 19, 2014, https://www.theatlantic.com/entertainment/archive/2014/11/the-cosby-show/382891/.

29. Maureen Dowd, "This Is Why Uma Thurman Is Angry" (opinion), *New York Times*, February 3, 2018, https://www.nytimes.com/2018/02/03/opinion/sunday/this-is-why-uma-thurman-is-angry.html.

30. Salma Hayek, "Harvey Weinstein Is My Monster Too," *New York Times* (opinion), December 13, 2017, https://www.nytimes.com/2017/12/13/opinion/salma-hayek-weinstein.html.

31. Jia Tolentino, "The Whisper Network After Harvey Weinstein and 'Shitty Media Men,'" *New Yorker*, October 14, 2017, https://www.newyorker.com/news/news-desk/the-whisper-network-after-harvey-weinstein-and-shitty-media-men; Constance Grady, "Shitty Men List Creator Moira Donegan on the Year in #MeToo," *Vox*, October 16, 2018, https://www.vox.com/culture/2018/10/16/17955392/moira-donegan-interview-me-too-shitty-media-men-list.

32. Megan Twohey et al., "Weinstein's Complicity Machine," *New York Times*, December 5, 2017, https://www.nytimes.com/interactive/2017/12/05/us /harvey-weinstein-complicity.html.

33. Catherine Thorbecke and Sarah Kunin, "Damon, Clooney Say They Never Saw Weinstein's 'Darkness': Vow to Fight Sexual Misconduct," ABC News, October 23, 2017, https://abcnews.go.com/Entertainment/damon-clooney-weinsteins-darkness-vow-fight-sexual-misconduct/story?id=50647881.

34. Thorbecke and Kunin, "Damon, Clooney Say."

35. Paul Bond, "Meryl Streep Targeted by Street Artists with 'She Knew' Posters," *Hollywood Reporter,* December 19, 2017, https://www.hollywoodreporter. com/news/meryl-streep-targeted-by-street-artists-she-knew-posters-1069400.

36. Jess Joho, "Matt Damon Admits to Knowing about Weinstein's Sexual Harassment for Decades," *Mashable*, October 23, 2017, https://mashable.com /2017/10/23/matt-damon-gwyneth-paltrow-weinstein-sexual-assault/.

37. Heather Jo Flores, "I Refuse to Post 'MeToo' as My Facebook Status. How about Men Post 'I Ignored it, and I Won't Anymore' Instead," *The Independent*, October 17, 2017, https://www.independent.co.uk/voices/harvey-weinstein-facebook-me-too-sexual-assault-abuse-men-should-post-too-a8004631.html.

38. See, for example, Alan Dershowitz, *Guilt by Accusation: The Challenge of Proving Innocence in the Age of #MeToo* (Hot Books, 2019).

39. Matthew Goldstein, "JP Morgan to Pay $290 Million in Settlement with Epstein's Victims," *New York Times*, June 12, 2023, https://www.nytimes .com/2023/06/12/business/jpmorgan-settlement-jeffrey-epstein-victims.html.

40. BBC News, "Harvey Weinstein Sacked after Sexual Harassment Claims," October 9, 2017, http://www.bbc.com/news/business-41546694; Mike Miller, "Child Molesters, Human Rights Abusers, and Maybe Harvey Weinstein: What It Takes to Have the Queen Revoke Your Honorary Title," *People*, October 26, 2017,http://people.com/movies/child-molesters-human-rights-abusers-and-maybe-harvey-weinstein-what-it-takes-to-have-the-queen-revoke-your-honorary-title/; Erika Harwood, "Emmanuel Macron Plans to Revoke Harvey Weinstein's French Legion of Honor Award," *Vanity Fair.* October 16, 2017, https://www.vanityfair.com/style/2017/10/emmanuel-macron-harvey-weinstein-legion-of-honor-revoked.

41. At the time, Cosby's donation was the largest single donation ever given to a historically Black college or university. Jelani Cobb, "Harvey Weinstein, Bill Cosby, and the Cloak of Charity," *New Yorker,* October 14, 2017, https://www.newyorker.com/news/daily-comment/harvey-weinstein-bill-cosby-and-the-cloak-of-charity.

42. Cobb, "Harvey Weinstein, Bill Cosby."

43. Cobb, "Harvey Weinstein, Bill Cosby."

44. Rhonda Lieberman, "Painting Over the Dirty Truth," *New Republic*, September 23, 2019, https://newrepublic.com/article/154991/rich-art-museum-donors-exploit-identity-politics-launder-reputations-philanthropy; BBC News, "Harvey Weinstein Timeline: How the Scandal Unfolded," February 24, 2023, http://www.bbc.com/news/entertainment-arts-41594672.

45. Johnnetta B. Cole, "Why I Kept Open an Exhibit Featuring Art Owned by Bill Cosby," *The Root*, August 5, 2015, https://www.theroot.com/why-i-kept-open-an-exhibit-featuring-art-owned-by-bill-1790860731.

46. Tessa Solomon, "Hannah Gadsby Addresses Sackler Ties to Their Brooklyn Museum Show: 'There's a Problem with Money in the Art World,'" *ARTnews*, May 9, 2023, https://www.artnews.com/art-news/news/hannah-gadsby-addresses-sackler-ties-to-brooklyn-museum-show-1234667185/.

47. Solomon, "Hannah Gadsby Addresses Sackler Ties."

48. Patrick Radden Keefe, "The Family That Built an Empire of Pain," *New Yorker*, June 16, 2021, https://www.newyorker.com/magazine/2017/10/30/the-family-that-built-an-empire-of-pain.

49. Solomon, "Hannah Gadsby Addresses Sackler Ties."

50. Tom Seymour, "Tainted Gifts: As British Museum and the Met Disavow the Sackler Name, Museums Rethink Donation Deals," *Art Newspaper*, March 28, 2022, https://www.theartnewspaper.com/2022/03/28/tainted-gifts-museums-rethink-donation-deals.

51. Liz Manne, "First Person: Sexual Harassers Are Poisonous, and So Are the Companies That Protect Them," *Indie Wire*, October 27, 2017, https://www.indiewire.com/2017/10/harvey-weinstein-sexual-harrassment-new-line-cinema-1201891113/.

52. Vasundhara Prasad, "If Anyone Is Listening, #MeToo: Breaking the Culture of Silence Around Sexual Abuse Through Regulating Non-Disclosure Agreements," *Boston College Law Review* 59 (2018): 2507, 2509.

53. Alexia Fernandez Campbell, "NBC Will Now Let Former Employees talk about Sexual Harassment. Critics Say that's Not Enough," *Vox*, October 28, 2019, https://www.vox.com/identities/2019/10/28/20936150/nbc-lauer-weinstein-employees-sexual-harassment-nda.

54. Scott Altman, "Do Non-Disclosure Agreements Hurt or Help Women?," *The Hill*, November 12, 2019, https://thehill.com/opinion/judiciary/470013-do-non-disclosure-agreements-hurt-or-help-women.

55. An Act to provide for reconciliation pursuant to titles II and V of the concurrent resolution on the budget for fiscal year 2018, Public Law No: 115–97 (12/22/2017).

56. Christina Newland, "Hero's Welcome for Johnny Depp at Cannes Film Festival was an Ugly Spectacle," iNews UK, May 18, 2023, https://inews.co.uk /culture/film/johnny-depp-hero-welcome-cannes-film-festival-2350328.

57. Rebecca Keegan, "#MeToo, Five Years Later: Why Time's Up Imploded," *Hollywood Reporter*, October 3, 2022, https://www.hollywoodreporter.com /news/general-news/metoo-five-years-later-times-up-1235228096/.

58. Christina L.H. Traina, "'This Is the Year': Narratives of Structural Evil," *Journal of the Society of Christian Ethics* 37 (2017): 2–19, 5.

59. Bethany Albertson and Shana Kushner Gadarian, *Anxious Politics* (Cambridge University Press, 2015), xxi.

60. Albertson and Kushner Gadarian, *Anxious Politics*, xxi.

61. Fiona Harvey et al., "Cop27 Agrees Historic 'Loss and Damage' Fund for Climate Impact in Developing Countries, *The Guardian*, November 20, 2022, https://www.theguardian.com/environment/2022/nov/20/cop27-agrees-to-historic-loss-and-damage-fund-to-compensate-developing-countries-for-climate-impacts.

62. Harvey et al., "Cop27 Agrees Historic."

63. Naomi Oreskes, "Fossil-Fuel Money Will Undermine Stanford's New Sustainability School," *Scientific American*, October 1, 2022, https://www .scientificamerican.com/article/fossil-fuel-money-will-undermine-stanford-rsquo-s-new-sustainability-school/.

64. Geoffrey Supran and Naomi Oreskes, "Rhetoric and Frame Analysis of ExxonMobil's Climate Change Communications," *One Earth*, 4, 696–719, 697, 706–707 (emphasis mine).

65. Naomi Oreskes and Eric Conway, *Merchants of Doubt: How a Handful of Scientists Obscured the Truth on Issues from Tobacco Smoke to Climate Change* (Bloomsbury, 2011); Lisa Girion, "Johnson & Johnson Knew for Decades that Asbestos Lurked in Its Baby Powder: A Reuters Investigation," *Reuters* (December 14, 2018), https:// www.reuters.com/investigates/special-report/johnsonandjohnson-cancer/.

66. John Letzing, "Is Climate Denialism Dead?" *World Economic Forum*, August 15, 2022, https://www.weforum.org/agenda/2022/08/is-climate-denialism-dead/.

67. Amy Westervelt, "Big Oil Is Trying to Make Climate Change Your Problem to Solve. Don't Let Them," *Rolling Stone*, May 14, 2021, https://www

.rollingstone.com/politics/politics-news/climate-change-exxonmobil-harvard-study-1169682/; Supran and Oreskes, "Rhetoric and Frame Analysis," 706–708.

68. Mark Kaufman, "The Carbon Footprint Sham," Mashable, https://mashable.com/feature/carbon-footprint-pr-campaign-sham; Elisa Aaltola, "Defensive Over Climate Change? Climate Shame as a Method of Moral Cultivation," *Journal of Agricultural and Environmental Ethic* 34, no, 6 (2021).

69. Pat Saperstein, "Taylor Swift and Kylie Jenner Provoke Private Jet Controversy, but Does Climate Shaming Work?," *Variety*, August 3, 2022, https://variety.com/2022/politics/news/taylor-swift-kylie-jenner-private-jets-climate-change-1235331873/.

70. Amy Harder, "The Climate Footprints of the Rich and Activist," *Axios*, December 9, 2019, https://www.axios.com/2019/12/09/carbon-footprints-rich-activists.

71. As philosopher Douglas McLean observes, "Not only is [imposing individual liability for climate change] ... too incremental, it does not hold accountable those who are truly responsible." Douglas MacLean, "Climate Complicity and Individual Accountability," *The Monist* 102 (2019): 1, 2, 5.

72. Robert L. Rabin, "Enabling Torts," DePaul Law Review 49, 435, 437. Sarah Swan argues, similarly, that broadening the application of civil aiding and abetting can be a key tool in obtaining justice for victims. Sarah Swan, "Aiding and Abetting Matters," *Journal of Tort Law* 12 (2019): 255, 269–272.

73. Matthew Green, Valerie Volcovici, and Emma Farge, "Climate Battles Are Moving into the Courtroom, and Lawyers are Getting Creative, Reuters, July 2, 2020, https://www.reuters.com/article/us-climate-change-lawsuits-idUKKBN2433G5; Chris McGreal and Alvin Chang, "How Cities and States Could Finally Hold Fossil Fuel Companies Accountable," *The Guardian*, https://www.theguardian.com/environment/ng-interactive/2021/jun/30/climate-crimes-fossil-fuels-cities-states-interactive.

74. Karen Sokol, "Seeking (Some) Climate Justice in State Tort Law," *Washington Law Review* 5, no. 3 (2020): 1383–1440; Lauren Kirchner, "Massive Court Case Suggests 'Forever Chemical' Manufacturers Hid Health Risks for Decades," *Consumer Reports*, June 2, 2023, https://www.consumerreports.org/toxic-chemicals-substances/case-suggests-forever-chemical-manufacturers-hid-health-risk-a8896667936/.

75. Frederick Hewett, "States Took Big Tobacco to Court and Won. Can They Now Beat Big Oil?," *WBUR*, June 6, 2022, https://www.wbur.org/cognoscenti/2022/06/06/exxon-mobil-law-suit-climate-change-big-oil-frederick-hewett.

76. Ioan Grillo, "Mexico Is Right to Sue U.S. Gun Companies," *Foreign Policy* (argument), August 12, 2021, https://foreignpolicy.com/2021/08/12/mexico-guns-lawsuit-firearms-drug-cartels-exports-border-violence/; White House, "Statement from President Joe Biden on the Sandy Hook Settlement," February 15, 2022, https://www.whitehouse.gov/briefing-room/statements-releases/2022/02/15/statement-from-president-joe-biden-on-sandy-hook-settlement/.

77. Sebastian Kloving Skelton, "USA: Washington DC Court Dismisses Cobalt Mining Deaths' Case Against Five Major Technology Companies," *Computer Weekly*, November 12, 2021, https://www.business-humanrights.org/en/latest-news/usa-washington-dc-court-dismissed-cobalt-mining-deaths-case-against-five-major-technology-companies/; Brittany Chang, "A Lawsuit Is Accusing 7 Chocolate Makers of Complicity in Child Labor and Trafficking in the Cocoa Trade," *Insider*, February 12, 2021, https://www.businessinsider.com/cocoa-companies-child-labor-complicity-lawsuit-2021-2; Don-Alvin Adegeest, "Nike, Patagonia Named in European Lawsuit as being Complicit in 'Forced Labour' Practices in Xinjiang, China," *Fashion United*, December 6, 2021, https://fashionunited.com/news/fashion/nike-patagonia-named-in-european-lawsuit-as-being-complicit-in-forced-labour-practices-in-xinjiang-china/2021120644306.

78. Emily Olson, "A $1.6 Billion Lawsuit Alleges Facebook's Inaction Fueled Violence in Ethiopia," *NPR*, December 17, 2022, https://www.npr.org/2022/12/17/1142873282/facebook-meta-lawsuit-ethiopia-kenya-abrham-amare.

79. Gonzalez v. Google LLC: 598 U.S. ___ (2023).

80. White House, "Statement from President Joe Biden on the Sandy Hook Settlement."

81. Mary Douglas, *Risk and Blame* (Routledge, 1992), 10; Gerald M. Stern, *The Buffalo Creek Disaster* (Random House, 1977).

82. White House, "Statement from President Joe Biden on the Sandy Hook Settlement."

83. Samir Parikh, "Mass Exploitation," *University of Pennsylvania Law Review Online* (2022), https://scholarship.law.upenn.edu/penn_law_review_online/vol170/iss1/4.

84. Paige Sutherland and Megna Chakrabarty, "Behind the Bankruptcy Tactic Shielding Corporate Executives from Accountability," *WBUR*, December 15, 2022, https://www.wbur.org/onpoint/2022/12/15/corporate-liability-should-this-common-tactic-be-reined-in.

85. Brady Leonard, "First Time Gun Ownership Continues to Soar," *Catalyst*, July 22, 2022, https://catalyst.independent.org/2022/07/21/first-time-gun-ownership/.

86. David Yamane, Sebastian L. Ivory, and Paul Yamane, "The Rise of Self-Defense in Gun Advertising: The American Rifleman, 1918–2017, Session on 'Guns and Markets,'" University of Arizona Gun Studies Symposium, October 20, 2017, 20.

87. Amy Sepinwall, "Conscience and Complicity: Assessing Pleas for Religious Exemptions in 'Hobby Lobby's' Wake," *University of Chicago Law Review* 82 (2015): 1897, 1957 (emphasis mine).

88. Michael Dorf, "Federal Judge Accepts Extravagant Complicity Claim to Exempt Company from Obligation to Provide Lifesaving Medicine," Verdict, September 13, 2022, https://verdict.justia.com/2022/09/13/federal-judge-accepts-extravagant-complicity-claim-to-exempt-company-from-obligation-to-provide-lifesaving-medicine.

89. Perez v. Paragon Contractors, Corp., No. 2:13CV00281-DS, 2014 WL 4628572 (D. Utah Sept. 11, 2014); Braidwood Management v. EEOC, No. 22-10145 (5th Cir. 2023).

90. Douglas NeJaime and Reva Siegel, "Conscience Wars: Complicity-Based Conscience Claims in Religion and Politics," *Yale Law Journal* 124 (2014-2015): 2202–2679.

91. Dorf, "Federal Judge Accepts."

92. Jack Karp, "'Meme Stock,' 'Quiet Quitting' Among Top New Legal Terms," *Law360* December 13, 2022, https://www.law360.com/articles/1558033/-meme-stock-quiet-quitting-among-top-new-legal-terms.

THREE. WHERE THERE'S SMOKE, THERE'S FIRE

1. Guardian Staff, "Minneapolis Police Chief: All Four Officers Complicit in Floyd's Death," *The Guardian*, June 1, 2020, https://www.theguardian.com/us-news/2020/jun/01/george-floyd-death-minneapolis-police-chief-medaria-arradondo-officers-complicit.

2. Global Burden of Diseases (GBD), Injuries, and Risk Factors Study Collaborators, "Fatal Police Violence by Race and State in the USA, 1980–2019: A Network Meta-Regression," *The Lancet* 398 (2021): 1239–55 (hereinafter GBD Study).

3. GBD study, "Fatal Police Violence," 1239.

4. Since 2005, 139 US police officers have been arrested for murder or manslaughter, 44 were convicted of some crime, and only 7 were convicted of

murder. Mapping Police Violence, March 3, 2023, https://mappingpoliceviolence.org.

5. Graham v. Connor, 490 U.S. 386 (1989).

6. "Civil Rights Trial over George Floyd's Death: Ex-Officers Guilty in Federal Trial over George Floyd's Death," *New York Times*, February 24, 2022, https://www.nytimes.com/live/2022/02/24/us/george-floyd-trial-verdict; Libor Jany and Randy Furst, "Minneapolis Police Training Polices Under Microscope in Trial of 3 Ex-Cops in George Floyd's Death," Minneapolis Star Tribune, January 30, 2022, https://www.startribune.com/minneapolis-police-training-policies-under-microscope-in-trial-of-3-ex-cops-in-george-floyds-death/600141339/.

7. Paul Walsh and Kim Hyatt, "Tu Thao, Former MPD Officer Charged in George Floyd's Killing, Found Guilty," *Minneapolis Star Tribune*, May 2, 2023, https://www.startribune.com/hennepin-county-tou-thao-mpd-officer-george-floyd-killing-manslaughter-cahill-minneapolis-police/600271709/.

8. Ashoka Mukpo, "When the State Kills Those Who Didn't Kill," *ACLU*, July 11, 2019, https://www.aclu.org/issues/capital-punishment/when-state-kills-those-who-didnt-kill.

9. Andrew White, "The Scope of Accomplice Liability Under 18 U.S.C. 2(b)," *Case Western Reserve Law Review* 31 (1981): 386, 387–88.

10. White, "Scope of Accomplice Liability," 23–25.

11. Krista Johnson, "Accomplice Law Case of Lakeith Smith, Sentenced to 55 Years, Gains Renewed Interest," *Montgomery Advertiser*, June 11, 2020, https://www.montgomeryadvertiser.com/story/news/crime/2020/06/11/alabama-case-lakeith-smith-inmate-sentenced-55-years-gains-renewed-interest/5344257002/; Ed Runyan, "Accomplice Gets 23 Years to Life: Most Agree Sentence in West Side Killing Too Harsh," *The Vindicator*, June 11, 2020, https://www.vindy.com/news/local-news/2020/06/accomplice-gets-23-years-to-life/; Lauren Gill, "Alabama Executes Nathaniel Woods Despite Claims That He Was an 'Innocent Man,'" The Appeal, March 6, 2020, https://theappeal.org/alabama-executes-nathaniel-woods-despite-claims-that-he-was-an-innocent-man/.

12. See, for example, United Nations Office on Drugs and Crime, *Handbook on Criminal Justice Responses to Terrorism* (2009), 53, https://www.unodc.org/documents/terrorism/Handbook_on_Criminal_Justice_Responses_to_Terrorism_en.pdf (describing that "the use of criminal informants and accomplices is usually considered essential to the successful detection and prosecution of terrorism and organized crime" and that, "[b]ecause of the importance of 'accomplice testimony' in cases involving terrorism, ... means of eliciting

cooperation from criminal informants ... are intertwined with other measures such as plea bargaining, immunity from prosecution and reduced sentences"); Stalking Prevention, Awareness, and Resource Center, "A Prosecutor's Guide to Stalking," 11–12, https://www.stalkingawareness.org/wp-content/uploads/2020/01/SPA-19.005-Prosecutors-Guide-to-Stalking-00000002.pdf (noting that "the accomplice ... could potentially be an important source of evidence implicating the primary [perpetrator]").

13. See, for example, Joshua Dressler, "Reassessing the Theoretical Underpinnings of Accomplice Liability: New Solutions to an Old Problem," *Hastings Law Journal* 37 no. 1 (1986): 91, 102; Alexander Sarch, "Condoning the Crime: The Elusive Mens Rea for Complicity," *Loyola University of Chicago Law Journal* 47 (2015): 131, 134; Christopher Kutz, "Causeless Complicity," *Criminal Law & Philosophy* 1 (2007): 289, 305; Heidi M. Hurd and Michael S. Moore, "Untying the Gordian Knot of Mens Rea Requirements for Accomplices," *Social Philosophy and Policy* 32, no. 2 (2016): 161–183; Kit Kinports, "Rosemond, Mens Rea, and the Elements of Complicity," *San Diego Law Review* 52 (2015): 133; G. Ben Cohen, Justin D. Levinson, and Koichi Hioki, "Racial Bias, Accomplice Liability, and the Felony Murder Rule: A National Empirical Study," *Denver Law Review* (forthcoming 2023): 8.

14. Dressler, "Reassessing the Theoretical Underpinnings," 102, *citing* Wilcox v. Jeffery, (1951) 1 All E.R. 464, 466 (K.B.) ("concertgoer's appearing in the audience was enough to establish his accomplice liability for playing an unauthorized concert"); Alexander v. State, 102 So. 597, 598 (Ala. Ct. App. 1925).

15. Alexander v. State, 102 So. 597, 598 (Ala. Ct. App. 1925).

16. Walsh and Hyatt, "Tou Thao, Former MPD Officer Charged."

17. Walsh and Hyatt, "Tou Thao, Former MPD Officer Charged."

18. Walsh and Hyatt, "Tou Thao, Former MPD Officer Charged."

19. *Commonwealth vs. Timothy Brown*, 477 Mass. 805 (2017).

20. *Brown*, 477 Mass. 805 at 812, citing Commonwealth v. Zanetti, 454 Mass. 449, 466 (2009) (emphasis mine).

21. *Brown*, 477 Mass. 805 at 818.

22. The conviction was later reduced to second-degree murder based on concerns about the application of the felony murder doctrine. SJC-11669 (slip op.) (September 20, 2017).

23. Lisa Redmond, "Lowell Man Wants Murder Verdict Overturned," *The Sun*, February 14, 2017, https://www.lowellsun.com/2017/02/14/lowell-man-wants-murder-verdict-overturned/.

24. People v. Kessler, 57 Ill. 2d 493 (1974).

25. *Kessler, 57.* Ill. 2d 493 at 500. There was one dissenting judge who found it unjust to find the defendant guilty based on the set of facts at hand.

26. United States v. Peoni, 100 F.2d 401, 402 (2d Cir. 1938); Rosemond v. United States, 134 S. Ct. 1240, 1243 (2014).

27. United States v. Peoni, 100 F.2d, 402; Sarch, "Condoning the Crime," 338; Stephen P. Garvey, "Reading Rosemond," *Ohio State Law Journal* 233 (2014): 12; Kinports, "Rosemond, Mens Rea." 136.

28. Garvey, "Reading Rosemond."

29. 18 U.S.C. § 924(c).

30. Garvey, "Reading Rosemond,"

31. Garvey, "Reading Rosemond."

32. Garvey, "Reading Rosemond"; Kinports, "Rosemond, Mens Rea," 170; Sarch, "Condoning the Crime," 338; Kimberly Kessler Ferzan, "Conspiracy, Complicity, and the Scope of Contemplated Crime," *Arizona State Law Journal* (2017): 453, 460.

33. Paul H. Robinson, "Imputed Criminal Liability," *Yale Law Journal* 93 (1984): 609, 619–621, 634, citing Berness v State, 40 Ala App 198, 202–3 (1958).

34. Amy Forliti, "What's Next After Chauvin's Conviction on Three Counts," Associated Press, April 20, 2021, https://apnews.com/article/derek-chauvin-trial-charges-716fa235ecf6212foee4993110d959df.

35. Ted Sampsell-Jones, "Explaining the New Second Degree Murder Charge Against Derek Chauvin, The Dispatch, June 4, 2020, https://thedispatch.com/article/explaining-the-new-second-degree/.

36. Sampsell-Jones, "Explaining the New Second Degree Murder Charge."

37. Sampsell-Jones, "Explaining the New Second Degree Murder Charge."

38. Kutz, Christopher, "The Philosophical Foundations of Complicity Law," in the *Oxford Handbook of Philosophy of Criminal Law,* edited by John Deigh and David Dolinko (Oxford University Press, 2011), 51–152.

39. Kutz, "Philosophical Foundations of Complicity," 151–52.

40. Kutz, "Philosophical Foundations of Complicity," 151–52.

41. Kutz, "Causeless Complicity," 289, 305; Sanford H. Kadish, "Complicity, Cause and Blame: A Study in the Interpretation of Doctrine," California Law Review 73 (1985): 386–387.

42. *Brown,* 477 Mass. 805 at 813, citing Commonwealth v. Silanskas, 433 Mass. 678, 690 n. 13 (2001) ("[C]omplicity in the underlying felony is sufficient to establish guilt of [felony-murder] if the homicide followed naturally and probably from the carrying out of the joint enterprise" [citation omitted]);

Commonwealth v. Benitez, 464 Mass. 686, 690 n.6 (2013) ("a person need not be physically present at the scene of the crime in order to participate as a joint venturer").

43. Kadish, "Complicity, Cause and Blame," 323, 388.

44. Kadish, "Complicity, Cause and Blame," 388.

45. Joshua Dressler, "Reforming Complicity Law: Trivial Assistance as a Lesser Offense?," *Ohio State Law Journal* 5 (2008): 437, 441. Alexander Sarch similarly argues that accomplices should be divided into categories based on the "incremental" or "non-incremental" nature of their involvement. Sarch, "Condoning the Crime," 131, 134.

46. Dressler, "Reforming Complicity Law," 437, 441; Sarch, "Condoning the Crime," 134.

47. Robinson, "Imputed Criminal Liability," 613; Nicola Lacey, "In Search of the Responsible Subject: History, Philosophy and Social Sciences in Criminal Law Theory," *Modern Law Review* 64 (2003): 350, 351, 355 (noting that many offenses can be committed "with strongly objective negligence or even without fault").

48. Robinson, "Imputed Criminal Liability," 619–621.

49. Sarch, "Condoning the Crime," 358.

50. Joshua Kleinfeld, "Two Cultures of Punishment," *Stanford Law Review* 68 (2016): 933, 941. 943–944.

51. Nicola Lacey, *In Search of Criminal Responsibility: Ideas, Interests, and Institutions* (Oxford University Press, 2016).

52. Kinports, "Rosemond, Mens Rea," 136.

53. *Rosemond*, 572 U.S. at __.

54. Lacey, "In Search of the Responsible," 351.

55. Redmond, "Lowell Man Wants."

56. Cohen et al., 39.

57. Cohen et al., 43–44.

58. Dan Olson, "Justice in Black and White: The Justice Gap," Minnesota-Public Radio, April 13, 2000, http://news.minnesota.publicradio.org/features/200004/17_olsond_race/?refid = 0; Greg Egan, "Minnesota Needs to Change Its Felony-Murder Doctrine. Racial Inequities Are One Reason," *Twin Cities Pioneer Press,* June 28, 2020, https://www.twincities.com/2020/06/28/greg-egan-minnesota-needs-to-change-its-felony-murder-doctrine-racial-inequities-are-one-reason/; Jacob Gershman, "The Controversial Legal Doctrine at the Heart of the Floyd, Brooks, Arbery Cases," *Wall Street Journal,* July 9, 2020, https://www.wsj.com/articles/the-controversial-legal-doctrine-at-the-heart-

of-the-floyd-brooks-arbery-cases-11594295529; Vaidya Gullapalli, "'The 'Felony Murder Rule' as a Representation of What's Wrong with Our Criminal Justice System," The Appeal, September 23, 2019, https://theappeal.org/the-felony-murder-rule-as-a-representation-of-whats-wrong-in-our-criminal-legal-system/.

59. Andy Mannix, *"Minnesota's Other Prison Problem: Race,"* *Minnesota Post,* June 26, 2015, https://www.minnpost.com/politics-policy/2015/06/minnesotas-other-prison-problem-race/.

60. The Sentencing Project, "Felony-Murder: An On Ramp for Extreme Sentencing," April 2022, 5, https://www.sentencingproject.org/app/uploads/2022/10/Felony-Murder-An-On-Ramp-for-Extreme-Sentencing.pdf.

61. The Sentencing Project, "Fact Sheet: Incarcerated Women and Girls," https://www.sentencingproject.org/wp-content/uploads/2016/02/Incarcerated-Women-and-Girls.pdf.

62. American Civil Liberties Union, Break the Chains, and the Brennan Center, "Caught in the Net: The Impact of Drug Policies on Women and Families," https://www.brennancenter.org/sites/default/files/publications/Caught%20in%20the%20Net.pdf.

63. Marilyn Harrell, "Serving Time for Falling in Love: How the War on Drugs Operates to the Detriment of Women of Circumstance in Poor Urban Communities of Color," *Georgetown Journal of Law and Modern Critical Race Perspectives* 11 (2019): 139, 140; Cary Aspinwall, Kari Blakinger, and Joseph Neff, "What Women Dying in Prison from COVID-19 Tells Us about Female Incarceration," Marshall Project, May 14, 2020, https://www.themarshallproject.org/2020/05/14/what-women-dying-in-prison-from-covid-19-tell-us-about-female-incarceration.

64. Aspinwall, Blakinger, and Neff, "What Women Dying."

65. Jane Aiken, "Motherhood as Misogyny," *Georgetown Law Journal* 108 (2020): 19, 27; Alisa Bierria and Colby Lenz, "Battering Court Syndrome: A Structural Critique of Failure to Protect," in *The Politicization of Safety: A Structural Critique of Domestic Violence,* edited by Jane K. Stoever (NYU Press, 2019), 93.

66. Commonwealth v. Mojica, 1960 Philadelphia 1996 (1998); Samantha Melamed, "An Accomplice Will Die in Prison While the Killer Goes Free: The Strange Justice of Pennsylvania's Felony-Murder Rule," *Philadelphia Inquirer,* February 16, 2018), https://www.inquirer.com/philly/news/crime/375250-pennsylvania-philly-felony-murder-law-da-larry-krasner-criminal-justice-reform-20180216.html-2.

67. Melamed, "An Accomplice Will."

68. Johnson, "Accomplice Law Case."

69. Robin Kaiser-Schatzlein, "'Hand of One, Hand of All': 50 Years for a Teen who Didn't Pull the Trigger," The Appeal, January 7, 2021.

70. An-Li Herring, "Sentenced for Life, People Convicted of Felony-Murder Sue for Relief," WHYY, July 8, 2020, https://whyy.org/articles/sentenced-for-life-people-convicted-of-felony-murder-sue-for-chance-at-release/.

71. Herring, "Sentenced for Life."

72. Worldwide Women's Criminal Justice Network, "Menchie's Story," http://www.wcjn.org/Marie_Scott_files/mechie0027s-story.pdf.

73. The State of Texas v. Andrew James Cotto, No. 08–08–00056-CR (2010).

74. Claudia Lauer, "You Can Serve Life in Prison for Murder without Killing Anyone. Six Inmates Who Are Suing Pennsylvania for a Chance at Parole," Morning Call, July 8, 2020, https://www.mcall.com/news/pennsylvania/mc-nws-pa-parole-lawsuit-20200708-zwrb3bcgdfchzfbyku5dmvo4sm-story.html; Melamed, "An Accomplice Will."

75. Emma Andersson, "Why Low-Level Offenders Can Get Longer Sentences Than Airplane Hijackers," ACLU, May 24, 2018, https://www.aclu.org/blog/smart-justice/sentencing-reform/why-low-level-offenders-can-get-longer-sentences-airplane.

76. 567 U.S. 460 (2012).

77. The Campaign for the Fair Sentencing of Youth, *Facts About Juvenile Life Without Parole*, https://www.fairsentencingofyouth.org/media-resources/facts-infographics/.

78. Avani Mehta Sood, "Attempted Justice: Misunderstanding and Bias in Psychological Constructions of Criminal Attempt," *Stanford Law Review* 71 (2019): 593, 597–598, 602.

79. Ferzan, "Conspiracy, Complicity, and the Scope," 1280, 1281.

80. Paul Marcus, "Criminal Conspiracy Law: Time to Turn Back from an Ever Expanding, Ever More Troubling Area," *William & Mary Bill of Rights Journal* 1 (1992): 1, 8, 14.

81. Liat Levanon, "Criminal Prohibitions on Membership in Terrorist Organizations," *New Criminal Law Review* 15 (2012): 224, 249–250.

82. David Alan Slansky, *A Pattern of Violence* (Harvard University Press, 2021).

83. Haidar Aviram, *Cheap on Crime: Recession Area Politics and the Transformation of American Punishment* (University of California Press, 2015).

84. Nicholas Zimmerman, "Attempted Stalking: An Attempt-To-Almost-Attempt-To Act," *Northern Illinois University Law Review* 20 (2000): 219, 220, citing Ira P. Robbins, "Double Inchoate Crimes," *Harvard Journal on Legislation* 26 (1989) 1, 5; US Department of Justice, Criminal Resource Manual (2401–2499, 2480)."Attempt to Aid and Abet."https://www.justice.gov/archives/jm/criminal-resource-manual-2480-attempt-aid-and-abet, citing United States v. Cartlidge, 808 F.2d 1064, 1068–69 (5th Cir. 1987).

85. Zimmerman, "Attempted Stalking," 219, 220, citing Ira P. Robbins, *Double Inchoate Crimes, Harvard Journal on Legislation* 26 (1989): 1, 5.

86. Kutz, "Causeless Complicity," 289, 305; Kadish, "Complicity, Cause and Blame," 386–387.

87. Merriam-Webster, "A Brief History of Complicit," https://www.merriam-webster.com/words-at-play/a-brief-history-of-complicit.

FOUR. ACCESSORIES

1. Delia Cai, "We Know Which 'Big Little Lies' Character You Are Based on How You Handle Conflict," Buzzfeed.com, June 10, 2018, https://www.buzzfeed.com/deliacai/which-big-little-lies-mom-you-are-based-on-how-you.

2. Victor Turner, "Betwixt and Between: The Liminal Period in Rites of Passage," in *The Forest of Symbols* (Ithaca, NY: Cornell University Press, 1967): 93-111; Mary Douglas, *Purity and Danger* (Frederick A. Praeger, 1966).

3. See, e.g., Stephanie E. Jones-Rogers, *They Were Her Property: White Women as Slave Owners in the American South* (Yale University Press, 2020).

4. Felicia Morris, "Beautiful Monsters," *Legacy* 11 (2011); Patricia Pearson, *When She Was Bad: Violent Women and the Myth of Innocence* (Viking, 1997); John W. Howard III and Laura Prividera, "The Fallen Woman Archetype: Media Representations of Lynndie England, Gender, and the (Ab)uses of U.S. Female Soldiers," *Women's Studies in Communication* 31 (2010): 287.

5. M. Kimberly MacLin and Vivian Herrera, "The Criminal Stereotype," *North American Journal of Psychology* 8, no. 2 (2006): 197–207, 98, 204.

6. Nira Yuval-Davis, *Woman-Nation-State* (Springer, 1989).

7. Pew Research Center, "The Challenge of Knowing What Is Offensive," June 19, 2019, https://www.pewresearch.org/politics/2019/06/19/the-challenge-of-knowing-whats-offensive/.

8. Jenna Johnson, "Trump Apologizes for 'Foolish' Comments about Women, Then Attacks the Clintons," *Washington Post*, October 8, 2016, https://www.washingtonpost.com/news/post-politics/wp/2016/10/08/trump-apologizes-for-foolish-comments-about-women-then-attacks-the-clintons/?utm_term = .e55906295cod.

9. Avery Anapol, "Trump Supporters Chant 'Lock Her Up' at Campaign Rally," *The Hill*, December 8, 2017, http://thehill.com/homenews/administration /364062-trump-supporters-chant-lock-her-up-at-campaign-rally.

10. Daniel Lavelle, "From 'Slimeball Comey' to 'Crooked Hillary,' Why Trump Loves to Brand His Enemies," *The Guardian*, April 17, 2018, https://www.theguardian.com/us-news/shortcuts/2018/apr/17/presidents-nicknames-slimeball-comey-former-fbi-director.

11. Susan Bordo, "The Destruction of Hillary Clinton: Sexism, Sanders and the Millennial Feminists," *The Guardian*, April 2, 2017, https://www.theguardian.com/us-news/commentisfree/2017/apr/03/the-destruction-of-hillary-clinton-sexism-sanders-and-the-millennial-feminists.

12. Michael Walsh, "How Corporate America Bought Hillary Clinton for $21M," *New York Post*, May 22, 2016, https://nypost.com/2016/05/22/how-corporate-america-bought-hillary-clinton-for-21m/.

13. Miles Surrey, "Hillary Clinton's Role in Benghazi: What You Need to Know," *Yahoo!News*, January 26, 2016, https://news.yahoo.com/hillary-clinton-role-benghazi-know-195600379.html.

14. Amy Chozick, "Clinton Defends Her Handling of a Rape Case in 1975," *New York Times*, July 7, 2014, http://www.nytimes.com/2014/07/08/us/08clinton .html.

15. Bordo, "Destruction of Hillary Clinton,"

16. Andrea Mitchell and Alastair Jamieson, "Trump Planned Debate 'Stunt,' Invited Clinton Accusers to Rattle Hillary," NBC News, October 10, 2016, https://www.nbcnews.com/storyline/2016-presidential-debates/trump-planned-debate-stunt-invited-bill-clinton-accusers-rattle-hillary-n663481; Rich Lowry, "Yes, Hillary Was an Enabler," *Politico*, May 26, 2016, https://www.politico.com/magazine/story/2016/05/yes-hillary-was-an-enabler-213919/.

17. Lowry, "Yes, Hillary Was an Enabler."

18. Marie Solia, "Did Hillary Clinton Help Bill Clinton Intimidate His Rape and Sexual Misconduct Accusers?," *Newsweek*, November 17, 2017, https://www.newsweek.com/did-hillary-clinton-help-bill-clinton-intimidate-and-discredit-his-accusers-714636.

19. Naomi Klein, "Trump Defeated Clinton, Not Women," *New York Times*, November 16, 2016, https://www.nytimes.com/2016/11/16/opinion/trump-defeated-clinton-not-women.html

20. Michael Sebastian and Gabrielle Bruney, "Years After Being Debunked, Interest in Pizzagate Is Rising—Again," *Esquire*, July 24, 2020, https://www.esquire.com/news-politics/news/a51268/what-is-pizzagate/.

21. Brandy Zadrozny, "An Old Hillary Clinton Conspiracy Theory Finds New Life in Jeffrey Epstein News," NBC News, July 25, 2019, https://www.nbcnews.com/tech/tech-news/old-clinton-conspiracy-theory-finds-new-life-jeffrey-epstein-news-n1034741.

22. Saturday Night Live, "Complicit," YouTube, March 12, 2017, https://www.youtube.com/watch?v=F7040MKbStE.

23. Sarah Lyall, "The Trump Women, Trying to Help Trump with Women," *New York Times*, August 28, 2020, https://www.nytimes.com/2020/08/28/us/politics/tiffany-trump-kimberly-guilfoyle-rnc.html.

24. Anita Kumar, "Trump Taps Ivanka for a Rescue Mission: Win Back Suburban Women," *Politico*, October 21, 2020, https://www.politico.com/news/2020/10/21/ivanka-suburban-women-11th-hour-430784; Carol Costello, "All the President's Women Are Complicit," CNN, December 5, 2017, https://www.cnn.com/2017/12/04/opinions/ivanka-trump-women-complicit-opinion-costello/index.html; Maureen Dowd, "The Princess vs. the Portrait in the Trump World" (opinion), *New York Times*, August 29, 2020, https://www.nytimes.com/2020/08/29/opinion/sunday/ivanka-melania-trump-2020.html.

25. Arwa Mahdawi, "Ivanka Trump Is Complicit in her Dad's Mission to Get Rich at the U.S.'s Expense" (op-ed), *The Guardian*, March 14, 2017, https://www.theguardian.com/commentisfree/2017/mar/14/ivanka-trump-complicit-dads-mission-get-rich-us-expense-trumps-heartland-appeasing-liberals.

26. Tim Cushing, "Ivanka Trump, Jared Kushner Threaten Defamation Suit Over Lincoln Project's Non-Defamatory Billboards," Techdirt, October 26, 2020, https://www.techdirt.com/articles/20201024/13110445574/ivanka-trump-jared-kushner-threaten-defamation-suit-over-lincoln-projects-non-defamatory-billboards.shtml.

27. Cushing, "Ivanka Trump, Jared Kushner."

28. Cushing, "Ivanka Trump, Jared Kushner."

29. Emily Tannenbaum, "Ivanka Trump Is 'Complicit' in Her Father's 'Collision of Cruelty and Incompetence'" Says Chelsea Clinton" *Glamour*, October 2, 2020, https://www.glamour.com/story/ivanka-trump-complicit-chelsea-clinton.

30. Jemima McEvoy, "What Does It Mean That Amy Coney Barrett Served as a "Handmaid" in a Religious Group," *Forbes*, October 7, 2020, https://www.forbes.com/sites/jemimamcevoy/2020/10/07/what-does-it-mean-that-amy-coney-barrett-served-as-a-handmaid-in-a-religious-group/?sh = 7eac9438932d; Constance Grady, "The False Link Between Amy Coney Barrett and The Handmaid's Tale, Explained," *Vox*, October. 27, 2020, https://www.vox.com/culture/21453103/amy-coney-barrett-handmaids-tale-supreme-court; Jill Filipovic, "What Amy Coney Barrett's Supreme Court Nomination Means for Women," *Medium*, September 25, 2020, https://gen.medium.com/what-amy-coney-barretts-supreme-court-nomination-means-for-women-88cf0d4149e9.

31. McEvoy, "What Does It Mean"; Grady, "The False Link."

32. Sophie Gilbert, "When Women Are Accused of Complicity," *The Atlantic*, August 17, 2019, https://www.theatlantic.com/entertainment/archive/2019/08/ghislaine-maxwell-jeffrey-epstein-roger-ailes-judy-laterza-serena-waterford-handmaids-tale/596236/; Olivia Beres, "Stop Comparing Amy Coney Barrett to a Handmaid. She Would Be a Wife." *Slate*, October 23, 2020, https://slate.com/news-and-politics/2020/10/amy-coney-barrett-wife-not-handmaid.html; Rachel Dodes, "Amy Coney Barrett's Judgment Day," *Vanity Fair*, October 7, 2020, https://www.vanityfair.com/style/2020/10/amy-coney-barretts-judgment-day.

33. Carla Herreria Russo, "Melania Trump Knows It's Ironic That She Advocates Against Bullying," *Huffington Post*, November 15, 2018, https://www.huffpost.com/entry/melania-trump-irony-anti-bullying_n_5bede64ee4b0c19de3fe04a5.

34. Cara Kelly and Erin Jensen, "Intentional or Not, Melania's Gucci Pussy-Bow Blouse Made A Statement at the Debate," *USA Today*, October 10, 2016, https://www.usatoday.com/story/life/entertainthis/2016/10/10/melania-trump-gucci-pussy-bow-blouse-presidential-debate/91845914/.

35. BBC News, "Melania Trump Says 'Don't Care' Jacket Was a Message," October 14, 2018, https://www.bbc.com/news/world-us-canada-45853364.

36. William Saletan, "Mr. Complicit," Slate, May 22, 2017, https://slate.com/news-and-politics/2017/05/mike-pence-is-complicit.html; Timothy Egan, "What Makes Mike Pence's Complicity So Chilling," *New York Times*, October 9, 2020, https://www.nytimes.com/2020/10/09/opinion/mike-pence-debate.html; Anne Applebaum, "History Will Judge the Complicit," *The Atlantic*, July/August 2020, https://www.theatlantic.com/magazine/archive/2020/07/trumps-collaborators/612250/.

37. Jane Lavender, "Mike Pence Calls his Wife Karen 'Mother' and Refuses to Drink Booze Without Her," *The Mirror*, September 23, 2020, https://www.mirror.co.uk/news/politics/mike-pence-calls-wife-karen-22716769; Judy Kurtz,

"Does Pence Really Call His Wife 'Mother'? Aide Says It's a 'Myth That Drives Me Crazy,'" *The Hill*, September 9, 2021, https://thehill.com/blogs/in-the-know/571408-does-pence-really-call-his-wife-mother-aide-says-its-a-myth-that-drives-me; William Saletan, "Mr. Complicit," Slate, May 22, 2017, https://slate.com/news-and-politics/2017/05/mike-pence-is-complicit.html.

38. Saletan, "Mr. Complicit."

39. Lavender, "Mike Pence Calls."

40. John Henry Wigmore, *A Treatise on the Anglo-American System of Evidence in Trials at Common Law*, 3rd ed. (Indiana University, 1940), §924a, 459.

41. Leigh Gilmore, "It Wasn't Just 'Fake News' Presenting a Fake Hillary Clinton: She Was Held to Impossible Standards," Salon, November 26, 2016, https://www.salon.com/2016/11/26/it-wasnt-just-fake-news-presenting-a-fake-hillary-clinton-she-was-held-to-impossible-standards_partner/.

42. Mahdawi, "Ivanka Trump Is Complicit."

43. Klein, "Trump Defeated Clinton, Not Women."

44. Mary Louise Fellows and Sherene Razack, "The Race to Innocence: Confronting Hierarchical Relations Among Women," *Journal of Gender, Race, and Justice* 1 (1998): 338.

45. Alana Abramson, "Ivanka: 'I Don't Know What It Means to Be Complicit,'" *Fortune*, April 4, 2017, http://fortune.com/2017/04/04/ivanka-trump-cbs-interview-complicit-donald/.

46. Abramson, "Ivanka: 'I Don't Know What.'"

47. Debarati Sanyal, *Memory and Complicity: Migrations of Holocaust Remembrance* (Fordham University Press, 2015), 11.

48. Hillary Hoffower, "Ellen DeGeneres Is Coming under Fire for Accusations of Rude Behavior Behind the Scenes of Her Beloved Talk Show. Take a Look at How She Became the Highest-paid Comedian in the World—and What She Spends Her $330 Million Fortune On," *Business Insider*, February 28, 2020, https://www.businessinsider.com/ellen-degeneres-net-worth-fortune-spending-2020-2.

49. Noel Gutierrez-Morfin, "Ellen DeGeneres to Receive Presidential Medal of Freedom," NBC News, November 16, 2016, https://www.nbcnews.com/feature/nbc-out/ellen-degeneres-receive-presidential-medal-freedom-n684926.

50. Gutierrez-Morfin, "Ellen DeGeneres to Receive."

51. Joan Raymond, "Who Is the Nicest Celebrity? The NBC News State of Kindness Survey Says …," Today, November 13, 2015, https://www.today.com/kindness/who-nicest-celebrity-nbc-news-state-kindness-survey-says-t55651.

52. Raymond, "Who Is the Nicest Celebrity?"

53. Ellen Shop, "Be Kind to One Another Collection," https://www
.ellenshop.com/collections/ellen-degeneres-be-kind-collection (last accessed
January 1, 2022).

54. Gina Vivinetto, "Here's How Ellen DeGeneres Inspired the Role of Dory
in Finding Nemo," *Today*, June 26, 2020, https://www.today.com/popculture
/here-s-how-ellen-degeneres-inspired-role-dory-finding-nemo-t185342.

55. Christin Cauterucci and June Thomas, "What to Do about Ellen,"
Slate, August 12, 2020, https://slate.com/human-interest/2020/08/ellen-degeneres-
homophobia-sexism-controversy.html.

56. Spencer Kornhaber, "Ellen's Celebrity Defenders Aren't Helping Her,"
The Atlantic, August 6, 2020, https://www.theatlantic.com/culture/archive/2020
/08/ellens-celebrity-defenders-arent-helping-her/614998/; Karen Ocamb,
"Deconstructing the Ellen DeGeneres Cover Up of Kevin Hart's Latent
Homophobia," *Los Angeles Blade*, January 4, 2019, https://www.losangelesblade
.com/2019/01/04/deconstructing-the-ellen-degeneres-cover-up-of-kevin-harts-
latent-homophobia/; Ira Madison III, "Ellen DeGeneres' Interview with
Kevin Hart Was an Insult to the Black LGBTQ Community" (guest column),
Hollywood Reporter. January 4, 2019, https://www.hollywoodreporter.com/news
/ellen-degeneres-kevin-hart-interview-was-an-insult-black-lgbtq-community-
1173419.

57. Kornhaber, "Ellen's Celebrity Defenders."

58. Christina Nunn, "Ellen DeGeneres Is Accused of Using Her Show
Platform for Homophobia Apologists," *Showbiz Cheat Sheet*. August 19, 2020,
https://www.cheatsheet.com/entertainment/ellen-degeneres-is-accused-of-using-
her-show-platform-for-homophobia-apologists.html/; Kornhaber, "Ellen's
Celebrity Defenders."

59. Joan Summers, "The Making of Ellen DeGeneres, The Nicest Person
on Television," *Jezebel*, August 24, 2020, https://jezebel.com/the-making-
of-ellen-degeneres-the-nicest-person-on-tel-1844626291.

60. John Koblin, "Ellen DeGeneres Loses 1 Million Viewers After Apologies
for Toxic Workplace," *New York Times*, March 22, 2021, https://www.nytimes
.com/2021/03/22/business/media/ellen-degeneres-ratings-decline.html.

61. Osagie K. Obasogie and Zachary Newman, "Black Lives Matter and
Respectability Politics in Local News Accounts of Officer-Involved Civilian
Deaths: An Early Empirical Assessment," *Wisconsin Law Review* 3 (2016): 543;
Mark Simpson, "Respectability is the New Closet," *The Guardian*, June 2, 2009,

https://www.theguardian.com/commentisfree/2009/jun/02/gay-stonewall-respectability-closet.

62. Jennifer Reed, "Ellen DeGeneres: Public Lesbian Number One," *Feminist Media Studies* 5 (2005): 23.

63. Helene Shugart, "Performing Ambiguity: The Passing of Ellen DeGeneres," *Text and Performance Quarterly* 23 (2003): 30.

64. Lou Papineau, "Hello, Dolly—Again! Parton Enjoying Career Resurgence," The Current, March 19, 2020, https://www.thecurrent.org/feature/2020/03/19/dolly-parton-career-resurgence; Janice Williams, "Dolly Parton Isn't the Only Person to Turn Down the Medal of Freedom—There Are Others," *Newsweek*, February 2, 2021, https://www.newsweek.com/dolly-parton-medal-freedom-1566244.

65. Martha Ross, "Mariah Carey Says Miscarriages Happened After Ellen DeGeneres Needled Her About Pregnancy," *Detroit News*, September 2, 2020, https://www.detroitnews.com/story/entertainment/2020/09/02/mariah-carey-ellen-degeneres-miscarriage-needled-pregnancy/113649366/; Web Desk, "Ellen DeGeneres Accused by Louisiana Man of Bullying Him as an 11-Year-Old," *The News*, August 8, 2020, https://www.thenews.com.pk/latest/697698-ellen-degeneres-accused-by.

66. Nicole Lyn Pesce, "Ellen DeGeneres Says Being Known as the 'Be Kind' Lady is 'Tricky' in her Embattled Show's Season Premier," *Market Watch*, September 21, 2020, https://www.marketwatch.com/story/ellen-degeneres-says-being-known-as-the-be-kind-lady-is-tricky-in-her-embattled-shows-season-premiere-2020-09-21.

67. *The Good Place,* NBC.

68. Nick Haslam, "Concept Creep: Psychology's Expanding Concepts of Harm and Pathology," *Psychological Inquiry* 27 (2016): 1, 7–10; Elizabeth Bernstein, "Toxic Positivity Is Very Real, and Very Annoying," *Wall Street Journal*, November 2, 2021, https://www.wsj.com/articles/tired-of-being-told-cheer-up-the-problem-of-toxic-positivity-11635858001?mod = wsjhp_columnists_pos2.

69. Rachel E. Greenspan, "How the Name Karen Became a Stand-In for Problematic White Women and Hugely Popular Meme," Insider, October 26, 2020, https://www.insider.com/karen-meme-origin-the-history-of-calling-women-karen-white-2020-5; Cady Lang, "How the 'Karen Meme' Confronts the Violent History of White Womanhood," *Time*, July 6, 2020, https://time.com/5857023/karen-meme-history-meaning/; Helen Lewis, "The Mythology of Karen," *The Atlantic*, August 19, 2020, https://www.theatlantic.com/international

/archive/2020/08/karen-meme-coronavirus/615355/; Henry Goldblatt, "A Brief History of Karen," *New York Times*, July 31, 2020, https://www.nytimes .com/2020/07/31/style/karen-name-meme-history.html.

70. Fuck You, Karen, https://www.reddit.com/r/FuckYouKaren/top/. https:// www.reddit.com/r/FuckYouKaren/comments/chjbh8/question_im_thinking_ of_dressing_up_like_a_karen/.

71. Upjoke, "Karen Jokes," https://upjoke.com/karen-jokes (last accessed January 1, 2022); Bored Panda, "People Sick of Entitled Women Are Posting These 'Karen' Jokes as Revenge for Their Behavior," https://www .boredpanda.com/funny-karen-jokes/?utm_source = google&utm_medium = organic&utm_campaign = organic (last accessed January 1, 2022).

72. Sarah Maslin Nir, "White Woman Is Fired After Calling Police on Black Man in Central Park," *New York Times*, May 26, 2020, https://www .nytimes.com/2020/05/26/nyregion/amy-cooper-dog-central-park.html.

73. Lang, "How the 'Karen Meme.'"

74. National Museum: Private Snafu, https://www.nationalww2museum .org/war/articles/private-snafu-cartoon-series.

75. Celia Ridgeway, *Framed by Gender: How Gender Inequality Persists in the Modern World* (Oxford University Press, 2011).

76. Ridgeway, *Framed by Gender.*

77. Kaitlyn Tiffany, "How Karen Became a Coronavirus Villain," *The Atlantic*, May 6, 2020, https://www.theatlantic.com/technology/archive/2020/05 /coronavirus-karen-memes-reddit-twitter-carolyn-goodman/611104/.

78. Peggy MacIntosh, "White Privilege: Unpacking the Invisible Knapsack," *Peace and Freedom* (July 1989).

79. Reddit, "r/FuckYouKaren," https://www.reddit.com/r/FuckYouKaren /comments/chjbh8/question_im_thinking_of_dressing_up_like_a_karen/.

80. Iris Marion Young, *Responsibility for Justice,* 144–145.

81. Nir, "White Woman Is Fired."

82. Nir, "White Woman Is Fired."

83. Nir, "White Woman Is Fired."

84. Sheila Weller, "How Author Timothy Tyson Found the Woman at the Center of the Emmett Till Case," *Vanity Fair,* January 26, 2017, https://www .vanityfair.com/news/2017/01/how-author-timothy-tyson-found-the-woman-at-the-center-of-the-emmett-till-case?mbid = social_twitter.

85. Weller, "How Author Timothy Tyson Found."

86. Julia Carrie Wong, "The Year of Karen: How a Meme Changed the Way Americans Talked About Racism," *The Guardian*, December 27, 2020,

https://www.theguardian.com/world/2020/dec/27/karen-race-white-women-black-americans-racism; Stephanie Jones-Rogers, *They Were Her Property: White Women as Slave Owners in the American South* (Yale University Press, 2019).

87. Charles M. Blow, "How White Women Use Themselves as Instruments of Terror," *Salt Lake City Tribune*, May 29, 2020, https://www.sltrib.com/opinion /commentary/2020/05/29/charles-m-blow-how-white/; Mia Brett, "Amy Cooper Played the Damsel in Distress. That Trope Has a Troubling History," *Washington Post*, May 28, 2020, https://www.washingtonpost.com/outlook/2020 /05/28/amy-cooper-played-damsel-distress-troubling-history-this-trope/.

88. Ryan W. Miller, "Charges Dismissed Against Amy Cooper, White Woman Who Called 911 on Black Birdwatcher," *USA Today*, February 16, 2021, https://www.usatoday.com/story/news/nation/2021/02/16/amy-cooper-charges-dropped-central-park-911-call/6763384002/ (emphasis mine).

89. Tiffany, "How Karen Became."

90. Karyn Stricker, "The Truth About Karens" (opinion), *The Hill*, July 1, 2020, https://thehill.com/opinion/civil-rights/505489-the-truth-about-karens.

91. Corwin Aragon and Alison M. Jaggar, "Agency, Complicity, and the Responsibility to Resist Structural Injustice," *Journal of Structural Philosophy* 49, no. 3 (2018): 439, 451.

FIVE. ASSUMPTIONS OF RISK

1. Malcolm Gladwell, *The Tipping Point: How Little Things Can Make a Big Difference* (Back Bay Books, 2002), 12.

2. Deborah Lupton, *Risk*, 2nd ed. (Routledge, 2013) 77; Gabe Mythen, "The Critical Theory of World Risk Society: A Retrospective Analysis," *Risk Analysis* 41 (2018): 533; George S. Rigakos and Richard W. Hadden, "Crime, Capitalism, and the 'Risk Society': Towards the Same Olde Modernity?" *Theoretical Criminology* 5 (2001): 61; Anthony Giddens, Modernity and Self-Identity (Stanford University Press, 1991).

3. Daniel Yeager, "Helping, Doing, and the Grammar of Complicity," *Criminal Justice Ethics* 15, no. 1 (1996): 25; Christopher Kutz, "Philosophical Foundations of Complicity," in *The Oxford Handbook of Philosophy of Criminal Law*, edited by John Deigh and David Dolinko (Oxford University Press, 2011), 151.

4. Ulrich Beck, "Emancipatory Catastrophism: What Does it Mean to Climate Change and the Risk Society?" *Current Sociology* 63 (2015): 77.

5. Beck, "Emancipatory Catastrophism," 75, 77.

6. Alec Karakatsanis, *Usual Cruelty: The Complicity of Lawyers in the Criminal Justice System* (New Press, 2019).

7. Monica Anderson and Skye Toor, "How Social Media Users Have Discussed Sexual Harassment Since #MeToo Went Viral," *Pew Research Trust*, October 11, 2018, https://www.pewresearch.org/fact-tank/2018/10/11/how-social-media-users-have-discussed-sexual-harassment-since-metoo-went-viral/.

8. Michelle S. Phelps, "Discourses of Mass Probation: From Managing Risk to Ending Human Warehousing in Michigan," *British Journal of Criminology* 58 (2018): 1107; Pat O'Malley, "Experiments in Risk and Criminal Justice," *Theoretical Criminology* 12 (2008): 451; Robert Werth, "Risk and Punishment: The Recent History and Uncertain Future of Actuarial, Algorithmic, and 'Evidence-Based' Penal Techniques," *Sociological Compass* 13 (2019).

9. Werth, "Risk and Punishment," 9.

10. Nicole Martinez Martin, "Psychiatric Genetics in a Risk Society," *American Journal of Bioethics* 17 (2017): 1–2, https://www.ncbi.nlm.nih.gov/pmc/articles/PMC6634988/, reviewing C. Kong, M. Dunn, and M. Parker, "Psychiatric Genomics and Mental Health Treatment: Setting the Ethical Agenda," *American Journal of Bioethics* 17 (2017): 3.

11. ABA News, "The Good, Bad and Ugly of New Risk Assessment Tech in Criminal Justice," *American Bar Association News*, February 16, 2020, https://www.americanbar.org/news/abanews/aba-news-archives/2020/02/the-good--bad-and-ugly-of-new-risk-assessment-tech-in-criminal-j/.

12. Lupton, *Risk*, 163; Stefan Vogler, "Constituting the 'Sexually Violent Predator': Law, Forensic Psychology, and the Adjudication of Risk," *Theoretical Criminology* 23 (2019): 509, 510.

13. Laura Eichelberger, "SARS and New York's Chinatown: The Politics of Blame During an Epidemic of Fear," *Science and Medicine* 65 (2007): 1284, 1291, 1293–1294.

14. Rigakos and Hadden, "Crime, Capitalism, and the 'Risk Society,'" 63.

15. Martinez Martin, "Psychiatric Genetics in a Risk Society," 3; Annie Stopford and Llewellyn Smith, "Mass Incarceration and the 'New Jim Crow': An Interview with Michelle Alexander," *Psychoanalysis, Culture & Society* 19 (2014): 379, 387.

16. Terry v. Ohio, 392 U.S., 1 (1968).

17. Terry v. Ohio, 392 U.S., 27 (1968).

18. Ta-Nehisi Coates, "The Dubious Math Behind Stop and Frisk," *The Atlantic*, July 24, 2013, https://www.theatlantic.com/national/archive/2013/07/the-dubious-math-behind-stop-and-frisk/278065/.

19. Coates, "The Dubious Math."

20. Coates, "The Dubious Math."

21. Emily Badger, "The Lasting Effects of Stop-and-Frisk in Bloomberg's New York," *New York Times*, March 2, 2020, https://www.nytimes.com/2020/03/02/upshot/stop-and-frisk-bloomberg.html.

22. Vera Institute of Justice, "Study Reveals Stop and Frisk Significantly Impacts Trust in New York City Police" (press release), September 19, 2013, https://www.vera.org/newsroom/study-reveals-stop-and-frisk-significantly-impacts-trust-in-new-york-city-police.

23. Floyd v. City of New York, 959 F. Supp. 2d 540 (S.D.N.Y. 2013).

24. Tatyana Monnay, "States Approved Nearly 300 Bills Affecting Policing in the Wake of George Floyd's Murder," Howard Center for Investigative Journalism, October 28, 2022, https://cnsmaryland.org/2022/10/28/states-approved-nearly-300-bills-affecting-policing-in-wake-of-george-floyds-murder/.

25. Monnay, "States Approved Nearly 300 Bills"; Jamiles Lartey, "New York Tried to Get Rid of Bail. Then the Backlash Came," *Politico*, April 23, 2020, https://www.politico.com/news/magazine/2020/04/23/bail-reform-coronavirus-new-york-backlash-148299; Editorial Board, "The 'No Bail' Fiasco in New York," *Wall Street Journal*, March 6, 2020., https://www.wsj.com/articles/the-no-bail-fiasco-in-new-yorkthe-no-bail-fiasco-in-new-york-11583534248.

26. Tom Nolan, "What Policing During the Pandemic Reveals about Crime Rates and Arrests," *PBS News Hour*, April 15, 2020, https://www.pbs.org/newshour/nation/what-policing-during-the-pandemic-reveals-about-crime-rates-and-arrests; Tom Nolan, "'Arresting Developments': The Pandemic Is Undermining Cops' Main Tool Against Crime," Newsone, April 16, 2020, https://newsone.com/3929015/coronavirus-arrests-criminal-justice-effect/.

27. Eric Westervelt, "Removing Cops from Behavioral Crisis Calls: 'We Need to Change the Model'," NPR, October 19, 2020, https://www.npr.org/2020/10/19/924146486/removing-cops-from-behavioral-crisis-calls-we-need-to-change-the-model.

28. Ronald Brownstein, "What's Really Going on with the Crime Rate?" The Atlantic, October 20, 2022, https://www.theatlantic.com/politics/archive/2022/10/crime-rate-justice-republicans-2022-elections/671800/.

29. Editorial Board, "Voters Cancel the War on Police," *Wall Street Journal*, November 3, 2021, https://www.wsj.com/articles/minneapolis-election-results-police-vote-11635979356?mod = hp_opin_pos_1; Fola Akkinibi, "Biden Scorns 'Defund the Police' as Cities Rush to Spend on Cops," *Bloomberg*, March 2, 2022, https://www.bloomberg.com/news/articles/2022-03-02/biden-calls-to-fund-

the-police-in-state-of-the-union; J. David Goodman, "A Year After'Defund' Police Get Their Money Back," *New York Times,* October 10, 2021, https://www.nytimes.com/2021/10/10/us/dallas-police-defund.html; Bryce Covert, "Where 'Defund' Isn't Dead," *The Nation*, November 16, 2021, https://www.thenation.com/article/society/police-reform-defund/.

30. NAACP Legal Defense Fund, "LDF Issues Statement on the Failure to Advance the George Floyd Justice in Policing Act of 2021," September 22, 2021, https://www.naacpldf.org/press-release/ldf-issues-statement-on-the-failure-to-advance-the-george-floyd-justice-in-policing-act-of-2021/; Ilya Somin, "The Volokh Conspiracy: Qualified Immunity Reform Stalls in the States—and the Courts," Reason, October 19, 2021, https://reason.com/volokh/2021/10/19/qualified-immunity-reform-stalls-in-the-states-and-in-the-supreme-court/; Cope v. Cogdill, 597 U.S. ___ (2022) (cert. denied).

31. WBZ News, "Starbucks CEO Says 'There Are Going to be Many More Store Closings," July 20, 2022, https://www.cbsnews.com/boston/news/starbucks-store-closings-safety/; Nathaniel Meyersohn, "Why Walmart Is Closing Half Its Stores in Chicago," *CNN*, April 13, 2023, https://www.cnn.com/2023/04/12/business/walmart-chicago-stores-closing/index.html.

32. Martin Kaste, "Minneapolis Voters Reject A Measure to Replace the Police Department," NPR, November 3, 2021, https://www.npr.org/2021/11/02/1051617581/minneapolis-police-vote.

33. Caitlin Dickerson, "A Minneapolis Neighborhood Vowed to Check Its Privilege. It's Already Being Tested" *New York Times,* June 24, 2020, https://www.nytimes.com/2020/06/24/us/minneapolis-george-floyd-police.html.

34. Dickerson, "A Minneapolis Neighborhood."

35. Brad Heath, "After Floyd's Killing, Minneapolis Police Retreated, Data Shows," Reuters, September 13, 2021, https://www.reuters.com/investigates/special-report/usa-policing-minneapolis/.

36. Katie Meyer, "Will Ongoing Gun Violence Bring a Stop-and-Frisk Resurgence to Philly? It Wouldn't be the First Time," July 15, 2022, *WHYY,* https://whyy.org/articles/philly-gun-violence-police-stop-and-frisk/.

37. Texas House Bill No. 1900, https://capitol.texas.gov/tlodocs/87R/billtext/html/HB01900F.htm; Texas Senate Bill No. 23, https://capitol.texas.gov/tlodocs/87R/billtext/html/SB00023F.htm.

38. Maryclaire Dale and Michael R. Sisak, "'I Was Frozen': Cosby Accuser Says She Was Drugged, Groped," Associated Press, June 6, 2017, https://apnews.com/article/5b019ff898da48d2a2bbbc2f1afeb321.

39. Associated Press, "Cosby Lawyers Say Prosecutors Using 'Casting Couch' Cliché," *VOA News*, November 1, 2016, https://www.voanews.com /a/bill-cosby-sexual-assault-trial-lawyers-prosecutors-casting-couch-cliche /3574708.html.

40. Associated Press, "Cosby Lawyers Say."

41. Associated Press, "Cosby Lawyers Say."

42. Chris Goddard et al., "The Rapist's Camouflage: 'Child Prostitution,'" *Child Abuse Review* 14 (2005): 275, 278.

43. Marlene D. Beckman, "The White Slave Traffic Act: The Historical Impact of a Criminal Law on Women," *Georgetown Law Review* 72 (1984): 1111.

44. Beckman, "White Slave Traffic Act," 1114–1115.

45. United States v. Holte, 236 U.S. 140 (1915).

46. Beckman, "White Slave Traffic Act," 1120.

47. Beckman, "White Slave Traffic Act," 1120.

48. Carol Bleser, *In Joy and in Sorrow: Women, Family, and Marriage in the Victorian South, 1830–1900* (Oxford University Press, 1991).

49. Bleser, *In Joy and in Sorrow*, 47.

50. State of Tennessee v. Dewayne Collier a/k/a Patrick Collier (TN S. Ct.), No. W2010–01606–SC–R11–CD, August 12, 2013, citing Shelley v. State, 31 S.W. 492, 492–93 (TN. 1895) (conviction reversed because "a consenting victim to incest qualified as an accomplice and that corroborative evidence was essential to uphold the verdict"), Sherrill v. State, 321 S.W.2d 811, 812–813 (1959) (conviction for sodomy with ten and eleven-year-old boys reversed due to uncorroborated testimony of the crime).

51. John Robert Phelps v. The State of Texas, No. 06–16–00116-CR (April 10, 2017), citing Alexander v. State, 72 S.W.2d 1080, 1082 (Tex. Crim. App. 1934).

52. Bolin v. State, 505 S.W.2d 912, 913 (Tex. Crim. App. 1974) (citations omitted). ("It is the established rule that a female who consents to or voluntarily enters into an incestuous intercourse is an accomplice witness.... If such female is found to be an accomplice witness, then there must be other evidence tending to connect the accused with the offense. If such corroboration is lacking, the evidence will be held insufficient to support the conviction.")

53. John Robert Phelps v. The State of Texas, No. 06–16–00116-CR (April 10, 2017), citing Alexander v. State, 72 S.W.2d 1080, 1082 (TX. Crim. App. 1934).

54. John Robert Phelps v. The State of Texas, No. 06–16–00116-CR (April 10, 2017).

55. Michelle Oberman, "Turning Girls into Women: Re-Evaluating Modern Statutory Rape Law," *Journal of Criminal Law and Criminology* 85 (1994): 15, 25, 35.

56. Oberman, "Turning Girls into Women," 25, 26.

57. Glanville Williams, "Victims and Other Exempt Parties in Crime," *Legal Studies* 10 (1990): 245.

58. Oberman, "Turning Girls into Women," 33.

59. Oberman, "Turning Girls into Women," 33.

60. State of Tennessee v. Dewayne Collier a/k/a Patrick Collier (TN S. Ct.), No. W2010–01606–SC–R11–CD, August 12, 2013.

61. Oberman, "Turning Girls into Women," 18.

62. Luis Martinez, "Pentagon Chief Supports Removing Chain of Command from Sexual Assault Cases," *ABC News*, June 22, 2021, https://abcnews.go.com/Politics/pentagon-chief-supports-removing-chain-command-sexual-assault/story?id=78430459.

63. Jackson Lewis P.C., "California Further Limits NDAs and Settlement Agreements in Terms of Employment Cases," National Law Review, October 8, 2021, https://www.natlawreview.com/article/california-further-limits-ndas-and-settlement-agreement-terms-employment-cases; Tom Spiggle, "Congress Passes New Law Ending Forced Arbitration for Sexual Harassment and Assault Claims," *Forbes*, February 16, 2022, https://www.forbes.com/sites/tomspiggle/2022/02/16/congress-passes-new-law-ending-forced-arbitration-for-sexual-harassment-and-assault-claims/?sh = 7e14c5b02289.

64. Katie J.M. Baker, "Here's the Powerful Letter the Stanford Victim Read to Her Attacker," BuzzFeedNews, June 3, 2016, https://www.buzzfeednews.com/article/katiejmbaker/heres-the-powerful-letter-the-stanford-victim-read-to-her-ra.

65. German Lopez, "Voters Recall Judge Who Sentenced Brock Turner to 6 Months in Jail for Sexual Assault," Vox, June 6, 2018, https://www.vox.com/policy-and-politics/2018/6/6/17433576/judge-aaron-persky-recall-brock-turner-results; Tracey Kaplan, "Recall Aftermath: Will the Removal of Judge Aaron Persky Prompt a New Legal Battle?," *Mercury News*, June 6, 2018, https://www.mercurynews.com/2018/06/06/judge-persky/.

66. Carrie N. Baker, "#MeToo Update: States Enact New Sexual Harassment Laws—But More is Needed," *Ms.*, October 13, 2020, https://msmagazine.com/2020/10/13/metoo-update-states-enact-new-sexual-harassment-laws-but-more-is-needed/.

67. Sarah L. Swan, "Bystander Interventions," *Wisconsin Law Review* 975 (2015): 1035.

68. Terry L. Schell et al., "The Relationship Between Sexual Assault and sexual Harassment in the U.S. Military: Findings from the RAND Military Workplace Study," RAND Corporation (2021): x, xi.

69. Stephanie Zacharek, Eliana Dockterman, and Haley Sweetland Edwards, "The Silence Breakers," *Time*, December 2017, http://time.com /time-person-of-the-year-2017-silence-breakers/.

70. Roee Levy and Martin Mattsson, "The Effects of Social Movements: Evidence from #MeToo," SSRN, August 6, 2021.

71. Genevieve Guenther, "Who Is the We in 'We Are Causing Climate Change?'" Slate, October 10, 2018, https://slate.com/technology/2018/10/who-is-we-causing-climate-change.html.

72. Gloria Allred, "Opinion: Gloria Allred: Assault Victims Have Every Right to Keep Their Trauma and Their Settlements Private" *Los Angeles Times*, September 24, 2019, https://www.latimes.com/opinion/story/2019-09-23 /metoo-sexual-abuse-victims-confidential-settlements-lawsuits.

73. Kristin Bumiller, *The Civil Rights Society: The Social Construction of Victims* (Johns Hopkins University Press, 1992), 62, 72.

74. Nils Christie, "The Ideal Victim," in *From Crime Policy to Victim Policy*, edited by A. Fattah (Palgrave Macmillan, 1986), 17.

75. Booth v. Maryland, 482 U.S. 496 (1987), overruled by Payne v. Tennessee, 501 U.S. 808 (1991).

76. Jill Lepore, "The Rise of the Victims'-Rights Movement," *New Yorker*, May 21, 2018, https://www.newyorker.com/magazine/2018/05/21/the-rise-of-the-victims-rights-movement.

77. Danielle C. Slakoff and Pauline K. Brennan, "The Differential Representation of Latina and Black Female Victims in Front-Page News Stories: A Qualitative Document Analysis," *Feminist Criminology* 14 (2019): 488, 493, 508.

78. Zachary D. Kaufman, "Protectors of Predators or Prey: Bystanders and Upstanders Amid Sexual Crimes," *Southern California Law Review* 92 (2019): 1317.

79. Sam Levin, "Armed Anarchists Rally at Brock Turner's Home: 'Try This Again and We'll Shoot You!,'" *The Guardian*, September 6, 2016, https:// www.theguardian.com/us-news/2016/sep/06/brock-turner-stanford-sexual-assault-case-ohio-armed-protest.

80. Mary Douglas, *Risk and Blame* (Routledge, 1992), 77.

81. Executive Order No. 13950, "Executive Order on Combating Race and Sex Stereotyping," September 22, 2020, revoked by E.O. 13985, January 20, 2021.

82. Aziz Huq, "The Conservative Case Against Banning Critical Race Theory," *Time*, July 13, 2021, https://time.com/6079716/conservative-case-against-banning-critical-race-theory/.

83. House Bill No. 1775, 58th Leg., 1st Sess. (OK 2021) (as approved by Gov. Stitt, May 7, 2021).

84. House Bill No. 5097, 101st Leg., (MI 2021).

85. Ananda Abeysekara, *Colors of the Robe: Religion, Identity and Difference*, (University of South Carolina Press, 2002), 4, fn. 10.

SIX. BEYOND COMPLICITY

1. Martin Gansberg, "37 Who Saw Murder Didn't Call the Police," *New York Times*, March 27, 1964, https://www.nytimes.com/1964/03/27/archives/37-who-saw-murder-didnt-call-the-police-apathy-at-stabbing-of.html.

2. Jim Rasenberger, "Kitty, 40 Years Later," *New York Times*, February 8, 2004, https://www.nytimes.com/2004/02/08/nyregion/kitty-40-years-later.html.

3. Loudon Wainwright, "The Dying Girl That No One Helped," *Life*, April 10, 1964.

4. Rachel Manning, Mark Levine, and Alan Collins, "The Kitty Genovese Murder and the Social Psychology of Helping: The Parable of the 38 Witnesses," *American Psychologist* 62 (2007): 555.

5. John M. Darley and Bibb Latané, "Bystander Intervention in Emergencies: Diffusion of Responsibility," *Journal of Personality and Social Psychology* 8 (1968).

6. Darley and Latane, "Bystander Intervention in Emergencies."

7. Bibb Latané and John M. Darley, "Bystander 'Apathy,'" *American Scientist* (1969): 244, 260 (1969).

8. Jackson Arn, "Thinking the Worst of Ourselves," *Hedgehog Review* 23 (2021).

9. Arn, "Thinking the Worst."

10. Geraldine Schwarz, *Those Who Forget: My Family's Story in Nazi Europe—A Memoir, A History, A Warning* (Scribner 2007), 45–46; Maryla Hopfinger, "We Are all Witnesses, Instead of an Introduction," in *The Holocaust Bystander in Polish Culture, 1945–2015: The Story of Innocence*, edited by Maryla Hopfinger and Tomasz Zukowski (Palgrave, 2021), 3.

11. Peter C. Baker, "Missing the Story," *The Nation*, April 8, 2014, https://www.thenation.com/article/archive/missing-story/.

12. Baker, "Missing the Story."

13. Tommy Beer, *Trust in Fellow Americans Hits All-Time Low, Survey Shows, Forbes*, October 7, 2021, https://www.forbes.com/sites/tommybeer/2021/10/07/trust-in-fellow-americans-hits-all-time-low-survey-shows/?sh = 6de95e9a70cf.

14. Dan Vallone et al., "Two Stories of Distrust in America," More in Common (2021): 5.

15. Vallone et al., "Two Stories of Distrust," 36.

16. Arn, "Thinking the Worst," 23.

17. Richard G. Tedeschi and Lawrence Calhoun, "Posttraumatic Growth: A New Perspective on Psychotraumatology," *Psychiatric Times* 21, no. 4 (2004), https://www.psychiatrictimes.com/view/posttraumatic-growth-new-perspective-psychotraumatology; George A. Bonnano, "Loss, Trauma, and Human Resilience," *American Psychologist* 59. no. 1 (January 2004): 20–28; Chiara Baiano et al., "Empathy through the Pandemic: Changes of Different Emphatic Dimensions during the Covid-19 Outbreak," *International Journal of Environmental Research and Public Health* 4, no. 19 (2022): 2435, https://www.ncbi.nlm.nih.gov/pmc/articles/PMC8872216/.

18. Beryl Leiff Benderly, "Psychology's Tall Tales," American Psychological Association, accessed January 7, 2022, https://www.apa.org/gradpsych/2012/09/tall-tales; Rasenberger, "The Kitty Genovese Murder"; Manning et al., "The Kitty Genovese Murder," 558.

19. David W. Dunlap, "How Many Witnessed the Murder of Kitty Genovese?" *New York Times*, April 6, 2016, https://www.nytimes.com/2016/04/06/insider/1964-how-many-witnessed-the-murder-of-kitty-genovese.html;

20. Robert D. McFadden, "Winston Moseley, Who Killed Kitty Genovese, Dies in Prison at 81," *New York Times*, April 4, 2016, https://www.nytimes.com/2016/04/05/nyregion/winston-moseley-81-killer-of-kitty-genovese-dies-in-prison.html.

21. Catherine Pelonero, *Kitty Genovese: A True Account of a Public Murder and Its Private Consequences* 81 (Skyhorse Publishing, 2014)

22. Pelonero, *Kitty Genovese: A True Account*, 82.

23. Pelonero, *Kitty Genovese: A True Account*, 17, 18; Sam Roberts, "Sophia Farrar Dies at 92; Belied Indifference to Kitty Genovese Attack," *New York Times*, September 2, 2020, https://www.nytimes.com/2020/09/02/nyregion/sophia-farrar-dead.html; McFadden, "Winston Moseley, Who Killed Kitty."

24. Saul Kassin, "The Killing of Kitty Genovese: What Else Does this Case Tell Us?," *Perspectives on Psychological Science* 12 (2017): 374, 379.

25. Kassin, "The Killing of Kitty Genovese," 375.

26. Carrie Rentschler, "An Urban Physiognomy of the 1964 Kitty Genovese Murder," *Space and Culture* 14, no. 3 (2011).

27. Benderly, "Psychology's Tall Tales."

28. Rutger Bregman, *Humankind: A Hopeful History* (Little Brown, 2019), 152–153.

29. Bregman, Humankind, 152–153.

30. Bregman, Humankind, 152–153.

31. Bregman, Humankind, 166.

32. Bregman, Humankind, 169, 170.

33. Bregman, Humankind, 169, 170.

34. Bregman, Humankind, 169, citing Gina Perry, *Behind the Shock Machine: The Untold Story of the Notorious Milgram Psychology Experiments* (Scribe, 2012), 70.

35. Adam M. Mastroianni and Daniel T. Gilbert, "The Illusion of Moral Decline," *Nature*, published online (June 7, 2023): 1–13, 1–2.

36. Mastroianni and Gilbert, 4–5.

37. Mastroianni and Gilbert, 4–5.

38. Mastroianni and Gilbert, 5.

39. Mastroianni and Gilbert, 2.

40. Mastroianni and Gilbert, 5.

41. Richard Philpot et al., "Would I Be helped? Cross-National CCTV Footage Shows That Intervention Is the Norm in Public Conflicts," *American Psychologist* 75, no. 1 (2020): 66–75.

42. Philpot et al., "Would I Be Helped?"

43. Hannah Natanson, "Forget What You May Have Been Told. New Study Says Strangers Step in to Help 90 Percent of the Time," *Washington Post*, September 6, 2019, https://www.washingtonpost.com/lifestyle/2019/09/06/high-level-help-was-surprising-new-study-says-strangers-step-help-percent-time/.

44. Peter Fischer et al., "The Bystander-Effect: A Meta-Analytic Review on Bystander Intervention in Dangerous and Non-Dangerous Emergencies," *Psychology Bulletin* 137, no. 4 (2011): 517–537, 534; Latané and Darley, "Bystander 'Apathy,'" 253.

45. Pelonero, *Kitty Genovese: A True Account*, 185; John Eligon, "'I was Failing': Bystanders Carry Guilt from Watching George Floyd Die," *New York Times*,

April 3, 2021 (updated April 21, 2021), https://www.nytimes.com/2021/04/03/us /george-floyd-derek-chauvin-trial.html.

46. Manning et al., "The Kitty Genovese Murder," 558.

47. McFadden, "Winston Moseley, Who Killed Kitty"; Baker, "Missing the Story"; Manning et al., "The Kitty Genovese Murder."

48. Manning et al., "The Kitty Genovese Murder," 558.

49. Pelonero, *Kitty Genovese: A True Account*, 112, 184.

50. McFadden, "Winston Moseley, Who Killed Kitty."

51. Mark Levine and Simon Crowther, "The Responsive Bystander: How Social Group Membership and Group Size can Encourage as well as Inhibit Bystander Intervention. *Journal of Personality and Social Psychology* 95, no. 6 (2008): 1429–1439.

52. Baker, "Missing the Story."

53. Baker, "Missing the Story."

54. Baker, "Missing the Story."

55. Pelonero, *Kitty Genovese: A True Account*, 93.

56. Manning et al., "The Kitty Genovese Murder," 558.

57. Brent Curtis, "Woman Recalls Partner's Brutal Murder," *Rutland Herald*, October 17, 2018, https://www.rutlandherald.com/news/woman-recalls-partners-brutal-murder/article_961c557a-b46a-5413-80ff-9b9a9b4af939.html.

58. Baker, "Missing the Story."

59. Pelonero, *Kitty Genovese: A True Account*, 157.

60. Pelonero, *Kitty Genovese: A True Account*, 95.

61. Curtis, "Woman Recalls Partner's Brutal Murder."

62. Victoria J. Barnett, "The Changing View of the 'Bystander,'" in Holocaust Scholarship: Historical, Ethical, and Political Implications," *Utah Law Review* 4 (2017): 641.

63. Barnett, "The Changing View of the 'Bystander,'" 641.

64. Schwarz, *Those Who Forget*, 1, 4

65. Barnett, "The Changing View of the 'Bystander,'" 633, 641.

66. Owen Bowcott, "Rwanda Genocide: The Fight to Bring the Perpetrators to Justice," *The Guardian*, April 2, 2014. https://www.theguardian.com /world/2014/apr/02/rwanda-genocide-fight-justice; Daniel M. Greenfield, "The Crime of Complicity in Genocide: How the International Tribunals for Rwanda and Yugoslavia Got it Wrong, and Why it Matters," *Journal of Criminal Law and Criminology* 98 (2007–2008): 922.

67. Jason Beaubien, "Catholic Complicity and Rwanda Genocide," NPR, April 22, 2005, https://www.npr.org/templates/story/story.php?storyId=4615171;

Eleanor Beardsley, "Historians Say France Was Not Complicit in Rwanda Genocide, but Did Turn a Blind Eye.," *NPR*, April 7, 2021, https://www.npr .org/2021/04/07/985128514/historians-say-france-was-not-complicit-in-rwanda-genocide-but-did-turn-a-blind-.

68. OSCE, "A Race Against Time—Successes and Challenges in the Implementation of the National War Crimes Processing Strategy of Bosnia and Herzegovina," Organization for Security and Co-operation in Europe, June 24, 2022, https://www.osce.org/mission-to-bosnia-and-herzegovina/521149.

69. Martha Minow, *Between Vengeance and Forgiveness: Facing History after Genocide and Mass Violence* (Beacon Press, 1998), 15.

70. Borgen Staff, "How Fast Fashion Causes Environmental Poverty," October 25, 2020, Borgen Magazine, https://www.borgenmagazine.com/fast-fashion-causes-environmental-poverty/; Annie Kelly, "'Virtually Entire' Fashion Industry Complicit in Uighur Forced Labor, Say Rights Groups," *The Guardian*, July 23, 2020, https://www.theguardian.com/global-development/2020/jul/23 /virtually-entire-fashion-industry-complicit-in-uighur-forced-labour-say-rights-groups-china.

71. Schwarz, *Those Who Forget*, 45–46.

72. Michael Rothberg, *The Implicated Subject: Beyond Victims and Perpetrators* (Stanford University Press, 2019), 1.

73. William Drozdiak, "Panel Finds Switzerland Complicit in Holocaust," *Washington Post*, December 10, 1999, https://www.washingtonpost.com/wp-srv /pmextra/dec99/10/swiss.htm.

74. Sheldon Kirshner, "France's Struggle to Accept Its Complicity in the Holocaust," *National Post*, December 11, 2014, https://nationalpost.com/opinion /sheldon-kirshner-frances-struggle-to-accept-its-complicity-in-the-holocaust.

75. Mary Louise Roberts, *What Soldiers Do: Sex and the American GI in World War II France* (University of Chicago, 2013); William I. Hitchcock, *The Bitter Road to Freedom: The Human Cost of Allied Victory in WWII Europe* (Free Press, 2009).

76. Roberts, *What Soldiers Do*, 195.

77. Roberts, *What Soldiers Do*, 195; Hitchcock, *The Bitter Road to Freedom*. Besides overt racism, including French women's disproportionate identification of Black soldiers as responsible for rape, one reason for the skewed prosecutions is that Black soldiers were more likely to be assigned to service rather than combat units. This meant that Black soldiers were more likely to engage with French citizens and that, when accused, they did not have a defense of excuse based on combat exposure.

78. Roberts, *What Soldiers Do*, 224.

79. Alice Kaplan, "A Hidden Memorial to the Worst Aspects of our Jim Crow Army," *Chicago Tribune*, September 25, 2005, https://www.chicagotribune .com/news/ct-xpm-2005-09-25-0509250486-story.html.

80. Anna Noryskiewicz and Haley Ott, "97-Year Old Former Nazi Camp Secretary Found Guilty of Complicity in Over 10,000 Murders," CBS News, October 20, 2022, https://www.cbsnews.com/news/former-nazi-camp-secretary-irmgard-furchner-found-guilty-complicity-over-10500-murders/.

81. BBC News, "Nazi Stutthof Camp Secretary Flees as German Trial Starts," September 30, 2021, https://www.bbc.com/news/world-europe-58747082; Melissa Eddy, "Why German Prosecutes the Aged for Roles It Long Ignored," *New York Times*, February 9, 2021, https://www.nytimes.com/2021/02/09/world /europe/germany-nazi-prosecution-elderly.html.

82. Shoshana Felman, *The Juridical Unconscious: Trials and Traumas in the Twentieth Century* (Harvard University Press, 2002).

83. Schwarz, *Those Who Forget*, 1.

84. Schwarz, *Those Who Forget*, 2.

85. adrienne maree brown, *We Will Not Cancel Us and Other Dreams of Transformative Justice* (AK Press, 2020), 7–8.

86. Iris Marion Young, *Responsibility for Justice* (Oxford University Press, 2011), 11, 99.

87. Young, *Responsibility for Justice*, 102.

88. Danielle Sered, *Until We Reckon: Violence, Incarceration, and A Road to Repair* (New Press, 2019), 96, 111–112.

89. Maria Rotundo, Dung-Hanh Nguyen, and Paul R. Sackett, "A Meta-Analytic Review of Gender Differences in Perceptions of Sexual Harassment," *Journal of Applied Psychology* 86 (2001): 914, 919.

90. Cole Kazdin, "Psychologists Weigh in on the Teen Who Live-Streamed Her Best Friend's Rape," *Identity* (April 25, 2006).

91. Jin X. Goh et al., "Narrow Prototypes and Neglected Victims: Understanding Perceptions of Sexual Harassment," *Journal of Personality and Social Psychology* 122, no, 5 (2021): 1, 13.

92. Vallone et al., "Two Stories of Distrust."

BIBLIOGRAPHY

Eliza Aaltola. "Defensive over Climate Change? Climate Shame as a Method of Moral Cultivation." *Journal of Agricultural and Environmental Ethics* 34, no. 6 (2021).

ABA News. "The Good, Bad and Ugly of New Risk Assessment Tech in Criminal Justice." American Bar Association News, February 16, 2020. https://www.americanbar.org/news/abanews/aba-news-archives/2020/02/the-good—bad-and-ugly-of-new-risk-assessment-tech-in-criminal-j/.

Ananda Abeysekara. *Colors of the Robe: Religion, Identity and Difference* (University of South Carolina Press, 2002).

Alana Abramson. "Ivanka: 'I Don't Know What it Means to be Complicit.'" *Fortune*, April 4, 2017. http://fortune.com/2017/04/04/ivanka-trump-cbs-interview-complicit-donald/.

Don-Alvin Adegeest. "Nike, Patagonia Named in European Lawsuit as Being Complicit in 'Forced Labour' Practices in Xinjiang, China." *Fashion United*, December 6, 2021. https://fashionunited.com/news/fashion/nike-patagonia-named-in-european-lawsuit-as-being-complicit-in-forced-labour-practices-in-xinjiang-china/2021120644306.

Raag Agrawal. "Columbia's Crisis of Complicity." *Columbia Spectator*, October 1, 2019. https://www.columbiaspectator.com/opinion/2019/10/02/columbias-crisis-of-complicity/.

Jane Aiken. "Motherhood as Misogyny." *Georgetown Law Journal* (2020): 19, 27.

Fola Akkinibi. "Biden Scorns 'Defund the Police' as Cities Rush to Spend on Cops." Bloomberg, March 2, 2022. https://www.bloomberg.com/news/articles/2022–03–02/biden-calls-to-fund-the-police-in-state-of-the-union.

Bethany Albertson and Shana Kushner Gadarian. *Anxious Politics* (Cambridge University Press, 2015).

Michelle Alexander. "The Newest Jim Crow" (opinion). *New York Times*, November 8, 2018. https://www.nytimes.com/2018/11/08/opinion/sunday /criminal-justice-reforms-race-technology.html.

Scott T. Allison. "COVID-19 Pandemic Turns Heroism Upside Down." Heroes: What They Do and Why We Need Them, April 3, 2020. https:// blog.richmond.edu/heroes/2020/04/03/covid-19-pandemic-turns-heroism-upside-down/.

Gloria Allred. "Opinion: Gloria Allred: Assault Victims Have Every Right to Keep Their Trauma and their Settlements Private." *Los Angeles Times*, September 24, 2019. https://www.latimes.com/opinion/story/2019-09-23 /metoo-sexual-abuse-victims-confidential-settlements-lawsuits.

Scott Altman. "Do Non-Disclosure Agreements Hurt or Help Women?" The Hill, November 12, 2019. https://thehill.com/opinion/judiciary/470013-do-non-disclosure-agreements-hurt-or-help-women.

American Civil Liberties Union, Break the Chains, and the Brennan Center. "Caught in the Net: The Impact of Drug Policies on Women and Families." https://www.brennancenter.org/sites/default/files/publications/Caught% 20in%20the%20Net.pdf.

American Psychological Association. "APA Apologizes for Longstanding Contributions to Systemic Racism." October 29, 2021. https://www.apa.org /news/press/releases/2021/10/apology-systemic-racism.

Avery Anapol. "Trump Supporters Chant "Lock Her Up" at Campaign Rally." The Hill, December 8, 2017. http://thehill.com/homenews/administration /364062-trump-supporters-chant-lock-her-up-at-campaign-rally.

Monica Anderson and Skye Toor. "How Social Media Users Have Discussed Sexual Harassment Since #MeToo Went Viral." Pew Research Trust, October 11, 2018. https://www.pewresearch.org/fact-tank/2018/10/11/how-social-media-users-have-discussed-sexual-harassment-since-metoo-went-viral/.

Emma Andersson. "Why Low-Level Offenders Can Get Longer Sentences Than Airplane Hijackers." ACLU, May 24, 2018. https://www.aclu.org /blog/smart-justice/sentencing-reform/why-low-level-offenders-can-get-longer-sentences-airplane.

Anne Applebaum. "History Will Judge the Complicit." *The Atlantic*, July/August 2020. https://www.theatlantic.com/magazine/archive/2020/07 /trumps-collaborators/612250/.

Corwin Aragon and Alison M. Jaggar. "Agency, Complicity, and the Responsibility to Resist Structural Injustice." *Journal of Structural Philosophy* 49, no. 3 (2018): 439–460.

David Armstrong. "Sealed Testimony Reveals Extent of Sackler's Complicity in Opioid Crisis." TruthDig, February 22, 2019. https://www.truthdig.com /articles/sealed-testimony-reveals-extent-of-sacklers-complicity-in-opioid-crisis/.

Jackson Arn. "Thinking the Worst of Ourselves." *Hedgehog Review* 23, no. 1 (2021).

Pamela Aronson and Islam Jaffal. "Zoom Memes for Self-Quaranteens: Generational Humor, Identity, and Conflict during the Pandemic." *Emerging Adulthood* 10, no. 2 (2021). https://journals.sagepub.com/doi/full/10.1177 /21676968211058513.

Cary Aspinwall, Kari Blakinger, and Joseph Neff. "What Women Dying in Prison from COVID-19 Tells Us about Female Incarceration." Marshall Project, May 14, 2020. https://www.themarshallproject.org/2020/05/14/what-women-dying-in-prison-from-covid-19-tell-us-about-female-incarceration.

Associated Press. "Cosby Lawyers Say Prosecutors Using 'Casting Couch' Cliché." VOA News, November 1, 2016. https://www.voanews.com/a /bill-cosby-sexual-assault-trial-lawyers-prosecutors-casting-couch-cliche /3574708.html.

Haidar Aviram. *Cheap on Crime: Recession Area Politics and the Transformation of American Punishment* (University of California Press, 2015).

Emily Badger. "The Lasting Effects of Stop-and-Frisk in Bloomberg's New York." *New York Times,* March 2, 2020. https://www.nytimes.com/2020/03/02 /upshot/stop-and-frisk-bloomberg.html.

Chiara Baiano, Genarro Raimo, Isa Zappullo, Marialaura Marra, Roberto Cecere, Luigi Trojano, and Massimillano Conson. "Empathy through the Pandemic: Changes of Different Emphatic Dimensions during the Covid-19 Outbreak." *International Journal of Environmental Research and Public Health* 19, no. 4 (2022): 2435. https://www.ncbi.nlm.nih.gov/pmc/articles /PMC8872216/.

Carrie N. Baker. "#MeToo Update: States Enact New Sexual Harassment Laws—But More is Needed." *Ms.*, October 13, 2020. https://msmagazine .com/2020/10/13/metoo-update-states-enact-new-sexual-harassment-laws-but-more-is-needed/.

Katie J.M. Baker. "Here's the Powerful Letter the Stanford Victim Read to Her Attacker." BuzzFeed News, June 3, 2016. https://www.buzzfeednews

.com/article/katiejmbaker/heres-the-powerful-letter-the-stanford-victim-read-to-her-ra.

Peter C. Baker. "Missing the Story." *The Nation,* April 8, 2014. https://www.thenation.com/article/archive/missing-story/.

Borwin Bandelow and Sophie Michaelis. "Epidemiology of Anxiety Disorders in the 21st Century." *Dialogues in Clinical Neuroscience* 17, no. 3 (2015).

Ashlee Banks. "Amy Cooper Proves Once Again That White Privilege Prevails." *Essence,* February 17, 2021. https://www.essence.com/op-ed/amy-cooper-proves-once-again-that-white-privilege-prevails/.

Brooks Barnes. "After #MeToo Reckoning, A Fear That Hollywood is Regressing." *New York Times,* October 24, 2022. https://www.nytimes.com/2022/10/24/business/media/hollywood-metoo.html.

Victoria J. Barnett. "The Changing View of the 'Bystander' in Holocaust Scholarship: Historical, Ethical, and Political Implications." *Utah Law Review* 4 (2017): 633.

Bijan C. Bayne. "How 'Woke' Became the Least Woke Word in U.S. English" (opinion). *Washington Post,* February 2, 2022. https://www.washingtonpost.com/opinions/2022/02/02/black-history-woke-appropriation-misuse/.

Max H. Bazerman. *Complicit: How We Enable the Unethical and How to Stop* (Princeton University Press, 2022).

Max H. Bazerman and Ann E. Tenbrunsel. *Blind Spots: Why We Fail to Do What's Right and What to Do about It* (Princeton University Press, 2011).

BBC News. "George Floyd: What Happened in the Final Moments of His Life." BBC, July 16, 2020. https://www.bbc.com/news/world-us-canada-52861726.

———. "Harvey Weinstein Sacked After Sexual Harassment Claims." BBC, October 9, 2017. http://www.bbc.com/news/business-41546694.

———. "Harvey Weinstein Timeline: How the Scandal Unfolded." BBC, February 24, 2023. http://www.bbc.com/news/entertainment-arts-41594672.

———. "Melania Trump Says "Don't Care" Jacket Was a Message." BBC, October 14, 2018. https://www.bbc.com/news/world-us-canada-45853364.

———. "Nazi Stutthof Camp Secretary Flees as German Trial Starts." BBC, September 30, 2021. https://www.bbc.com/news/world-europe-58747082.

Eleanor Beardsley. "Historians Say France Was Not Complicit in Rwanda Genocide, but Did Turn a Blind Eye." *NPR,* April 7, 2021. https://www.npr.org/2021/04/07/985128514/historians-say-france-was-not-complicit-in-rwanda-genocide-but-did-turn-a-blind-.

Jason Beaubien. "Catholic Complicity and Rwanda Genocide." NPR, April 22, 2005. https://www.npr.org/templates/story/story.php?storyId=4615171.

Ulrich Beck. "Emancipatory Catastrophism: What Does it Mean to Climate Change and the Risk Society?" *Current Sociology* 63 (2015): 75.

———. *The Metamorphosis of the World* (Polity Press, 2016).

———. *Risk Society: Towards a New Modernity* (Sage, 1992).

Marlene D. Beckman. "The White Slave Traffic Act: The Historical Impact of a Criminal Law on Women." *Georgetown Law Review* 72 (1984): 1111.

Tommy Beer. "Trust in Fellow Americans Hits All-Time Low, Survey Shows." *Forbes*, October 7, 2021. https://www.forbes.com/sites/tommybeer/2021/10/07/trust-in-fellow-americans-hits-all-time-low-survey-shows/?sh = 6de95e9a70cf.

Beryl Leiff Benderly. "Psychology's Tall Tales." American Psychological Association, accessed January 7, 2022. https://www.apa.org/gradpsych/2012/09/tall-tales

Jessica Bennett and Maya Salam. "Harvey Weinstein 'Perp Walked' into the Future of #MeToo." *New York Times*, May 25, 2018. https://www.nytimes.com/2018/05/25/us/harvey-weinstein-perp-walk.html.

Tony Bennett, Lawrence Grossberg, and Meaghan Morris (eds.). *New Keywords: A Revised Vocabulary of Culture and Society* (Wiley-Blackwell, 2005).

Greg Bensinger. "Now Social Media Grows a Conscience?" (opinion). *New York Times*, January 13, 2021. https://www.nytimes.com/2021/01/13/opinion/capitol-attack-twitter-facebook.html.

Olivia Beres. "Stop Comparing Amy Coney Barrett to a Handmaid. She Would Be a Wife." Slate, October 23, 2020. https://slate.com/news-and-politics/2020/10/amy-coney-barrett-wife-not-handmaid.html.

Elizabeth Bernstein. "Toxic Positivity Is Very Real, and Very Annoying." *Wall Street Journal*, November 2, 2021. https://www.wsj.com/articles/tired-of-being-told-cheer-up-the-problem-of-toxic-positivity-11635858001?mod = wsjhp_columnists_pos2.

BET. "Christian Cooper's Sister Speaks Out on Him Refusing to Cooperate with Prosecuting Amy Cooper." BET, July 13, 2020. https://www.bet.com/article/4zc62l/christian-cooper-s-sister-speaks-out-on-amy-cooper.

Alisa Bierria and Colby Lenz. "Battering Court Syndrome: A Structural Critique of Failure to Protect." In *The Politicization of Safety: A Structural Critique of Domestic Violence*, edited by Jane K. Stoever (NYU Press, 2019), 93, 94.

William Blackstone. *Commentaries.*

Carol Bleser. *In Joy and in Sorrow: Women, Family, and Marriage in the Victorian South, 1830–1900* (Oxford University Press, 1991).

Zack Block. "When We Do Nothing in the Face of Racism and Brutality, We Represent Amy Cooper and Derek Chauvin. We are Complicit." Public-Source, June 3, 2020. https://www.publicsource.org/when-we-do-nothing-in-the-face-of-racism-and-brutality-we-represent-amy-cooper-and-derek-chauvin-we-are-complicit/.

Thomas Blount. "To the Reader." In *Glossographia: Or a Dictionary, Interpreting All Such Hard Words of Whatsoever Language, Now Used in Our Refined English Tongue; with Etymologies, Definitions, and Historical Observations on the Same* (Tho. Newcomb for George Sawbridge at the Bible on Ludgate Hill, 1661).

Charles M. Blow. "How White Women Use Themselves as Instruments of Terror." *Salt Lake City Tribune*, May 29, 2020. https://www.sltrib.com/opinion/commentary/2020/05/29/charles-m-blow-how-white/.

Paul Bond. "Meryl Streep Targeted by Street Artists with 'She Knew' Posters." *Hollywood Reporter*, December 19, 2017. https://www.hollywoodreporter.com/news/meryl-streep-targeted-by-street-artists-she-knew-posters-1069400.

George A. Bonnano. "Loss, Trauma, and Human Resilience." *American Psychologist* 59, no. 1 (January 2004): 20–28.

Susan Bordo, *The Destruction of Hillary Clinton* (Melville House, 2017).

Bored Panda. "People Sick of Entitled Women Are Posting These 'Karen' Jokes as Revenge for Their Behavior." https://www.boredpanda.com/funny-karen-jokes/?utm_source = google&utm_medium = organic&utm_campaign = organic.

Borgen Staff. "How Fast Fashion Causes Environmental Poverty." Borgen Magazine, October 25, 2020. https://www.borgenmagazine.com/fast-fashion-causes-environmental-poverty/.

Owen Bowcott. "Rwanda Genocide: The Fight to Bring the Perpetrators to Justice." *The Guardian*, April 2, 2014. https://www.theguardian.com/world/2014/apr/02/rwanda-genocide-fight-justice.

Hugh Breakey. "Acting Selfishly Has Consequences Right Now—Why Ethical Decision Making is Imperative in the Coronavirus Crisis." The Conversation, March 23, 2020. https://theconversation.com/acting-selfishly-has-consequences-right-now-why-ethical-decision-making-is-imperative-in-the-coronavirus-crisis-134350.

Rutger Bregman. *Humankind: A Hopeful History* (Little Brown, 2019).

Mia Brett. "Amy Cooper Played the Damsel in Distress. That Trope Has a Troubling History." *Washington Post*, May 28, 2020. https://www.washingtonpost.com/outlook/2020/05/28/amy-cooper-played-damsel-distress-troubling-history-this-trope/.

Elizabeth Breunig. "Stop Death Shaming." *The Atlantic*, September 2, 2021. https://www.theatlantic.com/ideas/archive/2021/09/stop-death-shaming/619939/.

Daniela Brighenti and David Yaffe-Belany. "Crowd Cries 'Free Corey'; Case Continued." *New Haven Independent*, July 12, 2016. https://www.newhavenindependent.org/index.php/article/menafee_court/.

David Brooks. "The Shame Culture" (opinion). *New York Times*, March 15, 2016. https://www.nytimes.com/2016/03/15/opinion/the-shame-culture.html.

adrienne maree brown. *We Will Not Cancel Us and Other Dreams of Transformative Justice* (AK Press, 2020).

Ronald Brownstein. "What's Really Going on with the Crime Rate?" *The Atlantic*, October 20, 2022. https://www.theatlantic.com/politics/archive/2022/10/crime-rate-justice-republicans-2022-elections/671800/.

Alex Bryan. "Structural Injustice: A Tool for Emancipatory Politics." ENA Institute for Alternative Policies (May 2020).

Kristin Bumiller. *The Civil Rights Society: The Social Construction of Victims* (Johns Hopkins University Press, 1992).

Bye Bye Job. https://www.reddit.com/r/byebyejob/.

Delia Cai. "We Know Which 'Big Little Lies' Character You Are Based on How You Handle Conflict." Buzzfeed.com, June 10, 2019. https://www.buzzfeed.com/deliacai/which-big-little-lies-mom-you-are-based-on-how-you.

Campaign for the Fair Sentencing of Youth. "Facts about Juvenile Life without Parole." https://www.fairsentencingofyouth.org/media-resources/facts-infographics/.

Jessica Campisi, Emily Smith, Eric Levenson, and Kimberly Hutcherson. "After Internet Mockery, 'Permit Patty' Resigns as CEO of Cannabis-Products Company." CNN, June 26, 2018. https://www.cnn.com/2018/06/25/us/permit-patty-san-francisco-trnd/index.html.

David Carr. "Calling Out Bill Cosby's Media Enablers, Including Myself." *New York Times*, November 24, 2014. https://www.nytimes.com/2014/11/25/business/media/calling-out-bill-cosbys-media-enablers-including-myself.html.

Ron Carucci and Ludmila Praslova. "Employees Are Sick of Being Asked to Make Moral Compromises." *Harvard Business Review*, February 21, 2021. https://hbr.org/2022/02/employees-are-sick-of-being-asked-to-make-moral-compromises.

Christin Cauterucci and June Thomas. "What to Do about Ellen." Slate, August 12, 2020. https://slate.com/human-interest/2020/08/ellen-degeneres-homophobia-sexism-controversy.html.

Celebrity Apology Generator. https://apologygenerator.com.

Brittany Chang. "A Lawsuit Is Accusing 7 Chocolate Makers of Complicity in Child Labor and Trafficking in the Cocoa Trade." Insider, February 12, 2021. https://www.businessinsider.com/cocoa-companies-child-labor-complicity-lawsuit-2021-2.

Bill Chappell. "'Complicit' Is the Word of the Year in 2017, Dictionary.com Says." *NPR*, November 27, 2017. https://www.npr.org/sections/thetwo-way/2017/11/27/566763885/complicit-is-the-word-of-the-year-in-2017-dictionary-com-says#:~:text=Race-,%27Complicit%27%20Is%20The%20Word%20Of%20The%20Year%20In%202017%2C,with%20others%3B%20having%20complicity.%22.

Katarzyna Chmielewska. "Constructing the Figure of the Polish Shoah Witness." In *The Holocaust Bystander in Polish Culture, 1945–2015: The Story of Innocence*, edited by Maryla Hopfinger and Tomasz Zukowski (Palgrave, 2021).

Carina Chocano. "Behind Every Villain Stands Someone 'Complicit,'" *New York Times*, January 17, 2018. https://www.nytimes.com/2018/01/17/magazine/behind-every-villain-stands-someone-complicit.html.

Amy Chozick. "Clinton Defends Her Handling of a Rape Case in 1975." *New York Times*, July 7, 2014. http://www.nytimes.com/2014/07/08/us/08clinton.html.

Nils Christie. "The Ideal Victim." In *From Crime Policy to Victim Policy*, edited by E. A. Fattah (Palgrave Macmillan, 1986).

"Civil Rights Trial over George Floyd's Death: Ex-Officers Guilty in Federal Trial over George Floyd's Death." *New York Times,* February 24, 2022. https://www.nytimes.com/live/2022/02/24/us/george-floyd-trial-verdict.

Katherine Clark. "Clark, Rogers Release Report Exposing Purdue Pharma's Corrupting Influence at the World Health Organization." Katherine Clark, 5th District of Massachusetts, May 22, 2019. https://katherineclark.house.gov/2019/5/clark-rogers-release-report-exposing-purdue-pharma-s-corrupting-influence-at-the-world-health-organization.

Nick Clegg. "Joe Biden on America under Trump: 'Silence Is Complicity—Our Children Are Listening.'" *Anger Management with Nick Clegg*, July 13, 2018. https://www.youtube.com/watch?v=qZlH1O9lU18.

Ta-Nehisi Coates. "The Cosby Show." *The Atlantic*, November 19, 2014. https://www.theatlantic.com/entertainment/archive/2014/11/the-cosby-show/382891/.

———. "The Dubious Math Behind Stop and Frisk." *The Atlantic*, July 24, 2013. https://www.theatlantic.com/national/archive/2013/07/the-dubious-math-behind-stop-and-frisk/278065/.

Jelani Cobb. "Harvey Weinstein, Bill Cosby, and the Cloak of Charity." *New Yorker*, October 14, 2017. https://www.newyorker.com/news/daily-comment/harvey-weinstein-bill-cosby-and-the-cloak-of-charity.

G. Ben Cohen, Justin D. Levinson, and Koichi Hioki. "Racial Bias, Accomplice Liability, and the Felony Murder Rule: A National Empirical Study." *Denver Law Review* (forthcoming 2023).

Johnnetta B. Cole. "Why I Kept Open an Exhibit Featuring Art Owned by Bill Cosby." The Root, August 5, 2015. https://www.theroot.com/why-i-kept-open-an-exhibit-featuring-art-owned-by-bill-1790860731.

Christian Cooper. "Why I Have Chosen Not to Aid the Investigation of Amy Cooper" (opinion). *Washington Post*, July 14, 2020. https://www.washingtonpost.com/opinions/christian-cooper-why-i-am-declining-to-be-involved-in-amy-coopers-prosecution/2020/07/14/1ba3a920-c5d4-11ea-b037-f9711f89ee46_story.html.

Carol Costello. "All the President's Women Are Complicit." CNN, December 5, 2017. https://www.cnn.com/2017/12/04/opinions/ivanka-trump-women-complicit-opinion-costello/index.html.

Bryce Covert. "Where 'Defund' Isn't Dead." *The Nation*, November 16, 2021. https://www.thenation.com/article/society/police-reform-defund/.

Charlie R. Crimston, Matthew J. Hornsey, Paul G. Bain, and Brock Bastian. "Toward a Psychology of Moral Expansiveness." *Current Directions in Psychological Science* 27, no. 1 (2018): 14–19, 17–18.

CRT Forward. https://crtforward.law.ucla.edu/about/.

Julianne Cuba. "Trek Bicycles Declines to Divest from NYPD Despite 'Abhorrent' Use of Bikes Against Protesters." StreetsBlogNYC, June 10, 2020. https://nyc.streetsblog.org/2020/06/10/trek-bicycles-declines-to-divest-from-nypd-despite-abhorrent-use-of-bikes-against-protesters/.

Brent Curtis. "Woman Recalls Partner's Brutal Murder." *Rutland Herald*, October 17, 2018. https://www.rutlandherald.com/news/woman-recalls-partners-brutal-murder/article_961c557a-b46a-5413-80ff-9b9a9b4af939.html.

Tim Cushing. "Ivanka Trump, Jared Kushner Threaten Defamation Suit Over Lincoln Project's Non-Defamatory Billboards." Techdirt, October 26, 2020. https://www.techdirt.com/articles/20201024/13110445574/ivanka-trump-jared-kushner-threaten-defamation-suit-over-lincoln-projects-non-defamatory-billboards.shtml.

Maryclaire Dale and Michael R. Sisak. "'I Was Frozen': Cosby Accuser Says She Was Drugged, Groped." Associated Press, June 6, 2017. https://apnews.com/article/5b019ff898da48d2a2bbbc2f1afeb321.

John M. Darley and Bibb Latane. "Bystander Intervention in Emergencies: Diffusion of Responsibility." *Journal of Personality and Social Psychology* 8 (1968).

Charles Davis. "Biden Condemns 'Russian State' for Poisoning of Alexei Navalny, Says Trump's 'Silence Is Complicity.'" *Business Insider*, September 3, 2020. https://www.businessinsider.com/biden-condemns-russian-state-for-poisoning-of-alexey-navalny-2020-9.

Eli Davis. "Central Park Karen (Amy Cooper) Should be Charged with Assault with a Deadly Weapon—Her Whiteness." Medium, May 27, 2020. https://medium.com/@ancestors400/central-park-karen-amy-cooper-should-be-charged-assault-with-a-deadly-weapon-whiteness-63f246fdba67.

Samantha Delouya. "Court Grants Sackler Family Immunity in Exchange for $6 Billion Opioid Settlement." *CNN*, May 30, 2023. https://www.cnn.com/2023/05/30/business/sackler-purdue-opioid-liability/index.html.

Department of Justice. "Opioid Manufacturer Purdue Pharma Pleads Guilty to Fraud and Kickback Conspiracies." November 24, 2020. https://www.justice.gov/opa/pr/opioid-manufacturer-purdue-pharma-pleads-guilty-fraud-and-kickback-conspiracies.

Alan Dershowitz. *Guilt by Accusation: The Challenge of Proving Innocence in the Age of #MeToo* (Hot Books, 2019).

Robin DiAngelo. *White Fragility: Why It's So Hard for White People to Talk About Racism* (Beacon Press, 2018).

Caitlin Dickerson. "A Minneapolis Neighborhood Vowed to Check Its Privilege. It's Already Being Tested." *New York Times*, June 24, 2020. https://www.nytimes.com/2020/06/24/us/minneapolis-george-floyd-police.html.

Thomas Docherty. *Complicity: Criticism Between Collaboration and Commitment* (Rowman & Littlefield 2016).

Rachel Dodes. "Amy Coney Barrett's Judgment Day." *Vanity Fair*, October 7, 2020. https://www.vanityfair.com/style/2020/10/amy-coney-barretts-judgment-day.

Matt Donnelly. "'We Were All Complicit': Three Bombshells from the Harvey Weinstein 'Frontline' Special." The Wrap, March 2, 2018. https://www.thewrap.com/harvey-weinstein-frontline-pbs-bombshells-complicit/.

Michael Dorf. "Federal Judge Accepts Extravagant Complicity Claim to Exempt Company from Obligation to Provide Lifesaving Medicine." Verdict, September 13, 2022. https://verdict.justia.com/2022/09/13/federal-judge-accepts-extravagant-complicity-claim-to-exempt-company-from-obligation-to-provide-lifesaving-medicine.

Mary Douglas. *Purity and Danger* (Frederick A. Praeger, 1966).

———. *Risk and Blame* (Routledge, 1992).

Maureen Dowd. "The Princess vs. the Portrait in the Trump World" (opinion). *New York Times*, August 29, 2020. https://www.nytimes.com/2020/08/29/opinion/sunday/ivanka-melania-trump-2020.html.

———. "This Is Why Uma Thurman Is Angry" (opinion). *New York Times*, February 3, 2018. https://www.nytimes.com/2018/02/03/opinion/sunday/this-is-why-uma-thurman-is-angry.html.

Joshua Dressler. "Reassessing the Theoretical Underpinnings of Accomplice Liability: New Solutions to an Old Problem." *Hastings Law Journal* 37 (1985): 91, 102.

———. "Reforming Complicity Law: Trivial Assistance as a Lesser Offense?" *Ohio State Law Journal* 5 (2008): 427, 433, citing Robert Weisberg, "Reappraising Complicity." *Buffalo Criminal Law Review* 4 (2000): 217, 224.

William Drozdiak. "Panel Finds Switzerland Complicit in Holocaust." *Washington Post*, December 10, 1999. https://www.washingtonpost.com/wp-srv/pmextra/dec99/10/swiss.htm.

Steve Dubb and Amy Costello. "The Sackler Family Made Billions from OxyContin. Why Do Top U.S. Colleges Take Money Tainted by the Opioid Crisis?" *The Guardian*, January 27, 2018. https://www.theguardian.com/us-news/2018/jan/27/universities-sackler-family-purdue-pharma-oxycontin-opioids.

David W. Dunlap. "How Many Witnessed the Murder of Kitty Genovese?" *New York Times*, April 6, 2016. https://www.nytimes.com/2016/04/06/insider/1964-how-many-witnessed-the-murder-of-kitty-genovese.html.

Chandelis R. Duster. "Yale Janitor's Act of Civil Disobedience: A Stand Against Racism." NBC News, July 19, 2018. https://www.nbcnews.com/news/nbcblk/yale-janitor-s-act-civil-disobedience-stand-against-racism-n610416.

Alisha Ebrahimji. "San Francisco Official Proposes 'CAREN Act,' Making Racially Biased 911 Calls Illegal." CNN, July 8, 2020. https://www.cnn.com/2020/07/08/us/caren-act-911-san-francisco-trnd/index.html.

Melissa Eddy. "Why German Prosecutes the Aged for Roles It Long Ignored." *New York Times,* February 9, 2021. https://www.nytimes.com/2021/02/09 /world/europe/germany-nazi-prosecution-elderly.html.

Editorial Board. "The 'No Bail' Fiasco in New York." *Wall Street Journal,* March 6, 2020. https://www.wsj.com/articles/the-no-bail-fiasco-in-new-yorkthe-no-bail-fiasco-in-new-york-11583534248.

———. "Voters Cancel the War on Police." *Wall Street Journal,* November 3, 2021.https://www.wsj.com/articles/minneapolis-election-results-police-vote-11635979356?mod = hp_opin_pos_1.

Greg Egan, "Deadly Force: How George Floyd's Killing Exposes Racial Inequities in Minnesota's Felony Murder Doctrine Among the Disenfranchised, the Powerful, and the Police." *Minnesota Journal of Law and Inequality* 4 (2021): 1, 5.

———. "Minnesota Needs to Change Its Felony-Murder Doctrine. Racial Inequities Are One Reason." *Twin Cities Pioneer Press,* June 28, 2020. https:// www.twincities.com/2020/06/28/greg-egan-minnesota-needs-to-change-its-felony-murder-doctrine-racial-inequities-are-one-reason/.

———. "What Makes Mike Pence's Complicity So Chilling." *New York Times,* October 9, 2020. https://www.nytimes.com/2020/10/09/opinion/mike-pence-debate.html.

Laura Eichelberger. "SARS and New York's Chinatown: The Politics of Blame During an Epidemic of Fear." *Science and Medicine 65* (2007): 1284.

John Eligon. "'I was Failing': Bystanders Carry Guilt from Watching George Floyd Die." *New York Times,* updated April 21, 2021. https://www.nytimes .com/2021/04/03/us/george-floyd-derek-chauvin-trial.html.

Ellen Shop. "Be Kind to One Another Collection." Accessed January 1, 2022. https://www.ellenshop.com/collections/ellen-degeneres-be-kind-collection.

Executive Order No. 13950. "Executive Order on Combating Race and Sex Stereotyping." September 22, 2020. Revoked by E.O. 13985, January 20, 2021.

"Ex-Officers Guilty in Federal Trial over George Floyd's Death." *New York Times,* February 24, 2022. https://www.nytimes.com/live/2022/02/24/us /george-floyd-trial-verdict.

Ronan Farrow. "From Aggressive Overtures to Sexual Assault: Harvey Weinstein's Accusers Tell Their Stories." *New Yorker,* October 23, 2017. https:// www.newyorker.com/news/news-desk/from-aggressive-overtures-to-sexual-assault-harvey-weinsteins-accusers-tell-their-stories.

Mary Louise Fellows and Sherene Razack. "The Race to Innocence: Confronting Hierarchical Relations Among Women." *Journal of Gender, Race, and Justice* 1 (1998): 338.

Shoshana Felman. *The Juridical Unconscious: Trials and Traumas in the Twentieth Century* (Harvard University Press, 2002).

Alexia Fernandez Campbell. "NBC Will Now Let Former Employees Talk about Sexual Harassment. Critics Say That's Not Enough." Vox, October 28, 2019. https://www.vox.com/identities/2019/10/28/20936150/nbc-lauer-weinstein-employees-sexual-harassment-nda.

Kimberly Kessler Ferzan. "Conspiracy, Complicity, and the Scope of Contemplated Crime." *Arizona State Law Journal* (2017): 453-475.

———. "Inchoate Crimes at the Prevention/Punishment Divide." *San Diego Law Review* 48 (2011): 1273.

Jill Filipovic. "What Amy Coney Barrett's Supreme Court Nomination Means for Women." Medium, September 25, 2020. https://gen.medium.com/what-amy-coney-barretts-supreme-court-nomination-means-for-women-88cf0d4149e9.

Avram Finkelstein. "SILENCE = DEATH: How an Iconic Poster Came into Being." LitHub, December 1, 2017. https://lithub.com/silence-death-how-an-iconic-protest-poster-came-into-being/.

Peter Fischer, Joachim I. Krueger, Tobias Greitemeyer, Claudia Vogrincic, Andreas Kastenmuller, Dieter Frey, Moritz Heene, Magdalena Wicher, and Martina Kainbacher. "The Bystander-Effect: A Meta-Analytic Review on Bystander Intervention in Dangerous and Non-Dangerous Emergencies." *Psychology Bulletin* 137, no. 4 (2011): 517–37.

Dana R. Fisher and Stella M. Rouse. "Intersectionality within the Racial Justice Movement in the Summer of 2020." PNAS 119, no. 30 (July 12, 2022).

Mike Fleming Jr. "'Beautiful Girls' Scribe Scott Rosenberg on a Complicated Legacy with Harvey Weinstein." Deadline, October 16, 2017. https://deadline.com/2017/10/scott-rosenberg-harvey-weinstein-miramax-beautiful-girls-guilt-over-sexual-assault-allegations-1202189525/.

Heather Jo Flores. "I Refuse to Post 'MeToo' as My Facebook Status. How about Men Post 'I Ignored it, and I Won't Anymore' Instead." The Independent, October 17, 2017. https://www.independent.co.uk/voices/harvey-weinstein-facebook-me-too-sexual-assault-abuse-men-should-post-too-a8004631.html.

Amy Forliti. "What's Next After Chauvin's Conviction on Three Counts." Associated Press, April 20, 2021. https://apnews.com/article/derek-chauvin-trial-charges-716fa235ecf6212f0ee4993110d959df.

Jennifer Freyd and Pamela Birrell. *Blind to Betrayal: Why We Fool Ourselves We Aren't Being Fooled* (John Wiley & Sons 2013).

Martin Gansberg. "37 Who Saw Murder Didn't Call the Police." *New York Times,* March 27, 1964. https://www.nytimes.com/1964/03/27/archives/37-who-saw-murder-didnt-call-the-police-apathy-at-stabbing-of.html.

Stephen P. Garvey. "Reading Rosemond." *Ohio State Law Journal* 12 (2014): 233.

Jacob Gershman. "The Controversial Legal Doctrine at the Heart of the Floyd, Brooks, Arbery Cases." *Wall Street Journal,* July 9, 2020. https://www.wsj.com/articles/the-controversial-legal-doctrine-at-the-heart-of-the-floyd-brooks-arbery-cases-11594295529.

Anthony Giddens. *Modernity and Self-Identity* (Stanford University Press, 1991).

Sophie Gilbert. "When Women Are Accused of Complicity." *The Atlantic,* August 17, 2019. https://www.theatlantic.com/entertainment/archive/2019/08/ghislaine-maxwell-jeffrey-epstein-roger-ailes-judy-laterza-serena-waterford-handmaids-tale/596236/.

Lauren Gill. "Alabama Executes Nathaniel Woods Despite Claims That He Was an 'Innocent Man.'" The Appeal, March 6, 2020. https://theappeal.org/alabama-executes-nathaniel-woods-despite-claims-that-he-was-an-innocent-man/.

Leigh Gilmore. "It Wasn't Just 'Fake News' Presenting a Fake Hillary Clinton: She Was Held to Impossible Standards." Salon, November 26, 2016. https://www.salon.com/2016/11/26/it-wasnt-just-fake-news-presenting-a-fake-hillary-clinton-she-was-held-to-impossible-standards_partner/.

Lisa Girion. "Johnson & Johnson Knew for Decades that Asbestos Lurked in Its Baby Powder: A Reuters Investigation." Reuters, December 14, 2018. https://www.reuters.com/investigates/special-report/johnsonandjohnson-cancer/.

Malcolm Gladwell. *The Tipping Point: How Little Things Can Make a Big Difference* (Back Bay Books, 2002).

Global Burden of Diseases, Injuries, and Risk Factors Study Collaborators. "Fatal Police Violence by Race and State in the USA, 1980–2019: A Network Meta-Regression." *The Lancet* 398 (2021): 1239–55.

Chris Goddard, Lilian DeBortoli, Bernadette J. Saunders, and Joe Tucci. "The Rapist's Camouflage: 'Child Prostitution.'" *Child Abuse Review* 14 (2005): 275, 278.

Jin X. Goh, Bryn Bandt-Law, Stacey Sinclair, and Cheryl R. Kaiser. "Narrow Prototypes and Neglected Victims: Understanding Perceptions of Sexual Harassment." *Journal of Personality and Social Psychology* 122, no. 5 (2021): 1, 13.

Henry Goldblatt. "A Brief History of 'Karen,'" *New York Times*, July 31, 2020. https://www.nytimes.com/2020/07/31/style/karen-name-meme-history.html.

Matthew Goldstein. "JP Morgan to Pay $290 Million in Settlement with Epstein's Victims." *New York Times*, June 12, 2023. https://www.nytimes.com/2023/06/12/business/jpmorgan-settlement-jeffrey-epstein-victims.html.

Lev Golinkin. "Why Do Stanford, Harvard, and NASA Continue to Still Honor a Nazi Past?" *New York Times*, December 13, 2022. https://www.nytimes.com/2022/12/13/opinion/stanford-harvard-nasa-nazi-scientists.html.

J. David Goodman. "A Year After 'Defund' Police Get Their Money Back." *New York Times*, October 10, 2021. https://www.nytimes.com/2021/10/10/us/dallas-police-defund.html.

Constance Grady. "Ellen DeGeneres, George W. Bush, and the Death of Uncritical Niceness." Vox, October 9, 2019. https://www.vox.com/culture/2019/10/9/20906371/ellen-degeneres-george-w-bush-controversy.

———. "The False Link Between Amy Coney Barrett and The Handmaid's Tale, Explained." Vox, October 27, 2020. https://www.vox.com/culture/21453103/amy-coney-barrett-handmaids-tale-supreme-court.

———. "Shitty Men List Creator Moira Donegan on the Year in #MeToo." Vox, October 16, 2018. https://www.vox.com/culture/2018/10/16/17955392/moira-donegan-interview-me-too-shitty-media-men-list.

Matthew Green, Valerie Volcovici, and Emma Farge. "Climate Battles Are Moving into the Courtroom, and Lawyers Are Getting Creative." Reuters, July 2, 2020. https://www.reuters.com/article/us-climate-change-lawsuits-idUKKBN2433G5.

Daniel M. Greenfield. "The Crime of Complicity in Genocide: How the International Tribunals for Rwanda and Yugoslavia Got It Wrong, and Why It Matters." *Journal of Criminal Law and Criminology* 98 (2007–2008): 922.

Rachel E. Greenspan. "How the Name Karen Became a Stand-In for Problematic White Women and Hugely Popular Meme." Insider, October 26, 2020. https://www.insider.com/karen-meme-origin-the-history-of-calling-women-karen-white-2020-5.

Ioan Grillo. "Mexico Is Right to Sue U.S. Gun Companies" (argument). *Foreign Policy*, August 12, 2021. https://foreignpolicy.com/2021/08/12/mexico-guns-lawsuit-firearms-drug-cartels-exports-border-violence/.

Aya Gruber. *The Feminist War on Crime: The Unexpected Role of Women's Liberation in Mass Incarceration* (University of California Press, 2020).

Guardian Staff. "Minneapolis Police Chief: All Four Officers Complicit in Floyd's Death." *The Guardian*, June 1, 2020. https://www.theguardian.com

/us-news/2020/jun/01/george-floyd-death-minneapolis-police-chief-medaria-arradondo-officers-complicit.

Genevieve Guenther. "Who Is the We in 'We Are Causing Climate Change?'" Slate, October 10, 2018. https://slate.com/technology/2018/10/who-is-we-causing-climate-change.html.

Amos Guiora. *Armies of Enablers: Survivor Stories of Complicity and Betrayal in Sexual Assaults* (American Bar Association, 2020).

Vaidya Gullapalli. "The 'Felony Murder Rule' as a Representation of What's Wrong with Our Criminal Justice System." The Appeal, September 23, 2019. https://theappeal.org/the-felony-murder-rule-as-a-representation-of-whats-wrong-in-our-criminal-legal-system/.

Noel Gutierrez-Morfin. "Ellen DeGeneres to Receive Presidential Medal of Freedom." NBC News, November 16, 2016. https://www.nbcnews.com/feature/nbc-out/ellen-degeneres-receive-presidential-medal-freedom-n684926.

Ruby Hamad. "How White Women Use Strategic Tears to Silence Women of Color." *The Guardian*, May 7, 2018. https://www.theguardian.com/commentisfree/2018/may/08/how-white-women-use-strategic-tears-to-avoid-accountability.

Amy Harder. "The Climate Footprints of the Rich and Activist." Axios, December 9, 2019. https://www.axios.com/2019/12/09/carbon-footprints-rich-activists.

Marilyn Harrell. "Serving Time for Falling in Love: How the War on Drugs Operates to the Detriment of Women of Circumstance in Poor Urban Communities of Color." *Georgetown Journal of Law and Modern Critical Race Perspectives* 11 (2019): 139, 140.

Fiona Harvey, Nina Lakhani, Oliver Milman, and Adam Morton. "Cop27 Agrees Historic 'Loss and Damage' Fund for Climate Impact in Developing Countries." *The Guardian*, November 20, 2022. https://www.theguardian.com/environment/2022/nov/20/cop27-agrees-to-historic-loss-and-damage-fund-to-compensate-developing-countries-for-climate-impacts.

Erika Harwood. "Emmanuel Macron Plans to Revoke Harvey Weinstein's French Legion of Honor Award." *Vanity Fair*, October 16, 2017. https://www.vanityfair.com/style/2017/10/emmanuel-macron-harvey-weinstein-legion-of-honor-revoked.

Thomas Haskell. "Capitalism and the Origins of Humanitarian Sentiment," pts. 1 and 2. *American Historical Review* 90, no. 2 (1985): 339–61, 547.

Nick Haslam. "Concept Creep: Psychology's Expanding Concepts of Harm and Pathology." *Psychological Inquiry* 27, no. 1 (2016): 1–17, 7–10.

Salma Hayek, "Harvey Weinstein Is My Monster Too" (opinion). *New York Times*, December 13, 2017. https://www.nytimes.com/2017/12/13/opinion /salma-hayek-weinstein.html.

Brad Heath. "After Floyd's Killing, Minneapolis Police Retreated, Data Shows." Reuters, September 13, 2021. https://www.reuters.com/investigates /special-report/usa-policing-minneapolis/.

Hecate. "Blake Lively and Ryan Reynolds Donate $200K to NAACP, Acknowledge Their Complicity.'" Celebitchy, June 2, 2020. https://www.celebitchy.com /666037/blake_lively_ryan_reynolds_donate_200k_to_naacp_acknowledge_ their_complicity/.

Jeet Heer. "Was Harvey Weinstein Sending a Message with the Books He Carried to His Arrest?" New Republic, May 25, 2018. https://newrepublic .com/article/148552/harvey-weinstein-sending-message-books-carried- arrest.

Rebecca Heilweil. "Target's History of Working with Police Is Not a Good Look Right Now." Vox, June 5, 2020. https://www.vox.com/recode/2020 /6/1/21277192/target-looting-police-george-floyd-protests.

Carla Herreria Russo. "Melania Trump Knows It's Ironic That She Advocates Against Bullying." *Huffington Post*, November 15, 2018. https://www .huffpost.com/entry/melania-trump-irony-anti-bullying_n_5bede64ee4 boc19de3fe04a5.

An-Li Herring. "Sentenced for Life, People Convicted of Felony-Murder Sue for Relief." WHYY, July 8, 2020. https://whyy.org/articles/sentenced-for- life-people-convicted-of-felony-murder-sue-for-chance-at-release/.

Amanda Hess. "The Pandemic Ad Salutes You." *New York Times*, May 22, 2020. https://www.nytimes.com/2020/05/22/arts/pandemic-ads-salute-you .html.

Kristy Hess and Lisa Waller. "The Digital Pillory: Media Shaming of 'Ordi- nary' People for Minor Crimes." *Continuum* 28, no. 1 (2014): 101–11.

Frederick Hewett. "States Took Big Tobacco to Court and Won. Can They Now Beat Big Oil?" WBUR, June 6, 2022. https://www.wbur.org/cognoscenti /2022/06/06/exxon-mobil-law-suit-climate-change-big-oil-frederick-hewett.

William I. Hitchcock. *The Bitter Road to Freedom: The Human Cost of Allied Victory in WWII Europe* (Free Press, 2009).

Hillary Hoffower. "Ellen DeGeneres Is Coming under Fire for Accusations of Rude Behavior behind the Scenes of Her Beloved Talk Show. Take a Look at How She Became the Highest-Paid Comedian in the World—and What She Spends Her $330 Million Fortune On." Business Insider, February 28,

2020. https://www.businessinsider.com/ellen-degeneres-net-worth-fortune-spending-2020-2.

Maryla Hopfinger. "We Are All Witnesses, Instead of an Introduction." In *The Holocaust Bystander in Polish Culture, 1945–2015: The Story of Innocence*, edited by Maryla Hopfinger and Tomasz Zukowski (Palgrave, 2021).

Rose Horowitch. "Florida's 'Stop WOKE' Law to Remain Blocked in Colleges, Appeals Court Rules." NBC News, March 17, 2023. https://www.nbcnews.com/politics/politics-news/floridas-stop-woke-law-remain-blocked-colleges-appeals-court-rules-rcna75455.

"How Did the Opioid Epidemic Overtake America? The Prevailing Narrative Offered Too Easy a Scapegoat...If Not Purdue, Who Drove the Epidemic?" Judge for Yourselves, May 2020. https://www.judgeforyourselves.info.

John W. Howard III and Laura Prividera. "The Fallen Woman Archetype: Media Representations of Lynndie England, Gender, and the (Ab)uses of U.S. Female Soldiers." *Women's Studies in Communication* 31 (2010): 287.

Aziz Huq. "The Conservative Case against Banning Critical Race Theory." *Time*, July 13, 2021. https://time.com/6079716/conservative-case-against-banning-critical-race-theory/.

Heidi M. Hurd and Michael S. Moore. "Untying the Gordian Knot of Mens Rea Requirements for Accomplices." *Social Philosophy and Policy* 32, no. 2 (2016): 161–83.

"I Never Thought Leopards Would Eat My Face." Reddit. https://www.reddit.com/r/LeopardsAteMyFace/.

Libor Jany and Randy Furst. "Minneapolis Police Training Polices under Microscope in Trial of 3 Ex-Cops in George Floyd's Death." *Minneapolis Star Tribune*, January 30, 2022. https://www.startribune.com/minneapolis-police-training-policies-under-microscope-in-trial-of-3-ex-cops-in-george-floyds-death/600141339/.

Scott Jaschik. "Harvard Latest Revoked Admissions Offer." Inside Higher Ed, June 24, 2019. https://www.insidehighered.com/admissions/article/2019/06/24/harvard-rescinds-admissions-offer-over-applicants-past-racist-writings.

Jenna Johnson. "Trump Apologizes for 'Foolish' Comments about Women; Then Attacks the Clintons." *Washington Post*, October 8, 2016. https://www.washingtonpost.com/news/post-politics/wp/2016/10/08/trump-apologizes-for-foolish-comments-about-women-then-attacks-the-clintons/?utm_term=.e55906295cod.

Krista Johnson. "Accomplice Law Case of Lakeith Smith, Sentenced to 55 Years, Gains Renewed Interest." *Montgomery Advertiser*, June 11, 2020. https://

www.montgomeryadvertiser.com/story/news/crime/2020/06/11/alabama-case-lakeith-smith-inmate-sentenced-55-years-gains-renewed-interest/5344257002/.

R. Skip Johnson. "Codependency and Codependent Relationships." BPD Family, May 13, 2018. https://www.bpdfamily.com/content/codependency-codependent-relationships.

Jess Joho. "Matt Damon Admits to Knowing about Weinstein's Sexual Harassment for Decades." Mashable, October 23, 2017. https://mashable.com/2017/10/23/matt-damon-gwyneth-paltrow-weinstein-sexual-assault/.

Tashara Jones. "Ellen 'Scandal' Put Pressure on Stephen 'tWitch' Boss, Says Pal Todrick Hall." Page Six, January 25, 2023. https://pagesix.com/2023/01/25/ellen-scandal-pressured-late-dj-twitch-says-pal-todrick-hall/.

Stephanie Jones-Rogers *They Were Her Property: White Women as Slave Owners in the American South* (Yale University Press, 2019).

Dearbail Jordan. "Is This America's Most Hated Family?" BBC News, March 22, 2018. https://www.bbc.com/news/business-47660040.

Sanford H. Kadish. "Complicity, Cause and Blame: A Study in the Interpretation of Doctrine." *California Law Review* 73 (1985): 323, 410.

Robin Kaiser-Schatzlein. "'Hand of One, Hand of All': 50 Years for a Teen Who Didn't Pull the Trigger." The Appeal, January 7, 2021.

Elizabeth Papp Kamali. "Felonia felonice facta: Felony and Intentionality in Medieval England." *Criminal Law and Philosophy* 9 (2015): 397–421, 414–15.

Jodi Kantor and Megan Twohey. *She Said: Breaking the Sexual Harassment Story That Helped Ignite a Movement* (Penguin Press, 2019).

Alice Kaplan. "A Hidden Memorial to the Worst Aspects of our Jim Crow Army." *Chicago Tribune*, September 25, 2005. https://www.chicagotribune.com/news/ct-xpm-2005-09-25-0509250486-story.html.

Tracey Kaplan. "Recall Aftermath: Will the Removal of Judge Aaron Persky Prompt a New Legal Battle?" *Mercury News*, June 6, 2018. https://www.mercurynews.com/2018/06/06/judge-persky/.

Alec Karakatsanis. *Usual Cruelty: The Complicity of Lawyers in the Criminal Injustice System* (New Press, 2019). https://www.npr.org/2021/11/02/1051617581/minneapolis-police-vote.

Jack Karp. "'Meme Stock,' 'Quiet Quitting' Among Top New Legal Terms." Law360. December 13, 2022. https://www.law360.com/articles/1558033/-meme-stock-quiet-quitting-among-top-new-legal-terms.

Mona Kasra. "Vigilantism, Public Shaming, and Social Media Hegemony: The Role of Digital-Networked Images in Humiliation and Sociopolitical Control." *Communication Review* 20, no. 3 (2017): 172–188.

Saul Kassin. "The Killing of Kitty Genovese: What Else Does This Case Tell Us?" *Perspectives on Psychological Science* 12 (2017): 374.

Martin Kaste. "Minneapolis Voters Reject a Measure to Replace the Police Department." NPR, November 3, 2021.

Josh Katz and Margot Sanger-Katz, "'It's Huge, It's Historic, It's Unheard-of': Drug Overdose Deaths Spike." *New York Times,* July 14, 2021. https://www .nytimes.com/interactive/2021/07/14/upshot/drug-overdose-deaths.html.

Mark Kaufman. "The Carbon Footprint Sham." Mashable. https://mashable. com/feature/carbon-footprint-pr-campaign-sham.

Zachary D. Kaufman. "Protectors of Predators or Prey: Bystanders and Upstanders Amid Sexual Crimes." *Southern California Law Review* 92 (2019): 1317.

Cole Kazdin. "Psychologists Weigh in on the Teen Who Live-Streamed Her Best Friend's Rape." *Identity*, April 25, 2006.

Patrick Radden Keefe. "The Family That Built an Empire of Pain." *New Yorker,* June 16, 2021. https://www.newyorker.com/magazine/2017/10/30/the-family-that-built-an-empire-of-pain.

Rebecca Keegan. "#MeToo, Five Years Later: Why Time's Up Imploded." *Hollywood Reporter,* October 3, 2022. https://www.hollywoodreporter.com/news /general-news/metoo-five-years-later-times-up-1235228096/.

Eric Kelderman. "The Plan to Dismantle DEI." *Chronicle of Higher Education,* January 20, 2023. https://www.chronicle.com/article/the-plan-to-dismantle-dei.

Adam Kelly and Will Norman. "Complicity Then and Now." *Comparative Literature Studies* 56 (2019): 673.

Annie Kelly. "'Virtually Entire' Fashion Industry Complicit in Uighur Forced Labor, Say Rights Groups." *The Guardian*, July 23, 2020. https://www .theguardian.com/global-development/2020/jul/23/virtually-entire-fashion-industry-complicit-in-uighur-forced-labour-say-rights-groups-china.

Cara Kelly and Erin Jensen. "Intentional of Not Melania's Gucci Pussy-Bow Blouse Made A Statement at the Debate." *USA Today*, October 10, 2016. https://www.usatoday.com/story/life/entertainthis/2016/10/10/melania-trump-gucci-pussy-bow-blouse-presidential-debate/91845914/.

Kit Kinports. "Rosemond, Mens Rea, and the Elements of Complicity." *San Diego Law Review* 52 (2015): 133.

Lauren Kirchner. "Massive Court Case Suggests 'Forever Chemical' Manufacturers Hid Health Risks for Decades." *Consumer Reports*, June 2, 2023.

https://www.consumerreports.org/toxic-chemicals-substances/case-suggests-forever-chemical-manufacturers-hid-health-risk-a8896667936/.

Sheldon Kirshner. "France's Struggle to Accept Its Complicity in the Holocaust." *National Post*, December 11, 2014. https://nationalpost.com/opinion/sheldon-kirshner-frances-struggle-to-accept-its-complicity-in-the-holocaust.

Naomi Klein. "Trump Defeated Clinton, Not Women." *New York Times*, November 16, 2016. https://www.nytimes.com/2016/11/16/opinion/trump-defeated-clinton-not-women.html.

Joshua Kleinfeld. "Two Cultures of Punishment." *Stanford Law Review* 68 (2016): 933, 943⁻44.

John Koblin. "Ellen DeGeneres Loses $1 Million Viewers After Apologies for Toxic Workplace." *New York Times*, March 22, 2021. https://www.nytimes.com/2021/03/22/business/media/ellen-degeneres-ratings-decline.html.

C. Kong, M. Dunn, and M. Parker. "Psychiatric Genomics and Mental Health Treatment: Setting the Ethical Agenda." *American Journal of Bioethics* 17 (2017): 3.

Andrew Koppelman. "American Evil: A Response to Kleinfeld on Punishment." *Arizona State Law Journal* (2012): 179, 181.

Spencer Kornhaber. "Ellen's Celebrity Defenders Aren't Helping Her." *The Atlantic*, August 6, 2020. https://www.theatlantic.com/culture/archive/2020/08/ellens-celebrity-defenders-arent-helping-her/614998/.

Alyson Krueger. "Summer's Here, and America Is Ready to Quarancheat." *New York Times*, June 26, 2020. https://www.nytimes.com/2020/06/25/style/coroanvirus-america-summer.html.

Anita Kumar. "Trump Taps Ivanka for a Rescue Mission: Win Back Suburban Women." *Politico*, October 21, 2020. https://www.politico.com/news/2020/10/21/ivanka-suburban-women-11th-hour-430784.

Judy Kurtz. "Does Pence Really Call His Wife 'Mother'? Aide Says It's a 'Myth That Drives Me Crazy.'" The Hill, September 9, 2021. https://thehill.com/blogs/in-the-know/571408-does-pence-really-call-his-wife-mother-aide-says-its-a-myth-that-drives-me.

Christopher Kutz. "Causeless Complicity." *Criminal Law and Philosophy* 1 (2007): 289, 305.

———. "The Philosophical Foundations of Complicity Law." In *The Oxford Handbook of Philosophy of Criminal Law*, edited by John Deigh and David Dolinko (Oxford University Press, 2011).

Nicola Lacey. *In Search of Criminal Responsibility: Ideas, Interests, and Institutions* (Oxford University Press, 2016).

———. "In Search of the Responsible Subject: History, Philosophy, and Social Sciences in Criminal Law Theory." *Modern Law Review* 64 (2003): 350, 351.

Stephen LaConte. "16 Actors Who Have Admitted They Regret Their Past Problematic Roles." Buzzfeed, April 2, 2021. https://www.buzzfeed.com/stephenlaconte/problematic-castings-actors-apologize.

Cady Lang. "How the 'Karen Meme' Confronts the Violent History of White Womanhood." *Time*, July 6, 2020. https://time.com/5857023/karen-meme-history-meaning/.

Jamiles Lartey. "New York Tried to Get Rid of Bail. Then the Backlash Came." *Politico*, April 23, 2020. https://www.politico.com/news/magazine/2020/04/23/bail-reform-coronavirus-new-york-backlash-148299.

Bibb Latané and John M. Darley. "Bystander 'Apathy.'" *American Scientist* 244 (1969): 260.

Claudia Lauer. "You Can Serve Life in Prison for Murder Without Killing Anyone. Six Inmates Who Are Suing Pennsylvania for a Chance at Parole." Morning Call, July 8, 2020. https://www.mcall.com/news/pennsylvania/mc-nws-pa-parole-lawsuit-20200708-zwrb3bcgdfchzfbyku5dmvo4sm-story.html.

Daniel Lavelle. "From 'Slimeball Comey' to 'Crooked Hillary,' Why Trump Loves to Brand His Enemies." *The Guardian*, April 17, 2018. https://www.theguardian.com/us-news/shortcuts/2018/apr/17/presidents-nicknames-slimeball-comey-former-fbi-director.

Jane Lavender. "Mike Pence Calls His Wife Karen "Mother" and Refuses to Drink Booze Without Her." The Mirror, September 23, 2020. https://www.mirror.co.uk/news/politics/mike-pence-calls-wife-karen-22716769.

Colin Lecher. "Microsoft Employees Are Protesting 'Complicity in the Climate Crisis.'" *The Verge*, September 19, 2019. https://www.theverge.com/2019/9/19/20874081/microsoft-employees-climate-change-letter-protest.

Nicholas Lemann. "A Call for Help: What the Genovese Story Really Means." *New Yorker*, March 2, 2014. https://www.newyorker.com/magazine/2014/03/10/a-call-for-help.

Brady Leonard. "First Time Gun Ownership Continues to Soar." *Catalyst*, July 22, 2022. https://catalyst.independent.org/2022/07/21/first-time-gun-ownership/.

Jill Lepore. "The Rise of the Victims'-Rights Movement." *New Yorker*, May 21, 2018. https://www.newyorker.com/magazine/2018/05/21/the-rise-of-the-victims-rights-movement.

John Letzing. "Is Climate Denialism Dead?" World Economic Forum, August 15, 2022. https://www.weforum.org/agenda/2022/08/is-climate-denialism-dead/.

Liat Levanon. "Criminal Prohibitions on Membership in Terrorist Organizations." *New Criminal Law Review* 15 (2012): 224, 249–250.

Dan Levin. "Colleges Rescinding Admissions Offers as Racist Social Media Posts Emerge." *New York Times*, July 2, 2020. https://www.nytimes.com/2020/07/02/us/racism-social-media-college-admissions.html.

Sam Levin. "Armed Anarchists Rally at Brock Turner's Home: 'Try This Again and We'll Shoot You!'" *The Guardian*, September 6, 2016. https://www.theguardian.com/us-news/2016/sep/06/brock-turner-stanford-sexual-assault-case-ohio-armed-protest.

———. "'It Never Stops': Killings by US Police Reach Record High in 2022." *The Guardian*, January 6, 2023. https://www.theguardian.com/us-news/2023/jan/06/us-police-killings-record-number-2022.

Mark Levine and Simon Crowther. "The Responsive Bystander: How Social Group Membership and Group Size Can Encourage as Well as Inhibit Bystander Intervention. *Journal of Personality and Social Psychology* 95, no. 6 (2008): 1429–39.

Roee Levy and Martin Mattsson. "The Effects of Social Movements: Evidence from #MeToo." SSRN, August 6, 2021.

Helen Lewis. "The Mythology of Karen." *The Atlantic*, August 19, 2020. https://www.theatlantic.com/international/archive/2020/08/karen-meme-coronavirus/615355/.

Jackson Lewis P.C. "California Further Limits NDAs and Settlement Agreements in Terms of Employment Cases." *National Law Review*, October 8, 2021. https://www.natlawreview.com/article/california-further-limits-ndas-and-settlement-agreement-terms-employment-cases.

Ruth Leys. *From Guilt to Shame: Auschwitz and After* (Princeton University Press, 2007).

Rhonda Lieberman. "Painting Over the Dirty Truth." *New Republic*, September 23, 2019. https://newrepublic.com/article/154991/rich-art-museum-donors-exploit-identity-politics-launder-reputations-philanthropy.

German Lopez. "Voters Recall Judge Who Sentenced Brock Turner to 6 Months in Jail for Sexual Assault." Vox, June 6, 2018. https://www.vox.com/policy-and-politics/2018/6/6/17433576/judge-aaron-persky-recall-brock-turner-results.

Rich Lowry. "Yes, Hillary Was an Enabler." *Politico*, May 26, 2016. https://www.politico.com/magazine/story/2016/05/yes-hillary-was-an-enabler-213919/.

Deborah Lupton. *Risk*. 2nd ed. (Routledge, 2013).

Sarah Lyall. "The Trump Women, Trying to Help Trump with Women." *New York Times*, August 28, 2020. https://www.nytimes.com/2020/08/28/us/politics/tiffany-trump-kimberly-guilfoyle-rnc.html.

William MacAskill. *What We Owe the Future* (Basic Books, 2022).

Peggy MacIntosh. "White Privilege: Unpacking the Invisible Knapsack." *Peace and Freedom* (1989).

MacIver Institute. "A Hysterical Senate Speech Accidentally Reveals the Truth about Critical Race Theory." October 1, 2021. https://www.maciverinstitute.com/2021/10/a-hysterical-senate-speech-accidentally-reveals-the-truth-about-critical-race-theory/.

Douglas MacLean. "Climate Complicity and Individual Accountability." *The Monist* 102 (2019) 1, 2, 5.

M. Kimberly MacLin and Vivian Herrera. "The Criminal Stereotype." *North American Journal of Psychology* 8, no. 2 (2006): 197–207, 98, 204.

Ira Madison III. "Ellen DeGeneres' Interview with Kevin Hart Was an Insult to the Black LGBTQ Community" (guest column). *Hollywood Reporter*, January 4, 2019. https://www.hollywoodreporter.com/news/ellen-degeneres-kevin-hart-interview-was-an-insult-black-lgbtq-community-1173419.

Arwa Mahdawi. "Ivanka Trump Is Complicit in Her Dad's Mission to Get Rich at the U.S.'s Expense" (op-ed). *The Guardian*, March 14, 2017. https://www.theguardian.com/commentisfree/2017/mar/14/ivanka-trump-complicit-dads-mission-get-rich-us-expense-trumps-heartland-appeasing-liberals.

Liz Manne. "First Person: Sexual Harassers are Poisonous, and So Are the Companies That Protect Them." Indie Wire, October 27, 2017. https://www.indiewire.com/2017/10/harvey-weinstein-sexual-harrassment-new-line-cinema-1201891113/.

Rachel Manning, Mark Levine, and Alan Collins. "The Kitty Genovese Murder and the Social Psychology of Helping: The Parable of the 38 Witnesses." *American Psychologist* 62 (2007): 555.

Andy Mannix. "Minnesota's Other Prison Problem: Race." *Minnesota Post*, June 26, 2015. https://www.minnpost.com/politics-policy/2015/06/minnesotas-other-prison-problem-race/.

Mapping Police Violence. https://mappingpoliceviolence.org.

Paul Marcus. "Criminal Conspiracy Law: Time to Turn Back From an Ever Expanding, Ever More Troubling Area." *William & Mary Bill of Rights Journal* 1 (1992): 1, 8, 14.

Nikki Marczak, Sherizaan Minwalla, and Johanna E. Foster. "On Their Own Terms: A Survivor-Centered Approach to Sexual Violence in Conflict." WMC Women Under Siege, May 7, 2019. https://womensmediacenter.com/women-under-siege/on-their-own-terms-a-survivor-centered-approach-to-sexual-violence-in-conflict.

Alex Marshall. "Museums Cut Ties with Sacklers as Outrage Over Opioid Crisis Grows." *New York Times,* March 25, 2019. https://www.nytimes.com/2019/03/25/arts/design/sackler-museums-donations-oxycontin.html.

Luis Martinez. "Pentagon Chief Supports Removing Chain of Command from Sexual Assault Cases." ABC News, June 22, 2021. https://abcnews.go.com/Politics/pentagon-chief-supports-removing-chain-command-sexual-assault/story?id=78430459.

Nicole Martinez Martin. "Psychiatric Genetics in a Risk Society." *American Journal of Bioethics* 17 (2017): 1–2. https://www.ncbi.nlm.nih.gov/pmc/articles/PMC6634988/.

Adam M. Mastroianni and Daniel T. Gilbert. "The Illusion of Moral Decline." *Nature,* June 7, 2023: 1–13, 1–2.

Jemima McEvoy. "The Internet Cringes over Celebrity #ITakeResponsibility Social Media Campaign." *Forbes,* June 11, 2020. https://www.forbes.com/sites/jemimamcevoy/2020/06/11/the-internet-cringes-over-celebrity-itakeresponsibility-social-media-campaign/?sh = 67a585733701.

———. "What Does It Mean That Amy Coney Barrett Served as a 'Handmaid' in a Religious Group." *Forbes,* October 7, 2020. https://www.forbes.com/sites/jemimamcevoy/2020/10/07/what-does-it-mean-that-amy-coney-barrett-served-as-a-handmaid-in-a-religious-group/?sh = 7eac9438932d.

Robert D. McFadden. "Winston Moseley, Who Killed Kitty Genovese, Dies in Prison at 81." *New York Times,* April 4, 2016. https://www.nytimes.com/2016/04/05/nyregion/winston-moseley-81-killer-of-kitty-genovese-dies-in-prison.html.

Chris McGreal and Alvin Chang. "How Cities and States Could Finally Hold Fossil Fuel Companies Accountable." *The Guardian,* n.d. https://www.theguardian.com/environment/ng-interactive/2021/jun/30/climate-crimes-fossil-fuels-cities-states-interactive.

"McKinsey Settles with US Local Governments Over Opioid Consulting Work." Consulting.us, October 28, 2022. https://www.consulting.us/news/8330 /mckinsey-settles-with-us-local-governments-over-opioid-consulting-work.

Tressie McMillan Cottom. "The Limits of My Empathy for Covid Deniers." *New York Times,* September 10, 2021. https://www.nytimes.com/2021/09/10 /opinion/covid-empathy-grief.html.

————. "What's Shame Got to Do with It" (opinion). *New York Times,* April 12, 2022. https://www.nytimes.com/2022/04/12/opinion/whats-shame-got-to-do-with-it.html.

John McWhorter. "Racist Is a Tough Little Word." *The Atlantic,* July 24, 2019. https://www.theatlantic.com/ideas/archive/2019/07/racism-concept-change /594526/.

Samantha Melamed. "An Accomplice Will Die in Prison While the Killer Goes Free: The Strange Justice of Pennsylvania's Felony-Murder Rule." *Philadelphia Inquirer,* February 16, 2018. https://www.inquirer.com/philly /news/crime/375250-pennsylvania-philly-felony-murder-law-da-larry-krasner-criminal-justice-reform-20180216.html-2.

Gregory Mellema. *Complicity and Moral Accountability* (University of Notre Dame Press, 2016).

MeToo. Accessed December 30, 2022. https://metoomvmt.org/get-to-know-us/tarana-burke-founder/.

Katie Meyer. "Will Ongoing Gun Violence Bring a Stop-and-Frisk Resurgence to Philly? It Wouldn't Be the First Time." WHYY, July 15, 2022. https://whyy.org/articles/philly-gun-violence-police-stop-and-frisk/.

Nathaniel Meyersohn. "Why Walmart Is Closing Half Its Stores in Chicago." *CNN,* April 13, 2023. https://www.cnn.com/2023/04/12/business/walmart-chicago-stores-closing/index.html.

Mike Miller. "Child Molesters, Human Rights Abusers, and Maybe Harvey Weinstein: What It Takes to Have the Queen Revoke Your Honorary Title." *People,* October 26, 2017. http://people.com/movies/child-molesters-human-rights-abusers-and-maybe-harvey-weinstein-what-it-takes-to-have-the-queen-revoke-your-honorary-title/.

Ryan W. Miller. "Charges Dismissed Against Amy Cooper, White Woman Who Called 911 on Black Birdwatcher." *USA Today,* February 16, 2021. https://www.usatoday.com/story/news/nation/2021/02/16/amy-cooper-charges-dropped-central-park-911-call/6763384002/.

Martha Minow. *Between Vengeance and Forgiveness: Facing History after Genocide and Mass Violence* (Beacon Press, 1998).

David Mislin. "How a 1905 Debate about 'Tainted' Rockefeller Money Is a Reminder of Ethical Dilemmas Today." Associated Press, October 2, 2019. https://apnews.com/article/972b8e37aef3dfoa17751bd4fa42f308.

Andrea Mitchell and Alastair Jamieson. "Trump Planned Debate 'Stunt,' Invited Clinton Accusers to Rattle Hillary." NBC News, October 10, 2016. https://www.nbcnews.com/storyline/2016-presidential-debates/trump-planned-debate-stunt-invited-bill-clinton-accusers-rattle-hillary-n663481.

Tatyana Monnay. "States Approved Nearly 300 Bills Affecting Policing in the Wake of George Floyd's Murder." Howard Center for Investigative Journalism, October 28, 2022. https://cnsmaryland.org/2022/10/28/states-approved-nearly-300-bills-affecting-policing-in-wake-of-george-floyds-murder/.

Felicia Morris. "Beautiful Monsters." *Legacy* 11 (2011).

Mette Mortensen. "Connective Witnessing: Reconfiguring the Relationship between the Individual and the Collective." *Information, Communication, and Society* 18 (2015): 1393.

Ashoka Mukpo. "When the State Kills Those Who Didn't Kill." ACLU, July 11, 2019. https://www.aclu.org/issues/capital-punishment/when-state-kills-those-who-didnt-kill.

Gabe Mythen. "The Critical Theory of World Risk Society: A Retrospective Analysis." *Risk Analysis* 41 (2018): 533.

Gabe Mythen and Sandra Walklate. "Not Knowing, Emancipatory Catastrophism, and Metamorphosis: Embracing the Spirit of Ulrich Beck." *Security Dialogue* 47 (2016): 403, 412.

NAACP Legal Defense Fund. "LDF Issues Statement on the Failure to Advance the George Floyd Justice in Policing Act of 2021." September 22, 2021. https://www.naacpldf.org/press-release/ldf-issues-statement-on-the-failure-to-advance-the-george-floyd-justice-in-policing-act-of-2021/.

Hannah Natanson. "Forget What You May Have Been Told. New Study Says Strangers Step in to Help 90 Percent of the Time." *Washington Post*, September 6, 2019. https://www.washingtonpost.com/lifestyle/2019/09/06/high-level-help-was-surprising-new-study-says-strangers-step-help-percent-time/.

National Museum: Private Snafu. https://www.nationalww2museum.org/war/articles/private-snafu-cartoon-series.

Douglas NeJaime and Reva Siegel. "Conscience Wars: Complicity-Based Conscience Claims in Religion and Politics." *Yale Law Journal* 124 (2014–2015): 2202–2679.

Christina Newland. "Hero's Welcome for Johnny Depp at Cannes Film Festival Was an Ugly Spectacle." iNews UK, May 18, 2023. https://inews.co.uk/culture/film/johnny-depp-hero-welcome-cannes-film-festival-2350328.

Sarah Maslin Nir. "White Woman Is Fired After Calling Police on Black Man in Central Park." *New York Times*, May 26, 2020. https://www.nytimes.com/2020/05/26/nyregion/amy-cooper-dog-central-park.html.

Tom Nolan. "'Arresting Developments': The Pandemic Is Undermining Cops' Main Tool Against Crime." Newsone, April 16, 2020. https://newsone.com/3929015/coronavirus-arrests-criminal-justice-effect/.

———. "What Policing During the Pandemic Reveals about Crime Rates and Arrests." PBS News Hour, April 15, 2020. https://www.pbs.org/newshour/nation/what-policing-during-the-pandemic-reveals-about-crime-rates-and-arrests.

Anna Noryskiewicz and Haley Ott. "97-Year Old Former Nazi Camp Secretary Found Guilty of Complicity in Over 10,000 Murders." CBS News, October 20, 2022. https://www.cbsnews.com/news/former-nazi-camp-secretary-irmgard-furchner-found-guilty-complicity-over-10500-murders/.

Christina Nunn. "Ellen DeGeneres Is Accused of Using Her Show Platform for Homophobia Apologists." Showbiz Cheat Sheet, August 19, 2020. https://www.cheatsheet.com/entertainment/ellen-degeneres-is-accused-of-using-her-show-platform-for-homophobia-apologists.html/.

Daniel Nussbaum. "SNL, Scarlett Johansson Mock Ivanka Trump with 'Complicit' Perfume Ad." Breitbart, March 12, 2017. https://www.breitbart.com/entertainment/2017/03/12/snl-scarlett-johansson-mock-ivanka-trump-complicit-perfume-ad/.

Osagie K. Obasogie and Zachary Newman. "Black Lives Matter and Respectability Politics in Local News Accounts of Officer-Involved Civilian Deaths: An Early Empirical Assessment." *Wisconsin Law Review* 3 (2016): 543.

Michelle Oberman. Turning Girls into Women: Re-Evaluating Modern Statutory Rape Law. *Journal of Criminal Law and Criminology* 85 (1994): 15, 25, 35.

Karen Ocamb. "Deconstructing the Ellen DeGeneres Cover Up of Kevin Hart's Latent Homophobia." *Los Angeles Blade,* January 4, 2019. https://www.losangelesblade.com/2019/01/04/deconstructing-the-ellen-degeneres-cover-up-of-kevin-harts-latent-homophobia/.

Sean O'Kane. "Ford Employees Ask the Company to Stop Making Police Cars." The Verge, July 8, 2020. https://www.theverge.com/2020/7/8/21317894/ford-employees-black-police-vehicles-law-enforcement-george-floyd.

Tyler G. Okimoto, Michael Wenzel, and Matthew J. Hornsey. "Apologies Demanded Yet Devalued: Normative Dilution in the Age of Apology." *Journal of Experimental Social Psychology* 60 (2016), 133–36.

Dan Olson. "Justice in Black and White: The Justice Gap." Minnesota Public Radio, April 13, 2000. http://news.minnesota.publicradio.org/features/200004 /17_olsond_race/?refid = 0.

Emily Olson. "A $1.6 Billion Lawsuit Alleges Facebook's Inaction Fueled Violence in Ethiopia." NPR, December 17, 2022. https://www.npr.org/2022/12 /17/1142873282/facebook-meta-lawsuit-ethiopia-kenya-abrham-amare.

Pat O'Malley. "Experiments in Risk and Criminal Justice." *Theoretical Criminology* 12 (2008): 451.

Naomi Oreskes. "Fossil-Fuel Money Will Undermine Stanford's New Sustainability School." *Scientific American*, October 1, 2022. https://www.scientificamerican.com/article/fossil-fuel-money-will-undermine-stanford-rsquo-s-new-sustainability-school/.

Naomi Oreskes and Eric Conway. *Merchants of Doubt: How a Handful of Scientists Obscured the Truth on Issues from Tobacco Smoke to Climate Change* (Bloomsbury, 2011).

OSCE. "A Race Against Time—Successes and Challenges in the Implementation of the National War Crimes Processing Strategy of Bosnia and Herzegovina." Organization for Security and Co-operation in Europe, June 24, 2022. https://www.osce.org/mission-to-bosnia-and-herzegovina/521149.

Lou Papineau. "Hello, Dolly—Again! Parton Enjoying Career Resurgence." The Current, March 19, 2020. https://www.thecurrent.org/feature/2020/03 /19/dolly-parton-career-resurgence.

Samir Parikh. "Mass Exploitation." *University of Pennsylvania Law Review* 170 (2022). https://scholarship.law.upenn.edu/penn_law_review_online/vol170 /iss1/4.

Catherine Pelonero. *Kitty Genovese: A True Account of a Public Murder and Its Private Consequences* (Skyhorse Publishing, 2014).

Nicole Lyn Pesce. "Ellen DeGeneres Says Being Known as the 'Be Kind' Lady Is 'Tricky' in Her Embattled Show's Season Premiere." MarketWatch, September 21, 2020. https://www.marketwatch.com/story/ellen-degeneres-says-being-known-as-the-be-kind-lady-is-tricky-in-her-embattled-shows-season-premiere-2020-09-21.

Pew Research Center. "The Challenge of Knowing What Is Offensive." June 19, 2019. https://www.pewresearch.org/politics/2019/06/19/the-challenge-of-knowing-whats-offensive/.

Michelle S. Phelps. "Discourses of Mass Probation: From Managing. Risk to Ending Human Warehousing in Michigan." *British Journal of Criminology* 58 (2018): 1107.

Richard Philpot, Lasse Suonpera Liebst, Mark Leving, Wim Bernasco, and Marie Rosenkrantz Lindengaard. "Would I Be helped? Cross-National CCTV Footage Shows That Intervention Is the Norm in Public Conflicts." *American Psychologist* 5, no. 1 (2020): 66–75.

Alison Phipps. "'Every Woman Knows a Weinstein': Political Whiteness and White Woundedness in #MeToo and Public Feminisms Around Sexual Violence." *Feminist Formations* 31 (2019): 1.

Linda Pitcher. "'The Divine Impatience': Ritual, Narrative, and Symbolization in the Practice of Martyrdom in Palestine." *Medical Anthropology Quarterly* 12, no. 1 (1998): 8–30, 17.

Vasundhara Prasad. "If Anyone Is Listening, #MeToo: Breaking the Culture of Silence around Sexual Abuse through Regulating Non-Disclosure Agreements." *Boston College Law Review* 59 (2018): 2507, 2508.

Robert L. Rabin. "Enabling Torts." *DePaul Law Review* 49, 435, 437.

Maya Rajamani. "Black Birdwatcher's Sister Supports Charging 'Central Park Karen,' Even Though He Doesn't." 1010 Wins, July 13, 2020. https://www.radio.com/1010wins/articles/christian-coopers-sister-supports-amy-cooper-charge.

Jan Ransom. "Case Against Amy Cooper Lacks Key Element: Victim's Cooperation." *New York Times*, July 7, 2020. https://www.nytimes.com/2020/07/07/nyregion/amy-cooper-central-park-false-report-charge.html.

Jim Rasenberger. "Kitty, 40 Years Later." *New York Times*, February 8, 2004. https://www.nytimes.com/2004/02/08/nyregion/kitty-40-years-later.html.

Victor Ray. *On Critical Race Theory: Why It Matters & Why You Should Care* (Random House, 2022).

Joan Raymond. "Who Is the Nicest Celebrity? The NBC News State of Kindness Survey Says ..." Today, November 13, 2015. https://www.today.com/kindness/who-nicest-celebrity-nbc-news-state-kindness-survey-says-t55651.

Reddit. "r/FuckYouKaren." https://www.reddit.com/r/FuckYouKaren/comments/chjbh8/question_im_thinking_of_dressing_up_like_a_karen/.

Lisa Redmond. "Lowell Man Wants Murder Verdict Overturned." *The Sun*, February 14, 2017. https://www.lowellsun.com/2017/02/14/lowell-man-wants-murder-verdict-overturned/.

Jennifer Reed. "Ellen DeGeneres: Public Lesbian Number One." *Feminist Media Studies* 5 (2005): 23.

Carlton Reid. "Trek Urged to Divest from Police Business after Bicycles Used against Black Lives Matter Protestors." *Forbes*, June 8, 2020. https://www.forbes.com/sites/carltonreid/2020/06/08/trek-urged-to-divest-from-police-business-after-bicycles-used-against-black-lives-matter-protestors/?sh = 22d057135ec8.

James Reinl. "Goodbye Anti-Bias Training! Amazon, Applebee's, and Twitter are among Companies DITCHING Woke Diversity Teams as They Cut Costs." *Daily Mail*, February 17, 2023. https://www.dailymail.co.uk/news/article-11724079/Goodbye-anti-bias-training-DEI-teams-axed-diversity-RECKONING.html.

Jarrett Renshaw. "Biden, Saying 'Silence Is Complicity,' Signs COVID Hate Crimes Bill into Law." Reuters, May 20, 2021. https://www.reuters.com/world/us/biden-saying-silence-is-complicity-signs-covid-hate-crimes-bill-into-law-2021-05-20/.

Carrie Rentschler. "An Urban Physiognomy of the 1964 Kitty Genovese Murder." *Space and Culture* 14, no. 3 (2011).

Paul Reynolds. "Complicity as Political Rhetoric: Some Ethical and Political Reflections." In *Exploring Complicity: Concepts, Cases and Critique,* edited by M. Neu, R. Dunford, and A. Afexentis (Rowman and Littlefield, 2017).

Celia Ridgeway. *Framed by Gender: How Gender Inequality Persists in the Modern World* (Oxford University Press, 2011).

George S. Rigakos and Richard W. Hadden. "Crime, Capitalism, and the 'Risk Society': Towards the Same Olde Modernity?" *Theoretical Criminology* 5 (2001): 61.

Ira P. Robbins. "Double Inchoate Crimes." *Harvard Journal of Legislation* 26 (1989): 1, 5.

Mary Louise Roberts. *What Soldiers Do: Sex and the American GI in World War II France* (University of Chicago, 2013).

Paul H. Robinson. "Imputed Criminal Liability." *Yale Law Journal* 93 (1984): 609, 619–21.

Taylor Rogers. "Companies Urged to Honour Racial Justice Pledges." *Financial Times*, January 18, 2022. https://www.ft.com/content/f29449c1-aa80-40b3-9794-5b02bb557019.

Aja Romano. A History of "Wokeness." Vox, October 9, 2020. https://www.vox.com/culture/21437879/stay-woke-wokeness-history-origin-evolution-controversy.

Meghan Roos. "'We Need to Take Back Our Tenderloin': SF Mayor London Breed Takes Aim at Crime Surge." *Newsweek*, December 14, 2021. https://www.newsweek.com/we-need-take-back-our-tenderloin-sf-mayor-london-breed-takes-aim-crime-surge-1659417.

Martha Ross. "Mariah Carey Says Miscarriages Happened after Ellen DeGeneres Needled Her about Pregnancy." *Detroit News*, September 2, 2020. https://www.detroitnews.com/story/entertainment/2020/09/02/mariah-carey-ellen-degeneres-miscarriage-needled-pregnancy/113649366/.

Michael Rothberg. *The Implicated Subject: Beyond Victims and Perpetrators* (Stanford University Press, 2019).

Maria Rotundo, Dung-Hanh Nguyen, and Paul R. Sackett. "A Meta-Analytic Review of Gender Differences in Perceptions of Sexual Harassment." *Journal of Applied Psychology* 86 (2001): 914.

Ananya Roy. "Serious About Racial Justice? Then Divest from Policing." KnockLA, June 22, 2020. https://knock-la.com/ucla-racial-justice-divest-policing-lapd-72b274924111 (emphasis mine).

Ed Runyan. "Accomplice Gets 23 Years to Life: Most Agree Sentence in West Side Killing Too Harsh." The Vindicator, June 11, 2020. https://www.vindy.com/news/local-news/2020/06/accomplice-gets-23-years-to-life/.

William Safire. "On Language; Empowering Out, Enabling In." *New York Times*, June 21, 1998. https://www.nytimes.com/1998/06/21/magazine/on-language-empowering-out-enabling-in.html.

William Saletan. "Mr. Complicit." Slate, May 22, 2017. https://slate.com/news-and-politics/2017/05/mike-pence-is-complicit.html.

Ted Sampsell-Jones. "Explaining the New Second Degree Murder Charge against Derek Chauvin." The Dispatch, June 4, 2020. https://thedispatch.com/article/explaining-the-new-second-degree/.

Debarati Sanyal. *Memory and Complicity: Migrations of Holocaust Remembrance* (Fordham University Press, 2015).

Pat Saperstein. "Taylor Swift and Kylie Jenner Provoke Private Jet Controversy, but Does Climate Shaming Work?" *Variety*, August 3, 2022. https://variety.com/2022/politics/news/taylor-swift-kylie-jenner-private-jets-climate-change-1235331873/.

Alexander Sarch. "Condoning the Crime: The Elusive Mens Rea for Complicity." *Loyola University of Chicago Law Review* 47 (2015): 131.

Terry L. Schell, Matthew Cefalu, Colleen Farris, and Andrew L. Morral. "The Relationship between Sexual Assault and Sexual Harassment in the

U.S. Military: Findings from the RAND Military Workplace Study."
RAND Corporation (2021): x, xi.

Stan Schroeder. "'Silence is Complicity': Facebook Workers Speak Out After
Zuckerberg Refuses to Take Action on Trump." Mashable, June 1, 2020. https://
mashable.com/article/facebook-employees-speak-out-zuckerberg-trump/.

Alyssa Schukar. "A Racial Slur, A Viral Video, and a Reckoning." *New
York Times*, December 26, 2020. https://www.nytimes.com/2020/12/26/us
/mimi-groves-jimmy-galligan-racial-slurs.html.

Karina Schumann and Gregory M. Walton. "Rehumanizing the Self after Victimization: The Roles of Forgiveness versus Revenge." *Journal of Personality
and Social Psychology* 122, no. 3 (2022): 469–92.

Geraldine Schwarz. *Those Who Forget: My Family's Story in Nazi Europe—A Memoir, A History, A Warning* (Scribner, 2007).

Michael Sebastian and Gabrielle Bruney. "Years After Being Debunked,
Interest in Pizzagate Is Rising—Again." *Esquire*, July 24, 2020. https://www
.esquire.com/news-politics/news/a51268/what-is-pizzagate/.

Amy Sepinwall. "Conscience and Complicity: Assessing Pleas for Religious
Exemptions in 'Hobby Lobby's' Wake." *University of Chicago Law Review* 82
(2015): 1897.

The Sentencing Project. "Fact Sheet: Incarcerated Women and Girls." https://
www.sentencingproject.org/wp-content/uploads/2016/02/Incarcerated-Women-
and-Girls.pdf.

Tom Seymour. "Tainted Gifts: As British Museum and the Met Disavow the
Sackler Name, Museums Rethink Donation Deals." Art Newspaper, March 28,
2022. https://www.theartnewspaper.com/2022/03/28/tainted-gifts-museums-
rethink-donation-deals.

Ari Shapiro. "There Is No Neutral: 'Nice White People' Can Still Be Complicit in a Racist Society." National Public Radio, June 9, 2020. https://
www.npr.org/2020/06/09/873375416/there-is-no-neutral-nice-white-people-
can-still-be-complicit-in-a-racist-society.

Helene Shugart. "Performing Ambiguity: The Passing of Ellen DeGeneres."
Text and Performance Quarterly 23 (2003): 30.

Jacob Silverman. "Workers of the Facebook, Unite!" *New Republic*, December
29, 2020. https://newrepublic.com/article/160687/facebook-workers-union-
labor-organizing.

Mark Simpson. "Respectability is the New Closet." *The Guardian*, June 2, 2009.
https://www.theguardian.com/commentisfree/2009/jun/02/gay-stonewall-
respectability-closet.

Sebastian Kloving Skelton. "USA: Washington DC Court Dismisses Cobalt Mining Deaths' Case against Five Major Technology Companies." Computer Weekly, November 12, 2021. https://www.business-humanrights.org /en/latest-news/usa-washington-dc-court-dismissed-cobalt-mining-deaths-case-against-five-major-technology-companies/.

Danielle C. Slakoff and Pauline K. Brennan. "The Differential Representation of Latina and Black Female Victims in Front-Page News Stories: A Qualitative Document Analysis." *Feminist Criminology* 14 (2019): 488, 493, 508.

David Alan Slansky. *A Pattern of Violence* (Harvard University Press, 2021).

Karen Sokol. "Seeking (Some) Climate Justice in State Tort Law." *Washington Law Review* 5, no. 3 (2020): 1383–1440.

Marie Solia. "Did Hillary Clinton Help Bill Clinton Intimidate His Rape and Sexual Misconduct Accusers?" *Newsweek*, November 17, 2017. https://www .newsweek.com/did-hillary-clinton-help-bill-clinton-intimidate-and-discredit-his-accusers-714636.

Tessa Solomon. "Hannah Gabsby Addresses Sackler Ties to Their Brooklyn Museum Show: 'There's a Problem with Money in the Art World.'" *ARTnews*, May 9, 2023. https://www.artnews.com/art-news/news/hannah-gadsby-addresses-sackler-ties-to-brooklyn-museum-show-1234667185/.

Ilya Somin. "The Volokh Conspiracy: Qualified Immunity Reform Stalls in the States—and the Courts." Reason, October 19, 2021. https://reason.com /volokh/2021/10/19/qualified-immunity-reform-stalls-in-the-states-and-in-the-supreme-court/.

Avani Mehta Sood. "Attempted Justice: Misunderstanding and Bias in Psychological Constructions of Criminal Attempt." *Stanford Law Review* 71 (2019): 593, 597–598, 602.

Tom Spiggle. "Congress Passes New Law Ending Forced Arbitration for Sexual Harassment and Assault Claims." *Forbes*, February 16, 2022. https:// www.forbes.com/sites/tomspiggle/2022/02/16/congress-passes-new-law-ending-forced-arbitration-for-sexual-harassment-and-assault-claims/?sh = 7e14c5b02289.

Gerald M. Stern. *The Buffalo Creek Disaster* (Random House, 1977).

Doreen St. Felix. "The Rush of Seeing Harvey Weinstein's Perp Walk." *New Yorker*, May 25, 2018. https://www.newyorker.com/culture/annals-of-appearances/the-rush-of-feeling-seeing-harvey-weinsteins-perp-walk-arrest.

Farah Stockman, Kate Kelly, and Jennifer Medina. "How Buying Beans Became A Political Statement." *New York Times,* July 19, 2020. https://www.nytimes.com/2020/07/19/us/goya-trump-hispanic-vote.html.

Annie Stopford and Llewellyn Smith. "Mass Incarceration and the 'New Jim Crow': An Interview with Michelle Alexander." *Psychoanalysis, Culture & Society* 19 (2014): 379, 387.

Karyn Stricker. "The Truth About Karens" (opinion). The Hill, July 1, 2020. https://thehill.com/opinion/civil-rights/505489-the-truth-about-karens.

Rosemary Sullivan. *The Betrayal of Anne Frank: A Cold Case Investigation* (Harper, 2022).

S.P. Sullivan. "N.J. Sues Billionaire Sackler Family for 'Fueling' Opioid Crisis." NJ.com, May 30, 2019. https://www.nj.com/news/2019/05/nj-sues-billionaire-sackler-family-for-fueling-opioid-crisis.html.

Joan Summers. "The Making of Ellen DeGeneres, The Nicest Person on Television." Jezebel, August 24, 2020. https://jezebel.com/the-making-of-ellen-degeneres-the-nicest-person-on-tel-1844626291.

Geoffrey Supran and Naomi Oreskes. "Rhetoric and Frame Analysis of ExxonMobil's Climate Change Communications." One Earth, 4, 696–719, 697, 706–707 (emphasis mine).

Miles Surrey. "Hillary Clinton's Role in Benghazi: What You Need to Know." Yahoo!News, January 26, 2016. https://news.yahoo.com/hillary-clinton-role-benghazi-know-195600379.html.

Paige Sutherland and Megna Chakrabarty. "Behind the Bankruptcy Tactic Shielding Corporate Executives from Accountability." WBUR, December 15, 2022. https://www.wbur.org/onpoint/2022/12/15/corporate-liability-should-this-common-tactic-be-reined-in.

Sarah L. Swan. "Aiding and Abetting Matters." *Journal of Tort Law* 12, no. 2 (2019): 255–82.

———. "Bystander Interventions." *Wisconsin Law Review* no. 6 (2015): 975–1047.

Emily Tannenbaum. "Ivanka Trump Is 'Complicit' in Her Father's 'Collision of Cruelty and Incompetence' Says Chelsea Clinton." *Glamour*, October 2, 2020. https://www.glamour.com/story/ivanka-trump-complicit-chelsea-clinton.

Richard G. Tedeschi and Lawrence Calhoun. "Posttraumatic Growth: A New Perspective on Psychotraumatology." *Psychiatric Times* 21, no. 4 (2004). https://www.psychiatrictimes.com/view/posttraumatic-growth-new-perspective-psychotraumatology.

Kat Tenbarge. "People Are Urging Influencers and Celebrities to Support Black Lives Matter Online or Stop Posting Entirely." Insider, June 1, 2020. https://www.insider.com/celebrities-influencers-support-black-lives-matter-stop-posting-instagram-2020-6.

Catherine Thorbecke and Sarah Kunin. "Damon, Clooney Say They Never Saw Weinstein's 'Darkness': Vow to Fight Sexual Misconduct." ABC News, October 23, 2017. https://abcnews.go.com/Entertainment/damon-clooney-weinsteins-darkness-vow-fight-sexual-misconduct/story?id=50647881.

S.E. Thorne (ed.). *Bracton on the Laws and Customs of England*, Vol. II (Cambridge, 1968).

Kaitlyn Tiffany. "How 'Karen' Became a Coronavirus Villain." *The Atlantic*, May 6, 2020. https://www.theatlantic.com/technology/archive/2020/05/coronavirus-karen-memes-reddit-twitter-carolyn-goodman/611104/.

Jia Tolentino. "The Whisper Network after Harvey Weinstein and 'Shitty Media Men.'" *New Yorker*, October 14, 2017. https://www.newyorker.com/news/news-desk/the-whisper-network-after-harvey-weinstein-and-shitty-media-men.

Adam Tooze. *Shutdown: How Covid Shook the World's Economy* (Viking, 2021).

Touré. "Condoleeza Rice's CRT Stance Proves She's a Footsoldier for White Supremacy." The Grio, October 22, 2021. https://thegrio.com/2021/10/22/condoleezza-rice-foot-solider-for-white-supremacy/.

Carol E. Tracy and Charlene Whitman. "Rape and Sexual Assault in the Legal System." *AEquitas Women's Law Project* (2013): 19.

Christina L.H. Traina. "'This Is the Year': Narratives of Structural Evil." *Journal of the Society of Christian Ethics* 37 (2017): 2–19.

Victor Turner. "Betwixt and Between: The Liminal Period in Rites of Passage." In *The Forest of Symbols* (Cornell University Press, 1967).

Megan Twohey, Jodi Kantor, Susan Dominus, Jim Rutenberg, and Steve Eder. "Weinstein's Complicity Machine." *New York Times*, December 5, 2017. https://www.nytimes.com/interactive/2017/12/05/us/harvey-weinstein-complicity.html?mtrref=undefined&_r=0.

United Nations Office on Drugs and Crime. *Handbook on Criminal Justice Responses to Terrorism* (2009). https://www.unodc.org/documents/terrorism/Handbook_on_Criminal_Justice_Responses_to_Terrorism_en.pdf.

Upjoke. "Karen Jokes." https://upjoke.com/karen-jokes.

US Department of Justice. Criminal Resource Manual (2401–99, 2480). "Attempt to Aid and Abet." https://www.justice.gov/archives/jm/criminal-resource-manual-2480-attempt-aid-and-abet.

Alanna Vagianos. "Larry Nassar Survivors Hoped the John Geddert Case Would Bring Answers. Then Geddert Killed Himself." *Huffington Post,* April 5, 2021. https://www.huffpost.com/entry/larry-nassar-john-geddert-gymnastics-abuse_n_6064db07c5b6adf599cc8d6c.

Dan Vallone, Stephen Hawkins, Noelle Malvar, Paul Oshinski, Taran Raghuran, and Daniel Yudkin. "Two Stories of Distrust in America." More in Common, May 2021. https://www.moreincommon.com/media/yfcbfmmp/mic_two-stories-of-distrust.pdf.

Art Van Zee. "The Promotion and Marketing of OxyContin: Commercial Triumph, Public Health Tragedy." *American Journal of Public Health* 99 (2009): 221, 222.

Vera Institute of Justice. "Study Reveals Stop and Frisk Significantly Impacts Trust in New York City Police" (press release). September 19, 2013. https://www.vera.org/newsroom/study-reveals-stop-and-frisk-significantly-impacts-trust-in-new-york-city-police.

James Vincent. "Blackout Tuesday Posts Are Drowning Out Vital Information Shared under the BLM Hashtag." The Verge, June 2, 2020. https://www.theverge.com/2020/6/2/21277852/blackout-tuesday-posts-hiding-information-blm-black-lives-matter-hashtag.

Gina Vivinetto. "Here's How Ellen DeGeneres Inspired the Role of Dory in Finding Nemo." Today, June 26, 2020. https://www.today.com/popculture/here-s-how-ellen-degeneres-inspired-role-dory-finding-nemo-t185342.

Stefan Vogler. "Constituting the 'Sexually Violent Predator': Law, Forensic Psychology, and the Adjudication of Risk." *Theoretical Criminology* 23 (2019): 509, 510.

Loudon Wainwright. "The Dying Girl That No One Helped." *Life*, April 10, 1964.

Michael Walsh. "How Corporate America Bought Hillary Clinton for $21M." *New York Post*, May 22, 2016. https://nypost.com/2016/05/22/how-corporate-america-bought-hillary-clinton-for-21m/.

Paul Walsh and Kim Hyatt. "Tu Thao, Former MPD Officer Charged in George Floyd's Killing, Found Guilty." *Minneapolis Star Tribune*, May 2, 2023. https://www.startribune.com/hennepin-county-tou-thao-mpd-officer-george-floyd-killing-manslaughter-cahill-minneapolis-police/600271709/.

Joanna Walters. "Sackler Family Members Face Mass Litigation and Criminal Investigations Over Opioid Crisis." *The Guardian*, November 19, 2018. https://www.theguardian.com/us-news/2018/nov/19/sackler-family-members-face-mass-litigation-criminal-investigations-over-opioids-crisis.

WBZ News. "Starbucks CEO Says 'There Are Going to be Many More Store Closings." July 20, 2022. https://www.cbsnews.com/boston/news/starbucks-store-closings-safety/.

Web Desk. "Ellen DeGeneres Accused by Louisiana Man of Bullying Him as an 11-Year-Old." The News, August 8, 2020, https://www.thenews.com.pk/latest/697698-ellen-degeneres-accused-by.

Sheila Weller. "How Author Timothy Tyson Found the Woman at the Center of the Emmett Till Case." *Vanity Fair,* January 26, 2017. https://www.vanityfair.com/news/2017/01/how-author-timothy-tyson-found-the-woman-at-the-center-of-the-emmett-till-case?mbid = social_twitter.

Robert Werth. "Risk and Punishment: The Recent History and Uncertain Future of Actuarial, Algorithmic, and 'Evidence-Based' Penal Techniques." *Sociological Compass* 13 (2019): 4.

Lindy West. "Trump's First Year in One Word." *New York Times*, November 29, 2017. https://www.nytimes.com/2017/11/29/opinion/complicity-word-of-the-year.html.

Amy Westervelt. "Big Oil Is Trying to Make Climate Change Your Problem to Solve. Don't Let Them." *Rolling Stone*, May 14, 2021. https://www.rollingstone.com/politics/politics-news/climate-change-exxonmobil-harvard-study-1169682/.

Eric Westervelt. "Removing Cops from Behavioral Crisis Calls: 'We Need to Change the Model.'" NPR, October 19, 2020. https://www.npr.org/2020/10/19/924146486/removing-cops-from-behavioral-crisis-calls-we-need-to-change-the-model.

Andrew White. "The Scope of Accomplice Liability Under 18 U.S.C. 2(b)." *Case Western Reserve Law Review* 31 (1981): 386, 387–88.

Martha C. White, Stephanie Rhule, and Charlie Herman. "Corporate America Faces Reckoning on Cost of Silence, Pauses Political Donations." NBC News, January 11, 2011. https://www.nbcnews.com/business/business-news/corporate-america-faces-reckoning-cost-silence-pauses-political-donations-n1253813.

White House. "FACT SHEET: President Biden's Safer America Plan." August 1, 2022. https://www.whitehouse.gov/briefing-room/statements-releases/2022/08/01/fact-sheet-president-bidens-safer-america-plan-2/.

———. "Statement from President Joe Biden on the Sandy Hook Settlement." February 15, 2022. https://www.whitehouse.gov/briefing-room/statements-releases/2022/02/15/statement-from-president-joe-biden-on-sandy-hook-settlement/.

John Henry Wigmore. *A Treatise on the Anglo-American System of Evidence in Trials at Common Law*, 3rd ed. (Indiana University, 1940).

Apryl Williams. "Black Memes Matter: #LivingWhileBlack With Becky and Karen." *Social Media + Society* 6, no. 4 (2020).

Glanville Williams. "Victims and Other Exempt Parties in Crime." *Legal Studies* 10 (1990): 245.

Janice Williams. "Dolly Parton Isn't the Only Person to Turn Down the Medal of Freedom—There Are Others." *Newsweek*, February 2, 2021. https://www.newsweek.com/dolly-parton-medal-freedom-1566244.

Raymond Williams. *Keywords: A Vocabulary of Culture and Society* (Oxford University Press, 1985).

John Wilson. "Shame, Guilt, and Moral Education." *Journal of Moral Education* 30: 71–81.

Alana Wise. "Biden Calls George Floyd Killing 'An Act of Brutality.'" NPR, May 29, 2020. https://www.npr.org/2020/05/29/865511082/biden-calls-george-floyd-killing-an-act-of-brutality.

Ilan Shor Wittstein. "Broken Heart Syndrome." Johns Hopkins Medicine. https://www.hopkinsmedicine.org/health/conditions-and-diseases/broken-heart-syndrome.

Julia Carrie Wong. "The Year of Karen: How a Meme Changed the Way Americans Talked About Racism." *The Guardian*, December 27, 2020. https://www.theguardian.com/world/2020/dec/27/karen-race-white-women-black-americans-racism.

Worldwide Women's Criminal Justice Network. "Menchie's Story." http://www.wcjn.org/Marie_Scott_files/mechie0027s-story.pdf.

David Yamane, Sebastian L. Ivory, and Paul Yamane. "The Rise of Self-Defense in Gun Advertising: The American Rifleman, 1918–2017, Session on 'Guns and Markets.'" University of Arizona Gun Studies Symposium (October 20, 2017), 20.

Daniel B. Yeager. "Helping, Doing, and the Grammar of Complicity." *Criminal Justice Ethics* 15, no. 1 (1996): 3.

Iris Marion Young, *Responsibility for Justice* (Oxford University Press, 2011).

Corey Rayburn Yung. "One of These Laws Is Not Like the Others: Why the Federal Sex Offender Registration and Notification Act Raises New Constitutional Questions." *Harvard Journal on Legislation* 46 (2009): 372.

Nira Yuval-Davis. *Woman-Nation-State* (Springer, 1989).

Stephanie Zacharek, Eliana Dockterman, and Haley Sweetland Edwards. "The Silence Breakers." *Time*, December 2017. http://time.com/time-person-of-the-year-2017-silence-breakers/.

Brandy Zadrozny. "An Old Hillary Clinton Conspiracy Theory Finds New Life in Jeffrey Epstein News." NBC News, July 25, 2019. https://www.nbcnews.com/tech/tech-news/old-clinton-conspiracy-theory-finds-new-life-jeffrey-epstein-news-n1034741.

Nicholas Zimmerman. "Attempted Stalking: An Attempt-To-Almost-Attempt-To Act." *Northern Illinois University Law Review* 20 (2000): 219, 220.

INDEX

Founded in 1893,
UNIVERSITY OF CALIFORNIA PRESS
publishes bold, progressive books and journals
on topics in the arts, humanities, social sciences,
and natural sciences—with a focus on social
justice issues—that inspire thought and action
among readers worldwide.

The UC PRESS FOUNDATION
raises funds to uphold the press's vital role
as an independent, nonprofit publisher, and
receives philanthropic support from a wide
range of individuals and institutions—and from
committed readers like you. To learn more, visit
ucpress.edu/supportus.